CHARLESTON
HISTORIC AND ROMANTIC

Uniform with this Volume

RICHMOND, ITS PEOPLE AND
ITS STORY

BY MARY NEWTON STANARD

ST. MICHAEL'S CHURCH AND THE PORTICO OF THE HALL OF
THE SOUTH CAROLINA SOCIETY

CHARLESTON
HISTORIC AND ROMANTIC

BY HARRIETTE KERSHAW LEIDING
AUTHOR OF "HISTORIC HOUSES OF SOUTH CAROLINA"

WITH 80 ILLUSTRATIONS

PHILADELPHIA & LONDON
J. B. LIPPINCOTT COMPANY
MCMXXXI

FOREWORD

CAROLINA and Charleston, the metropolis, did not spring fully built from the English Crown as did Minerva from the brain of Jove. Carolina and Charleston evolved.

We have become accustomed to thinking of Charleston (Charles Town until 1783) as though it were a growth indigenous to the soil, when in reality it was the focal point of a transplanted growth. The "Why" of Charleston can best be answered by realising that while its population is a blend of many nationalities its beginnings were English and its genius manifests itself in the ceaseless, perpetual, subtle struggle of the Roundhead versus the Cavalier spirit. As each succeeding generation throws the torch to the oncoming one, the drama, with new settings and new dramatic personages, repeats itself. Restraint versus self-expression, inhibitions that smack of inertia, have barred any liberty that borders on license. The struggle proceeds yet the soul of the city is the same—unconquerable except by itself. Invulnerable in spirit to alien influences we stand.

Charlestonians say they are accused of being of Chinese extraction because they "eat rice and worship their ancestors," but that is just one of their clever phrases, for Charleston is given to phrases, and shows its culture by the way it loves words: blest indeed is he who coins a new expression. There are those who ably dispose of disagreeable aspects of life— social and private—with an apropos remark, but if one does not speak "Charlestonese," he is apt to feel like a little child outside of a shop window or hearing grown people talk about things outside their ken.

Many contend that "B. C." to Charlestonians, means "Before Charleston," but that is pure spite. The *City Gazette* No. 1769, for May 5, 1791, furnishes the following, written evidently by someone left out of "The Know:" "Wanted as an assistant to a laureate, one who is dexterous in the operation of culling phrases from the classics to 'gild' the names of

5

eminent personages." So it was in the beginning and is now. Charleston not only used fine phrases in talk but in her life used them, and sometimes both humorously and gruesomely. As for example the phrase "Getting down to brass tacks" is carried out in the use of brass tacks to mark the initials on the coffin of "J. O. B., 1704," buried beneath the steps of old St. Michaels, [south side] discovered by workmen repairing the edifice. Charleston used to sell goods "by inch of candle" and one with keen ears may yet hear persons of the older generation speak of getting home "by early candle light"— several old advertisements mention events that are to take place at that hour.

Charleston according to various "Hoyles" has been more written about than written; like the muchly kissed girl, more kissed against than kissing, she is misunderstood. A review recently appeared in the New York *Times* of "A Tale of Charleston." The writer of this "Tale," for a little while perched himself in the "Pirate House" and gave the city the "once over," in modern language, and then gave this description of our city:

"Charleston is an old city, as cities go in America, combining within its boundaries the stench of the waterfront and the dry perfume of its aristocracy. Between these two extremes are the ordinary people who live ordinary lives, and the climbers, the women who emulate the old families and hem in their lives with the futile attempt to shine."

And "That is That"—because Charleston does not always keep her lights burning for a certain type of wayfarer; who it seems, would not be able to understand "Carolina Bourbons," for whom "Life moved on as in a trance" after the fall of the Southern Confederacy. Nor could they ever understand that old social gospel of ours wherein it has been said that Charleston women's names should never appear but twice in the newspapers—at marriage and at death. "Charleston women live for their epitaphs," said one of the clever phrasemakers to whom we must again refer for a short, witty epitome of our history.

To those of us who love her, appreciate her, and live in her historic confines it is futile to try to put Charleston into language. She is in many respects "a song without words," an evanescent atmosphere that refuses to be distilled. Nor can we penetrate those depths of thought and feeling of which we sometimes attain a flashing glimpse, or drag forth the informing motives to use as a pattern for coming generations. These can never be reduced to a formula—least of all the intellectual and spiritual life of our people.

The beginnings of our state and Charleston its capital lie far back in England, France and Spain. The emigrant as an individual repeated the old life, but in new surroundings to which he must adapt himself, perish, or return from whence he came. Return ofttimes being absolutely impossible, adaptation followed, and South Carolina is to-day the result of the various stages of immigration and their more or less successful absorption. Nevertheless in Charleston, character is clearly to be traced to the various lines of cleavage that obtained before the first shipload of bold adventurers left English shores. The old contest between Cavaliers and Roundheads is renewed at every election, with almost all the bitterness which marked the original struggle, to which is added ever and anon the familiar "No Popery" slogan of England of the Middle Years (of which cry no less a person than one of the Lords Proprietors made good political use when it served his purpose) so that the adherents of each ancient historical and political faction of the days when the embryonic idea of the Carolina colonization was yet unhatched, come fresh to the fray and lay about them with tongue and lampoon, seemingly not caring if Charleston perish, if only they can carry out the old idea of Rule or Ruin. Little do they dream that they are not acting under a high stimulus of patriotism, but are simply reacting to tradition.

The day for this is fast closing. Charlestonians *must* co-operate or dwindle, and so the spirit of *new* Charleston shows that just as colonies have sometimes exceeded the development of the mother country, so the younger generation of Charletsonians are putting by these issues and honestly co-operating for a Charleston even more worthy than in her glorious past.

To show why Charleston possesses its marked characteristics, to show its newer development, and to tell its story are the objects of this book.

HARRIETTE KERSHAW LEIDING

CHARLESTON
JUNE 1ST, 1931

CONTENTS

ILLUSTRATIONS

11

CHARLESTON
HISTORIC AND ROMANTIC

BOOK I

PROPRIETARY ADMINISTRATION
1670-1719

CHAPTER I

CHARLESTON'S romantic and historic story began in the days when two men of Genoa, Christopher Columbus and John Cabot startled the world with their discoveries. Columbus found the lands on the continent of South America and the Islands of the West Indies for Spain, and Cabot, sent out by Henry VII of England, explored the northern coast of America. His son Sebastian sailed to the southern part of the continent and upon his return to England told of a land where great lumps of gold were to be picked up in the fields or on the beaches, and so enthralled the merchants of Bristol that efforts were made to claim and colonize these rich regions. Other explorers from England later confirmed Cabot's claims, under which the British settlements of this country proceeded from the three nearly equi-distant points of New England, Virginia and Charlestown, which latter was for a hundred years as much Carolina as Paris is France.

It is not possible to review the Floridian land-falls of DeLeon, and his journeys on the American continent, nor is it necessary to more than mention De'Ayllon's quest for gold and Indian slaves which gave name and nationality to the Island of St. Helena. It is not possible to ignore the French claim to Carolina, established when French Protestants attempted to find an asylum from the religious persecutions of the sixteenth century on these unknown shores.

But commercial enterprise and Christian zeal failed alike to tame the wilderness. The story of man's inhumanity to man weaves dark shadows into the tale of golden romance and high adventure. Evil cruelties proceeded in the New World as they had done in the Old, and the shining sands

17

of Carolina were stained with the blood of those Huguenots who came with Ribault and Laudonnier. Their lives were snuffed out like candles in the wind. After 1567, when De Gourges made bloody retaliation upon the Spaniards, no further efforts were made to colonize the southern part of the continent of America and for long years history is silent concerning Carolina.

In 1629 Charles I granted lands on the continent of America to Sir Robert Heath. The region included all the land south of Virginia between the 36" and 31" northern latitudes extending from ocean to ocean. Heath made no effort to occupy his vast domain. The claim lapsed, but the ghost of the grant appeared thirty years later along with claims for grants in the Barbadoes.

Meanwhile England had undergone the trials of civil war. Many Royalists and Parliamentarians fled to the Barbadoes to escape the throes of the strife when Cavalier Charles I came to grips with Puritan Cromwell.

Eventually Charles lost his head and Cromwell his life. Cromwell's son failed to carry on his father's effort. England, left without a ruler, recalled Charles II from exile to be king, the plague came to London along with the king and the merry-makers and sellers of trinkets who swarmed over from the Continent to vend their wares and add to the festivies of the coronation. So many thousands perished of disease that pits were dug in the fields and bodies were buried wholesale. The great fire which consumed London followed. The Puritans regarded these troubles as the vengeance of God upon the gay Cavaliers. The irreconcilable differences in religion and outlook naturally became a part of Carolina's heritage when the colony came into being.

England, already depleted by civil war, pestilence and fire, was further distressed by the tremendous taxes levied to meet the extravagance of the "Merry Monarch". The Royal coffers were all but empty when the great speculative enterprise, known as the East Indian Bauble, burst. This disaster created such national and personal depression that the English statesmen feared an outbreak of serious proportion.

The king resolved to recoup his fortunes, pay his political debts, satisfy claims made by those who served his father, and divert public attention to "green fields and pastures new" by one bold stroke. Neither caprice nor unconsidered haste prompted Charles to give a large slice of the southern portion of the American continent to a group of his friends, and Charleston's history dates from this prodigal gesture made by the king in 1663.

Carolina was officially granted to Lord Clarendon and seven other noblemen of England who became known as the Lords Proprietors. Difficulties arose from the old Heath grant. Charles issued another document declaring the Heath grant void, and bestowed valid titles to the old territory on these same men, who became known as the "Second Lords Proprietors."* The king enlarged the first territory from the old bounds at the north end of the island called "Lucke" to the River Mathias at the south. He renamed the enlarged territory "Carolina" in honor of his father, and signified that the land was to be "had, used and enjoyed" with all it contained, in as ample manner as any Bishop of Durham, in the Kingdom of England. Thus the land became a Palatinate.

Virginia settlers straggling down in 1655 had built a few homes on the Chowan River, which region had been called Albemarle County in honor of the oldest Lord Proprietor. The region about Cape Fear was similarly called Clarendon County and a number of English people went there in 1664. As soon as the Counties of Albemarle and Clarendon were defined and that of Cartaret projected, Carolina began definitely to take shape and form.

The Barbadian influence again appears in the story of

* Action becoming necessary to secure the empire, to protect the rights of the Lords Proprietors and prevent questions of previous ownership from arising as to the rights and titles to the territory, on August 12, 1663, his Majesty summoned all pretenders to former grants to present or send their evidences of title to the Court at Whitehall and "took into consideration the state and present condition of the Province or Region called Carolina in America." Under his grant of the same date, Letters Patent, bearing the Great Seal of England, confirmed valid titles to the Lords Proprietors, who thus became known as the "Second Lords Proprietors."

this city where so many Barbadian habits, forms and influences are found. When Charles II came to the throne he re-established royal authority in the Barbadoes, bestowed titles upon certain gentlemen, but failed to relieve the traders from Cromwell's stifling enactments. By excessive taxes he virtually confiscated the estates of the planters. Through Modyford and Peter Colleton these discontented Barbadians requested room in the new settlement in Carolina and proposed a scheme of government which they wished to put into operation there. Without waiting for official sanction they dispatched Captain Hilton to view the land.

Though the Barbadian venture came to naught yet the pamphlet published by Hilton contained maps of the region that he had visited and served to stimulate interest in Carolina. Shortly after this Robert Sandford was sent out to be Chief Register and Secretary for Clarendon County. Governor Berkeley of Virginia, one of the Lords Proprietors, was made Governor of the province of Carolina. Shortly after, Sir John Yeamans of Barbadoes was commissioned to be Governor of the Cape Fear settlement. He brought a number of colonists with him, but the venture failed, the colony was gradually abandoned and finally disappeared.

Meanwhile, Yeaman's return to the Barbadoes was followed by Sandford's expedition to the South. Landing near the Edisto River, Sandford took possession by "Turffe and Twigge" in the name of the King and for the use of the Proprietors, visited the site of the ancient French settlement at Port Royal, made friends with the Indians, left Woodward as a hostage, and, taking seven savages with him, returned to the Cape Fear settlements.

Sandford's recommendations concerning Port Royal and his glowing accounts of the territory were seconded by William Sayle, who was sent out from the Bermudas to check Sandford's report. Sayle suggested that the Proprietors should secure grants in some of the islands of the Bahamas, and thus obtain a base of supplies close to the projected colony.

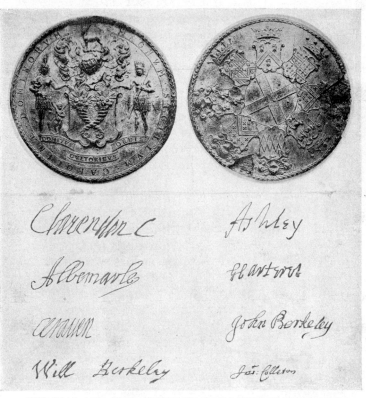

THE SEAL AND SIGNATURES OF THE LORDS PROPRIETORS

A New
DISCRIPTION OF
CAROLINA
By Order of the
Lords Proprietors.
1672.

The Lords Proprietors had, in the meantime, organized, adopted a seal, raised money by subscriptions, formed a stock company, and, in 1669, seven years after the King had given them the country, they proceeded to settlement by securing ships and starting an expedition to Carolina.

After seven months of vexatious delays the colonists arrived on its coast, attempted to build a town at Port Royal, were dislodged by unfriendly Spaniards, and, accepting the invitation of the Cacique of Kiawah, settled on Albemarle Point, and, in 1670 founded a town on the western branch of the Kiawah river, which they called Charles-Town in honor of their king.

Old Town was but a transient dream of which nothing remains except a few forgotten graves on Ghost Island, a deep ditch marking where a fort once stood, and a pair of tabby steps, that led, perhaps, into the governor's mansion of long ago. Some ancient deeds are recorded in old leather-bound books in the Probate Court; these deeds have outlasted by two hundred years the hands that penned them. The persons who made them might have been forgotten except for the little granite marker erected over the site of the first settlement, and tablets, hatchments and gravestones found in old St. Andrew's or over at Goose Creek Church.

The first actual conflict for the soil occurred when a Charleston-bound vessel which stopped at the Florida settlement of Santa Catalina was attacked as an enemy intruder and several of her crew killed. John Rivers and William Carr were held captives. Governor William Sayle's messengers Joseph Bailey and John Collins, who were dispatched to threaten vengeance, were also captured and taken to St. Augustine, the Spanish stronghold. Spain's effort to destroy the English settlement was one of the determining factors in the selection of a naturally fortified site for the chief port of Carolina, after a Spanish fleet was sent to attack the settlers on the western bank of the Ashley. Shaftesbury, Patron Saint of the settlement, made a gesture of buying the land from its Indian owners and for a few trinkets thus secured a color of title over a vast domain extending as far west as the Appalachian mountains.

The first inhabitants came from England and Ireland. The second direct accession arrived in 1671 with Captain Mathias Halstead in the ship Blessing. Three years later this same vessel, with the Phoenix, fetched people from Novia Belgia to colonize on James Island, but for protection these Dutch immigrants abandoned their town and moved near the other settlers.

The presence of savage Indians and the jealousy of the Spaniards who claimed the territory compelled the small outpost of the British empire to lead the existence of a garrison: men worked with an axe in one hand and a gun in the other. The great riches advertised as existing in Carolina did not fail to attract undesirables and adventurers, many of whom were found among the settlers. Some served the colony well enough but others treacherously hobnobbed with the Spaniards.

In order to encourage emigration a bounty of fourteen pounds currency was allowed to anyone who should bring over or import a healthy male British servant, anywhere from twelve to thirty years old, provided they were not criminals. Power conferred upon the holders of large estates was feudal in its extent. Those who were leetmen or vassals on the great estates were as much servitors as were their kinsmen on the English estates, but provision was made for impartial administration of justice. High-sounding titles were bestowed upon various officers of the court and minute directions were outlined for the actual government of the colony beginning with the first charter of 1663 and followed by that of 1665 and the first constitution of 1669 with its eighty-one articles.

Sayle's "instructions" of 1669 held fourteen additional articles and in 1670 the second constitution, issued as Locke's First Constitution, contained one hundred and twenty items. Carolina was never able to live up to the scheme of its numerous provisos, fashioned by the philosophic Locke, when he was Secretary to Lord Ashley Cooper. It is a moot question as to the exact amount of influence which Locke's Grand Model had upon the actual government of Carolina. His scheme included a colonial hereditary nobility of two orders, Landgrave and Caciques, whose dignity was supported by grants of large estates and secured by making those estates forever inseparable from the title and privileges of the respective orders.

Carolina was divided into counties, of eight seignories each, reserved for the eight Proprietors; eight baronies which should belong to the Provincial nobility; and four precincts of six colonies each reserved for the people. By this arrangement it was hoped to preserve the balance of power in favor of the aristocratic element.

Carolina was a wilderness. The nobles must have great estates, new settlers who were ambitious wanted land, and so the universal endeavor of those who came to Charlestown was to obtain and hold lands. They were encouraged in this by the Proprietors. The first administration concentrated on surveying lands and securing quit rents. It was all-desirable to build up the population, and population could only be secured by granting lands to prospective settlers. For many years after the first settlement all title deeds held an interesting clause which reserved certain rights in prospective mines of gold, silver and precious stones for the Proprietors.

Carolina was settled at a time marked by a strong belief in "legislative omnipotence." It was an age of bounties, encouragements and prohibitions: it was thought that formal legislation could establish a colony and provide colonists anxious to fell trees, clear fields and build houses, and all sorts of encouragements were offered. In a description of Cape Fear, in 1666, ladies were told that if they were under fifty and civil, husbands were forthcoming.

Temporary laws of 1672 embodied articles, resolutions and instructions, while agrarian laws of the same year were issued along with further instructions and six additional articles.

During the first popular election, held in 1672, and

during the first session of the Parliament created by this election, it was resolved on April 23d to issue a warrant to the Surveyor General for the laying out of three colonies of 12,000 acres each, one at Jamestown, one at Charlestown and the third at Oyster Point. In 1664, Sir John Yeamans had been appointed Governor of the Northern settlements but no colony was founded under him. Sayle, appointed by Yeamans for the Proprietors, settled Old Town on the Ashley, and being a soldier reserved land for a fort and possible town on the peninsula opposite the place where he elected to settle. He died before 1671 and was succeeded by Joseph West, elected by Council. West was but a temporary officer, and in 1672 the Palatine appointed Sir John Yeamans as Governor over the established colony and town on the banks of the Ashley. He was duly proclaimed Governor and when he came brought with him a commission appointing his friend Culpepper as Surveyor General of the colony to succeed Florence O'Sullivan, who had proven an unworthy official. The Proprietors, snug in England and not realizing the advantages of the location, resented the fact that Yeamans expended money to build forts, provide ammunition and arm inhabitants who had straggled over to the present site of Charleston.

Under his governorship the freemen in the colony were called together and elected a new Parliament. The Governor and his Council issued an order directing Culpepper to lay out a town on Oyster Point. Among the stragglers, who had crossed the river and taken up lands on the peninsula between the two Indian rivers, were certain far-sighted individuals, Henry Hughes and John Comings, who now came forward and volunteered to give up part of their lands to increase space for a town and commons of pasture. Culpepper was instructed to lay out the new town, it to include the original six hundred acres specified by Sayle and one hundred and fifty acres from the lands of Henry Hughes. John Comings' land was released, but the southern point of the town bore his name for many years, and his wife, Mrs. Affra Comings, later on, donated much land now in the

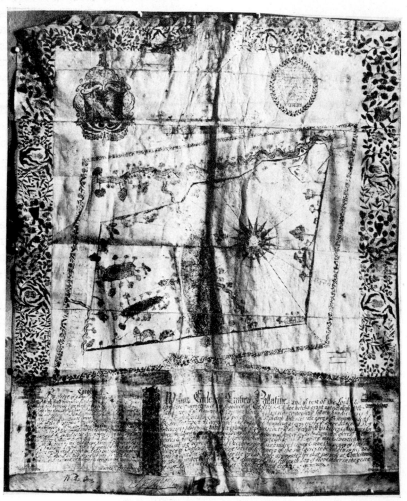

GRANT ISSUED TO JOSEPH WEST

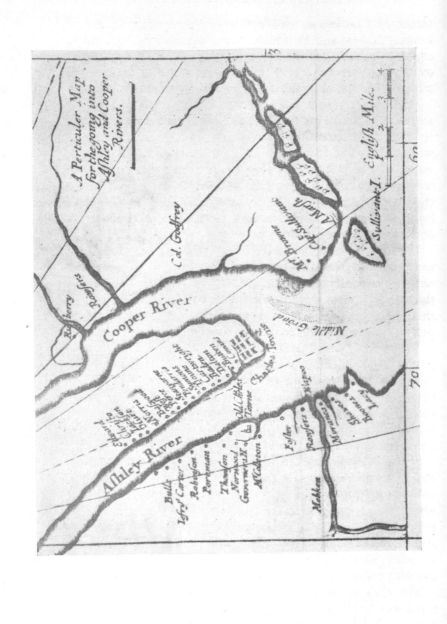

center of Charleston, easily recognizable in the streets of Coming, Glebe and St. Philip. She gave the land for Glebe, or Church land, and the street and the fine old brick house memoralise her generosity, although the parsonage was not erected until about 1732.

Shaftesbury gave the signal for the actual construction of a port town in the letter addressed to Secretary Dalton, who replying to Shaftesbury's specifications, said that the Council was looking out for things and that, as the world was not asleep nor the Spaniards less vengeful than formerly, the colony must have a town that was built for safety and so they had occupied the site considered of military value by Sayle, which commanded a view up and down the harbor and was like a key to open or shut the colony into safety.

He did not add, as well he might have done, that the town was situated at the narrow apex of a triangle and would eventually drain the trade of the whole hinterland through its streets and ship timber, rice, indigo, naval stores, thousands of skins of wild animals, and other Carolina products over her wharves.

When Yeamans had ordered Culpepper to lay out the town the documents were not recorded and Culpepper, who "illegally" departed out of the colony, created great confusion by his act. His plats and surveys were "whollie miscarried and lost." It is not therefore known if the town evolved according to the plan projected by Culpepper, assisted by Stephen Bull, who later helped to plan Savannah.

Shaftesbury pictured in his mind how he wished Charleston to look. He foresaw the time when the "void spaces" around the city would be filled with handsome buildings, lining the broad streets of sixty-six feet specified in his plans. The meanest alleys were to be not less than eight feet, and although these specifications may not now seem so prodigiously large, they were quite elaborate for that day and generation.

The *City Gazette* of August 29, 1799 furnishes a plain statement to the effect that the original plan of Charleston was supposed to have been kept in Craven's Bastion and lost during a great hurricane. A discussion arose during a meeting of sixteen commissioners of public lands who came together to decide on buying a public burying ground in the outskirts of the city. Several interesting statements are found in the minutes of this meeting of City Council. One says that when Charleston was first settled the whole neck of land to the westward of Mazych street appears to have been set apart and used as the burying ground of St. Philip's Parish which then, and for many years after, comprehended the whole of the town; but in 1698, when Mr. James Moore obtained a grant which surrounded this neck and covered nearly all the land within Allen, Archdale and Broad streets and the Old Town Line, now Beaufain street, extending a certain distance in the marsh, the Surveyor General marked off four acres for the church yard, on the above-mentioned neck, being such part of the square formed by Queen, Bache, and Mazych streets as was high land. The part that was marsh remained to the rest of the grant. The present city evolved from a small village which was partly on high ground, partly lowland.

In November, 1680, the present site was officially and legally accepted. The city of today is an enlargement of the original town and is situated on a long, narrow peninsula, between the Ashley and Cooper rivers, which unite at South Battery to form one of the most spacious harbors in America.

Charleston occupies a narrow, congested area, three and one-half miles in length by two in breadth, extending from the Battery and Murray Boulevard, which form the southern bounds, northward to Magnolia Crossing. Beyond the city, large phosphate, lumber and oil industries occupy a three-mile stretch of country, terminating, on the right, in the United States Navy Yard on the Cooper river, the town of North Charleston, and the Port Terminals. Beyond this, Yeamans Hall, an old plantation, now a winter club for resident millionaires, occupies the territory adjacent to and bordering upon Goose Creek. Between this development and Meeting Street road the Charleston Water Works Company's plant is situated. Across Meeting Street road is an unoccupied section of country, once the scene of fertilizer diggings and the site of Michaux's Botanical Garden, and a section once characteristically known as Hell's Half Acre. At Ten Mile Hill, Charleston has established her Air Port, and below this, leading toward town, are various industrial plants, which terminate at the northern end of the city in the Ashley Park and Magnolia Cemetery on the Cooper river.

The Cooper and Ashley rivers are spanned, East and West, by two great bridges. That across the Cooper connects the city with the mainland in Christ Church Parish. Here the road branches to permit a road to connect Mount Pleasant with Sullivan's Island and the Isle of Palms; while the main road traverses Coastal Highway No. 40, which follows the old King's Highway and proceeds to the Santee River settlements, various plantations below Georgetown, and through that historic place to Waccamaw, Myrtle Beach, over the border of the sister state, and on to the North.

The Ashley Memorial Bridge connects Charleston with St. Andrew's Parish, where the colony began in 1670. Here the road divides into three forks, to reach the Country Club on the left, various sub-divisions, Riverland Terrace, and Folly Island.

Returning from Folly by the same route, emerging from Charleston, the traveler who desires to go South would take, at Windemere, the center road which leads to Savannah and touches in its passage trucking lands near Meggett and Edisto Island. The main road proceeds through Adam's Run village, across Edisto river to the old rice fields and plantation estates near Beaufort, and through Yemassee to the South.

Back again at the Ashley river bridge the road to the right is traversed by those who desire to visit the first settlement, the Bull Plantations, St. Andrew's Church, old Bee's Ferry, and famous gardens along the river route. The plantations along this route include Drayton Hall, Magnolia Gardens, Runnymead, Middleton Gardens, Wragg Barony and Hannahan's estate, above which the road swings across Ashley river, at Bacon's Bridge, and goes on to old Dorchester and the Indian Fort there. One road back to town leads down by the old Middleton places, the Goose Creek settlements and so on into the city, to join another old road leading to Back River, the western branch of the Cooper, Mulberry, Dean Hall, Childsbury or to the Santee settlements. But in olden times the road led across Bacon's Bridge, and down the Ashley river, through great plantations which then lined its eastern shore. These places are all destroyed, and no vestige remains of these splendid mansions, once occupied by the Boones, the Warings, the Bakers and other grandees of Colonial Carolina. The plantations are now hunting preserves, their owners are dust, "their good swords rust, their souls are with the Lord, we trust."

In 1704, Edward Crisp made a chart of the town as it existed in that year. Crisp shows its limits as lying between Craven's Bastion on the North, where the Custom House is, and Market Street, and Granville's Bastion on the south, on the banks of a creek to which the name Vanderhorst was given before it was filled up and made into Water street. It was then the southern boundary of the city and was sometimes called South street. Before it was filled up it was crossed by a bridge called Young's Bridge, used by those who lived where South Battery is now and along Church street to reach their homes.

Book Q-6, M.C.O. contains a plat of the foundation of old walls adjacent to Granville's Bastion that were uncovered when East Bay street was to be widened. The Bastion was situated in the neighborhood of Stoll's alley, an ancient passage, extending from East Bay to Church street. Parts of the old walls of the city are said to be embraced within the old Teasdale property, now the Matthewes' residence, 43 East Battery. The second volume of Ramsay's History of South Carolina carries a reproduction of a survey of the city made by Edward Crisp, which is the oldest typographical delineation extant.

Fifteen buildings are marked as the most conspicuous in the town of 1704, and Charlestown radiated from a nucleus built in the center and occupying angles of the square formed

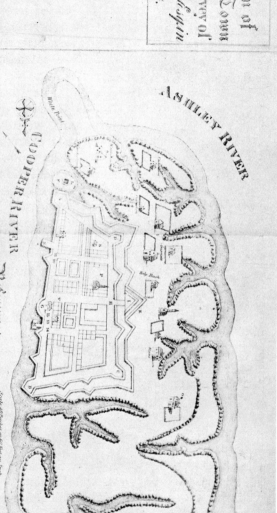

CRISP'S SURVEY OF CHARLESTOWN, 1704

Exterior

Interior

THE OLD MAGAZINE, CUMBERLAND STREET. ERECTED ABOUT
1704
The oldest building in the city still in use

by the intersection of Cooper, now Broad street, and Church, at that time the main street of the town. At first there were Pasquero and Garret's house at the northeast corner, Lansack's at the northwest, John Croskey's at the southwest and Chevelier's at the southeast. As the town grew efforts to prevent encroachments of the sea on the town caused a Curtain Line to be built on East Bay to keep out tide water. As the danger from the Indians and the Spaniards increased, the first crude forts were elaborated into real walls, which ran along from bastion to bastion. Starting with Granville's Bastion and proceeding along the banks of the creek, the town limits stopped at the present Meeting street. Near the present corner of Broad and King streets were gates to the city, which led through a horn work and crossed the outer ditch by a draw-bridge. It was used constantly by those who lived on the various outlying estates and by persons who had market gardens just outside of the fortifications. In a few years, planters who came into town by road, instead of river, entered through the narrow neck of land composing the peninsula. They came down the "Board Path" after passing the Quarter House, or crossed the ferry from "Dover to Calais" that led over into the lands across Cooper and Wando rivers, via Daniels Island, or over into St. Andrew's Parish by the ferry to Mr. Branford's Plantation, or at the ferry, now called Bee's Ferry, where forgotten Shem Town once stood on the banks of the Ashley above "Accabee" Woods.

When the first rough census had been taken of the town it included all masters and mistresses of households, all families living in their protection and all "freemen lodgers." Constables who made the lists included the houses of those who owned property in town but lived in the country. The actual construction of the town was accomplished by artisans who came out among the first settlers. Though listed as carpenters and sawyers, many of them were in reality skilled master-builders.

Captains of ships were encouraged to fetch stones for the sea-walls. Owners of low lots were required to fill them in. The town grew, and as it grew it was found desirable to close some of the creeks and fill in marsh land. Bridges were thrown across some of the smaller creeks to connect the "Out" portions of the town with the town proper. Soon these outer portions took the names of the owners and became known as boroughs. But for a long time Charlestown extended no farther north than Queen, then called Dock, street, and the northern bound of the town intersected the western bound, just north of the Circular Church. The line is obliterated.

The city was soon surrounded by a substantial wall, garrisoned, and fortified. It is strange to read of little children being taken to task because they passed to and fro over the walls just as little children of today will do. But the matter was so vital that the town authorities censured those who were accused of "daily defacing the fortifications" by their walks, and so a sentinel was placed at the town gate and bridge. His official duty was to challenge every colt, mare, cow, calf or ox that approached and, it is presumed that he also challenged the children. All live stock, except horses, were banished from the fortified area and a common pound was provided for vagrant cattle.

In 1680 the city was formally located in its present situation and by 1682 it contained a hundred houses, to which additions were constantly made. Samuel Wilson, Secretary to the Lords Proprietors, published an account of the Province and city. During the ten formative years the lands near the town had been cleared of valuable timber but was not ready for cultivation and was sold for twenty shillings an acre. Land prepared for planting and enclosed rented at ten shillings an acre, even though it was twenty miles from town.

As the population radiated from the city the horse became more and more valuable. Saddlers and stable keepers furnished places where visitors and traders coming into town could find entertainment for horses," at a widely advertised "horse hotel" on Old Church street, behind the church yard. Those who did not intend to leave quickly placed their beasts in various pastures situated near to the town.

The New Market Plantation seems to have been the favorite place; later on slave sales took place there, and, later again, horse-races were announced at "New Market" race course.

The commercial enterprises and trade relations that developed very early in Charleston were neither anticipated nor desired, as the city was not primarily a commercial venture but an agricultural experiment.

It cost five pounds to come from London and when each head of a family arrived he was to get fifty acres of land for himself and for each able-bodied son and male servant, and each marriageable daughter or woman servant. When the white indentured servants had served their time each one became a freeman and received fifty acres of land in his own right. All this property was to be enjoyed forever on the payment of a penny an acre quit rent, to begin two years after occupation. Land that was bought outright sold for fifty pounds a thousand acres, with a quit rent of a "pepper corn" upon demand.

It was the cherished design of the Proprietors to found a planting colony and early in 1684 they expressed their great displeasure at the large increase in stocks and cattle. Thousands of cows, hogs and sheep were found in a country that but a few years previously was almost destitute of cattle. It required many acts to keep the swine and goats out of Charlestown where they used to go loose in great numbers to "the prejudice and great annoyance of the inhabitants."

It would seem that in a country where wheat and rye, oats, peas, turnips, parsnips, potatoes and twenty kinds of beans could grow, the inhabitants would take kindly to planting, but such was not the case. Cattle found good forage on the low places in the country, called savannahs or meadow lands. The forest ranges supplied additional cattle-food in winter when meat was cured and as salt beef was shipped out to the Northern colonies. Hogs throve on abundant acorns and after being made into pork they were shipped to the Barbadoes, Jamaica and New England, so that it was scarcely to be expected that the early inhabitants of Charlestown would pay any attention to the repeated rebukes of the Proprietors, though they continued to supply the colony with seeds for planting and to bestow bounties upon native products, all to no effect. Charlestown, like the true Episcopal community that she was, continued as she was in the beginning, is now, and ever shall be, and did what she wanted.

As late as 1675 the Proprietors complained that they had expended £10,000 and were still charged with the care of five or six hundred people who were not yet self-supporting. Part of this expenditure went to arming the inhabitants, who had formed themselves into three companies for protection, and in 1680 had attacked the Spanish missions to the South. It is true that an effort was made to settle a buffer colony on the Edisto river, at Locke's Island. Andrew Percival was made Governor, but his settlement failed and he returned to Charlestown to become Register of Berkeley County. The names of the Lords Proprietors are preserved in the counties of the State, Albemarle, Berkeley, Cartaret, Clarendon, Colleton, Craven, while Ashley Cooper gave his name to the two great rivers surrounding the city of Charleston.

In 1682, a third constitution, composed of one hundred and twenty articles, was sent out to Charlestown. A fourth, of 120 items, followed it in August; a fifth, containing 41 articles, came over in 1698. It is sufficient to scan the list of laws to appreciate the fact that Charleston, long ago, for self-protection discarded her constitution and lived upon her by-laws.

Woodward, while serving as hostage to the Indians at the time of Sandford's voyage, had learned their habits and customs. Shaftesbury engaged him to act as an ambassador to the natives, to establish friendly relationships with them, interest them in developing the country and so permit resources being developed. He was partially successful.

Trade was diverted to the city, ships from all European ports frequented the harbor, and flags of various nations fluttered from the masts of vessels trading here, which came from all over the world. Settlers from the Barbadoes, Jamaica and the Caribbees reinforced the original colonists from England and Ireland. In 1680, French Huguenots came to Carolina, and in 1696 New Englanders from Dorchester, Mass. settled on Ashley river.

The settlers each brought their ideas from their old homes with them, but although the settlement was English in language and laws yet colonists from the West Indies greatly influenced the laws of Carolina in regard to the usage accorded to slaves, and they knew the climatic conditions of this region, and were familiar with the soil and its products. They knew also the type of architecture suitable for residences in a semi-tropical region. They have left a marked influence upon the life and civilization of Carolina, and there remain several buildings in Charleston which are quite similar to Barbadian structures.

CHAPTER II

CHARLES II ordered two small vessels to be provided at his expense to transport foreign Protestants to Carolina. Secretary Wilson's prospectus enumerated the products of Carolina as wine, "oyl," tobacco, indigo, cotton of the cyprus and smyrna sort, flax, hemp, pitch, tar, oak staves, sumac, woad, madder, jallop, sarsaparilla, turmeric, snake root and other herbs. Prospective settlers must bring linen, woolen and other stuffs with which to make clothes, (not omitting threads and buttons). A laborer needed an axe, broad bill, grubbing hoe, a cross cut and a whip saw, besides wedges, beetle rings, nails and hooks.

Hoping to counteract the passion for cattle-raising and desiring to build up the population, Thomas Ashe in 1680 came out as a clerk on board his Majesty's ship Richmond to bring a colony of French Protestants and supplies with which to establish silk culture in the Province. The experiment failed, the silkworms having died on the way over. These French Huguenots came from the South of France and were versed not only in silk culture but in raising olives and making wine. It was found that samples of wine made in Carolina and sent to England were equal to any produced on the continent and it was confidently predicted that Charlestown would soon be exporting wine to the whole of the West Indian Islands. Moreover, maize or corn that could be roasted or parched and boiled with milk was even then being made into "corn cordial" which was used in preference to a "noble" beverage made from casino-berry leaves.

Tradesmen and shop-keepers invested their earnings in cargoes and sent them out to the trade centers of the world. In this way they secured sufficient money to buy tracts of land and join the ranks of the land-holders, and thereby lose the stigma attached to those in trade. As lands near to Charleston were taken up these people secured grants for tracts in outlying districts. Charleston was, thus, continuously supplying settlers who pushed further and further afield.

Superb ship-timbers, masts and spars were easily obtained in the Carolina forests and were shipped to England with other commodities. Out of seventeen ships which sailed from Charleston in 1707 all arrived in England laden with tar, pitch, rice, beaver, bear, deer, fox, racoon, wild-cat skins and furs of great value.

In one year seventy thousand deer-skins alone were exported and this quantity had increased twenty years later to two hundred and fifty thousand, reaching by the middle of the century the enormous number of six hundred thousand skins.

The trade of Charlestown was a prize worth having, and while politics engrossed the gentlemen and crops absorbed the farmer class, the subject of Carolina commerce completely engrossed the Proprietors.

Indigo was among the crops raised later in Carolina and exported through the port of Charlestown. Then Colonel Lucas, who owned a plantation near the confluence of Wappoo Creek and Stono river, encouraged his daughter Eliza's fondness for planting by sending seeds and fruits to her from the West Indies to be tested in Carolina. Later on a Mr. Cromwell from the Island of Montserrat was brought to Carolina and stationed upon the Lucas plantation where he built the first vats in which Carolina Indigo was drawn. Until the Revolutionary War indigo found a ready market in Charlestown, but after this the British bounty was withdrawn, and in an open market it could not vie with rice and cotton and ceased to be planted. However, small cakes of indigo could be purchased here until 1867.

Meanwhile, lumber, meats, butter, cheese and maize had begun to be exported in the coastwise trade and to the West Indies, and the Indian trade assumed importance as Charlestown began to trade nearly a thousand miles into the continent.

The farmers brought their wares to town and "numerous disputes arose" between the merchants and inhabitants "for

want of ascertaining the rate of country produce", so that
a merchants' exchange was formed in the rough. Its activities centered, no doubt, around the little Watch House upon
the site of which was later erected the present Exchange
Building. The responsible task of surveying and weighing
produce was given to David Maybank and a public market
was soon erected at the northeast corner of Broad and
Meeting streets. In Charlestown, good, merchantable corn,
peas, beef, pork or tar at the market price were regarded
as being equal to money itself, and fines were frequently
paid in these articles.

In 1685 the first Collector of Customs was established at
Charlestown when the commerce of the City began to attract the notice of the world. In the same year the colonial
legislature passed "an act for the settling of a pilot." And
then, when the Captain of a slaver brought rice seeds to
Charlestown, the big crop that was soon to come was begun
and in 1696 the cultivation of rice was introduced on such
a large scale as to give great impetus to foreign trade.

From the first the colonists had fought for the Golden
Fleece of the Indian trade, and Spain was fighting for it
also. Contacts and antagonisms incurred during these early
days sowed the seed of Indian uprisings and conflicts with
Spain, or paved the way for smuggling and its first cousin,
piracy; the very suspicion of which deprived Charlestown of
just protection and gave the Lords Proprietors an excuse for
their failure properly to outfit and arm their colony in a
later attempt against Spain.

A picture of Charlestown in these stirring days would show
her wharves piled high with goods, her harbor alive with
picturesque vessels, her streets thronged with prosperous
citizens, Indian traders, and sailors from off the boats, all
passing in and out of the shops that lined Tradd and Elliott
streets and fronted the blue waters of the bay. On the
streets "victualers, vinters, cord-wainers, waggoners, hig-
glers and writing fellows or scriveners" cried their wares
as they had been wont to do in the streets of London town

and vied with the hawkers, peddlers and petty chapman who sold goods to passers-by.

While little boats, called perriaugers or wherries, ferried folk up and down the rivers, mariners from big ships scattered themselves in the town, searching for the crude entertainment to be found in the ale houses. Officers from the same boats seeking better class fare, patronized the coffee-houses or inns that flourished up and down the water-front of the small town or faced the narrow sidewalks of Tradd street.

On the city streets were various traders, some illicit and some licensed, who went about their business or regaled themselves at taverns. Mariners ogled the lesser folk of the town, while semi-piratical sailors from boats that cruised the Seven Seas made merry in a rough way with others of their kind and ordinary people were jostled by rough free-booters, who came to the colony when smuggling and other easy methods of making money became frequent.

Indian traders who penetrated beyond the mountain ranges and traveled paths beside the rivers soon found that Charlestown merchants gave good prices for their wares, and Charlestown itself was a good place to get supplies for their Indian clients. Rum, guns, beads and Indian cloth were imported for this class of trade.

Wealthy traders brought their wares into town by caravans of horses. The jangling of bells announced the coming of a string of twenty or thirty horses bearing packs of roots, herbs, deer- and bear-skins, which had been slowly gathered through long months in far-away Indian villages. When the caravan ended its weary journey at the counting-house of some great merchant prince and the Indian traders received their pay then the town awoke from its hum-drum existence for a while, as the "bucks" swaggered about enjoying the pleasure found in this outpost of civilization and spent their hard-earned money in wild drinking bouts.

Small traders who could not afford horses fetched their goods into Charlestown on the backs of Indian runners, who counted it no hardship to follow the young white men into the town. Often these men acted as spies and reported back to their tribes the strength or weakness of the colony and the number of guns and men in Charlestown. The Indians had learned many things since the coming of the white men to these shores. The first Indians had run out into the water to meet the white brothers, had given them "ye stroaking compliments of ye country" and had called them "Bonne comrado Anglais", but now the savages had learned wisdom. Commissioners were appointed to regulate the Indian trade: so once every year each trader presented himself in town to have his record investigated and his license reissued or revoked. Outside the quarters of the Commission squatted old Indian chiefs, who came to town to complain about the abuses practised upon them by the white men and incidentally to see for themselves the wonderful town. No doubt they made their way into the shops and fingered the goods that lined the shelves, or visited the water-front and inspected the boxes and bales of goods consigned to the Charlestown tailors and milliners. Colonial Charlestonians of wealth kept up with the English fashions, while poor folks bought goods in local shops. As there were no newspapers in the colony until 1730, recourse must be had to ancient inventories to find out precisely what was sold in the city, early in its history. As an example, the inventory of merchant Alexander Duprys, shows "twenty-three Buret hats, 349 yards of Ozinburgs, four pieces of coarse, and three quarters garlics for servants' wear," also "patterborns, calamancos, blew plains, burdet, some tape, some redcaddis and some silk galloon." Judging by early inventories, money was plentiful and of various kinds, as the colony had no specific circulating medium. Articles made of "coin" silver were sometimes used as reserved wealth: as was also wrought silver. Sometimes the inventories listed a half of a pistole as money—or a "lion dollar, or a Royal", but most of the money was found listed as Spanish, English, or French coins.

Wealthy folk made their wills and left their lands and family pictures and furniture and gold and silver, their horses and carriages and guns and swords and plantation supplies to their eldest son and thus kept the property intact. For when it came to the business of dying and making wills the early Charlestonians knew their minds. People of small importance generally died without making wills, and then persons were appointed to make a list of their belongings. A hurried glance through the old books at the probate court shows that besides looking glasses, "walnutt" chests, window curtains, and "vallions", table "cloaths" and napkins were prized possessions—as were beds and "cheers", "ceader" tables and "joynt stools". "Scrutore" desks came next, and lanthorns, candlesticks and slicers, and "save alls," were highly prized objects. Mention of Buccaneer-guns, canoes, wheelbarrows, carbines, stilettos, "cartouche boxes" and slaves occur frequently in the lists of men's belongings. One very sad little list that included "one poor old violen" in its pitiful contents calls to mind the picture of a homesick soul pouring out his feelings in the streets of the quaint, walled town, while little children stood around the steps of the house to hear the sound of an old English song played in the new land of Carolina.

The ordinary belongings of the frugal housewives of early Charleston included "sadirons, squellits, kneeding traughs, pots and pans, spits and trivits, flesh forcks, pot hooks, and crammels", for the kitchen, while the beds were made up with sheets and "pillow bears."

Soon the wealth and growing importance of the town made many new laws necessary. Money matters became involved. Public needs multiplied, companies of soldiers had to be raised and paid for. White servants arrived without contracts, and had to be taken into custody and placed out. Slaves ran away. These must be recaptured and corrected, and those who harbored them punished. Roads had to be constructed. Commissioners were appointed to see that these were properly run, so as to serve the great number of planters living on their estates in the winter and visiting town in summer. There were bridges to be built and ferries to be established. All these matters had to be looked after. All took time and money.

The town required many officials, and these in turn required clerks and helpers. Fat fees went with certain offices. Very early in the history of the City it was found needful to investigate this matter of government-fees. As the offices multiplied the fees increased. It became expensive to get things done according to law. The investigations finally reached into the offices of the "Clerk of the Peace, The Crown Coroner and the Clerk of the Parliament". Taxes were placed on all goods arriving and departing. Life became quite complicated.

One of the first laws passed in Carolina was to enforce the keeping of the Lord's day and to suppress idle, drunken and swearing persons. This may seem to reflect upon the inhabitants of Charleston, but the Spaniards had always had the run of St. George's Bay and no doubt people of Spanish sympathies still visited these waters. Moreover the renegade Brian Fitzpatrick had long ago formed a precedent by skipping off to the Spanish settlements near St. Augustine and giving information about the colony, since which time there had been a constant passage of those who had legitimate business and those who came to Carolina to induce the slaves to desert to the Spanish colors. St. Helena, by Port Royal, had been abandoned, but other missions operated and there were four in existence. Spain and England made a treaty recognizing occupation as the basis of ownership, but much of the territory remained debatable land. In 1696, Arthur Middleton as President of the Legislative Council attended a meeting of Governors to pass upon the question of ownership. He declared that Carolina had a right to erect a fort at the forks of the Altamaha river, as the territory was within the bounds of lands originally granted to the Proprietors and that Spain held no title to the spot, thus adhering to the geographical confines of the old Heath claim. Charleston was never quite free from the fear of Spanish attack, prowling Indians and slave insurrections. The local negroes were sometimes described as "playing rough at unreasonable hours," and were "caballing, pilfering and stealing", so that without stringent laws, which seemed to reflect upon the habits of the inhabitants and to encroach upon the personal rights of the colonies, this city, which was also a garrison town would have become a rendezvous for all sorts and conditions of men having no regard for the higher requirements of life.

Eleven years after the city was founded an act was passed to regulate trade, in which liquor was recognized as a leading import, with skins and furs as exports. Rum and gunpowder were important articles of traffic. The gunpowder was used in defense of the colony and the liquor was used in the Indian trade, although from numerous acts, regulating taverns and punch houses, it would appear that a fair amount was consumed in the town.

Many of the "bridges" referred to in the old laws were really nothing but wharves erected on land belonging to some of the first rich men of the colony. The South Carolina Historical and Genealogical Magazine publishes the reproduction of an early plan of Charleston. This valuable document was rescued from destruction by General Wilmot DeSaussure, and has been used to illustrate some articles dealing with the early history of Charleston written by the late Judge H. A. M. Smith. Inspection of this plan furnishes a valuable outline of the contour of the city and the number of lots it contained. Judge Smith's articles furnish a detailed and historically correct account of almost every foot of land now embraced in that portion of Charleston which comprised the first little walled city, set in the wilderness, on the banks of the Cooper river.

When the town was laid out, spaces were left for government offices, for a town hall, and for certain wharves and a church. The first Episcopal Church built in the colony was erected in Charlestown by the Established Church. It dates from the year 1681 old style, or 1682 new style, but little is known of the structure which occupied the position now held by St. Michael's beyond the fact that it was called the "English Church," and that the building was "large and stately", was constructed of black cypress, rested upon a brick foundation, and soon had a neat white fence around the yard.

At first the streets were described as the "Little Street that runneth by so-and-so's house," or "The Great Street that runs by the Market place," or "Leadeth to the River." Presently names emerged. The first male child born in the colony gave the name for Tradd street. William Elliott gave the Ana-Baptists a church yard and furnished the name for a street, famous in its day, now called "the Creek" by the negroes who live in its strange and interesting houses. Bedon's Alley was opened, and "Cooper" gave way to Broad street. Early acts for paving sidewalks with oyster shells, in 1698, locate streets "extending from Captain Risby's store house, fronting the harbor where Mary Cross lately lived, and from Hookley's to Tradd's house": both sides of the street from Garrett's house to Captain William Rhett's, Callyboff's Lane, and the Church, are mentioned.

In 1701, twenty feet on either side of the Half Moon was appropriated for two public landing-places. This was at the eastern end of the present Broad street. Public wharves where the people from the country came and landed free of charge gave the name to Dock street, now swallowed up in Queen, and a little street just inside the northern wall of the town quaintly called Amen Street is lost in the Cumberland street of today, which itself grew out of Moore's street of olden days, a portion of which still exists in Horlbeck's Alley.

The Council wrestled as best it might with local problems. Charlestown was the capital of the colony and had no municipal body corresponding to a Town Council. Charlestown made laws for the whole colony, aided by a distant board of managers. In this fact lies much of the puzzling tendency to centralize government which permeates the history of Carolina. As the colony grew, Charlestown enacted regulations for itself and the whole settlement. When the town was very young people were required to clear the streets in front of their own houses, grub up the young trees and keep the spaces in front of their small enclosures clear of weeds. No animals were allowed to roam the town.

Swine and goats running at large were "cried" at four different designated localities. If nobody claimed the animal
after its earmarks had been announced by beat of drum, the
person who had fetched it in became its new owner. There
were no local police. The town operated under constables.
In order to get watchmen to patrol the ramparts and streets
of the little city, constables had to summon six persons every
night, who served from ten until a half hour before sun-
rise. Everybody, rich or poor, high or low, had to serve or
provide a substitute. An able man must have a "well fixed"
gun, charged with powder and balls, as part of his equip-
ment. Human nature being always the same the poor complained to the Governor that they were more often called
upon to stand watch than the rich people. The complaint
was investigated. Any constable who extended favors or sat
too long in somebody's warm comfortable house was fined
two shillings and six pence. It soon became apparent that
a watch-house was needed.

Fires have always plagued Charleston. There have been
frequent conflagrations, which have virtually wiped out certain sections. Soon after the city was laid out the fire hazard
became so great that inhabitants were forbidden to build
houses with "wooden chimneys," and were made to keep
their chimneys well swept, just as English towns did. Until
recent years, Charleston houses were regularly visited by
black boys called "Roo-Roos," who for a few cents edged
their way up through the flues of the chimneys of the large
houses to sweep out the soot, just like the little people told
about in Kingsley's "Water Babies."

Early householders were required to keep as many buckets of water in the halls as there were rooms. Ladders
and fire-hooks had to be kept in some convenient place.
The town provided six ladders of various sizes, six fire-
hooks, and fifty leather buckets for "fire quenchings." All
sailors in the city were compelled to serve as volunteer
firemen, and any tavern-keeper who failed to turn mariners
out to fight fires was subject to stiff penalties. Fire masters
had the right to blow up buildings in the path of fires if this

became necessary to stop the flames. The cost of the buildings so destroyed was pro-rated and charged off against all property-owners in the town.

Men finding that they could secure tracts of land by bringing out additional settlers, imported large numbers of white indentured servants, who came, served their time and then received their apportionment of free land. Social lines, as always, were drawn and distinctions were made against those who came out as servants. The English caste system naturally obtained here. Those in trade were looked down upon until some of the great owners of estates took to trade, became merchant princes, were greatly esteemed, lived in fine brick residences, furnished their homes with family belongings brought over from England, and lived so nobly in their houses and gave such entertainments to strangers and all who came to visit that the early inn-keepers complained that their business was ruined by the hospitality of Carolinians.

Politics engaged the leisure moments of these wealthy traders who gathered together around the government offices or at the "Corner," to exchange news or to publish prices of various commodities. The government offices housed various commissioners, who looked after the welfare of the town and of the colony. They had the right to impress laborers and paid bricklayers, carpenters and craftsmen five shillings a day. The negroes received two and one-half Royals and the master provided the victuals and "found" the lime used in the walls along the sea front and in the defenses of the city.

Wherever the merchants congregated a discussion of what was being raised in the colony, the prices they would bring, and the things which were exported were discussed. Sugar, rum, molasses, chocolate, coconuts, slaves and money were imported from the West Indies, in exchange for meats, candles, soap, rice, and tar. Although silk was listed among the Carolina products and though Sir Nathaniel Johnson called his plantation Silk Hope and Mulberry Castle obtained its name from trees planted around the house, it never became a staple, and the inhabitants worked up silk into druggets mixed with wool, which formed an excellent wear for the country.

No effort was ever made to capitalize the fine fruits which grew in this country. Charlestown could have done a good business in exporting fruit in some of the vessels which sailed from this port. To be exact, seventeen vessels loaded here in 1706 for the foreign trade, beside several stragglers and other coastwise vessels. In 1710 regular sailings included twenty-two ships bound for England and sixty for other countries. Carolina imports amounted to £120,000 sterling, by the year 1723. One hundred thousand of this was credited to England. The wealthy traders of Charlestown built wharves in front of their houses and over these a stream of exports and imports continuously passed. The passage along the eastern part of town was called the Bay, and was the center, then as now, of the shipping trade. The only other street of any importance, stretching north and south, was Church street, which received its name from various houses of worship. Some of the old land titles are quite confusing because the deeds continually refer to old or new Church street. When the White Meeting House was built New Church Street became known as Meeting House Street. It is now Meeting Street.

The Huguenots arrived in 1680, and those who did not go out into the wilderness and settle built a church for themselves on Church street. The Quaker Meeting was on the far side of the draw-bridge, near "Holly Bush", the English Church, called by the distinctive name of St. Philip's, was just about opposite to the first market and the town gate. The most distant house outside of town was that of the minister, the site of which was donated by Affra Comings to St. Philip's Church. Her gift may be located by the present streets of St. Philip, Coming and Glebe.

Under the Fundamental Constitution the Church of England was the "Established Church". Other denominations, as such, could not hold property in the denominational name, hence the land for such churches had to be taken in the name of some member of the congregation. Charlestown soon presented the anachronism of a political center dominated by a religious hierarchy operating in an agricultural country. This condition produced a sense of unreality and made for disturbance and constant upheavals.

High and low, rich and poor, were required by law to observe the Sabbath day and contribute to the salary of the minister of the Church of England, and to conform to certain observances. Imagine the feelings of the Protestants and Dissenters who had left England to escape these identical demands: revolt against these laws was a foregone conclusion. Political prestige to be secured through passive resistance became the goal of those who were not members of the Church of England.

The Church of England being the established form of worship, validity of marriages performed among French inhabitants was sometimes attacked. Feeling ran high on the subject and a Huguenot registered a notice to say that "If any person or persons be any waies scrupulous concerning ye: Lawfulness of ye Marriage betwixt Mr.: Isaac Mazicq, and Mrs. Marianne Le Sarrurier, These are therefore to certifye that they were lawfully married upon ye fourteenth day of October in ye yeare of our Lord One Thousand Six Hundred Ninety. I say that they were then Lawfully married by me, Attkin Williamson, Minister of Ye: Gospell and Recorded ye: 17th October, 1693, by me Jno. Hamilton, Depty, Sec'ty."

Pastor Elias Prioleau simply presented a certificate of citizenship secured in London for himself, his wife and children, which he then had placed on record in the office of the Secretary of State.

Inside the Huguenot church, which still uses the original liturgy and chants, called by a ribald writer of olden times "Geneva Jigs," there may be seen a curious Carolina souvenir —a coffin-plate of Governor Glenn attached to a mural tablet.

In 1682, Morton, who was to become a Governor of the colony, came to Charlestown and brought with him many dissenting Scotch folk: there were a few members of the

Roman Catholic Church in the city: there were a few persons of Jewish descent: the Government Church was the English Church. All of these groups had held differing opinions in the old country. Many of them had left Europe in search of religious freedom. They differed in customs, habits, thoughts, feelings and politics. It is not to be wondered at that the early days of Charleston were exciting and sometimes turbulent. Differences had to be adjusted, social codes revised: Locke's great instrument was inadequate to the task of adjustment, and the Proprietors were still resentful of the fact that Carolina preferred cattle-grazing to agriculture, even though they profited by the money made in the flourishing colony.

Thrust together on a narrow peninsula, continually beset by Indians, threatened by Spaniards and fearful of the slaves, the majority of the colonists adjusted themselves to the unformulated democracy of the situation, submitted to their betters, formed a cohesive society and functioned under social codes and religious ideas which developed with the settlement, embraced ideas new to themselves and settled to their task of building up the colony. Besides which—the old order was changing in England, and Charlestown reflected in miniature those changes which were taking place in London, from whence they took their fashions, favors, laws—and life.

Chapter III

NOW followed the fateful years in English history when Charles II died and Catholic James came to the throne. Monmouth attempted an uprising in England. His attempt failed as did the Scottish uprising. Both rebellions were suppressed: vindictive measures were employed against those who took part. England was experiencing a religious persecution. Carolina politics mirrored the troubled state of England. When the "non-conformist" laws were strictly enforced against Dissenters and Scotch covenanters in England, the acts which caused the English Church to "sit down with sorrow in dust and ashes," did not in the least alter the Church's loyalty to the tenet that James was the legal successor to the throne.

This period of English history is entwined with the fortunes of the Church and with the political acts of those who sought to place William of Orange and his wife, Mary, upon the throne of England. William arrived in England and in November 1688 James fled to France; the revolution was accomplished without bloodshed. The church kept the golden mean between old forms and new innovations. James' daughter, Anne, joined the insurgents, allied herself with William of Orange and his wife, Mary, her aunt. They were childless, and England desired to have a Protestant ruler. Anne eventually became Queen of England and bravely fought the claims of her brother, the Pretender. The history of the Jacobites had its interesting sequel in the story of Charleston. Several "Goose Creek men" were supposedly in sympathy with the movement.

Persecutions raged in Scotland. In 1682-3 Lord Henry Cardross desired to secure an asylum in Carolina for his countrymen, and succeeded in having the fundamental constitution of Carolina altered to meet the views of Nonconformists. The Proprietors made every concession. They expected ten thousand colonists for the new settlement of

36,000 acres at Port Royal, which was to be independent of Charlestown. The Scots failed to realize that Port Royal was the place fought for by Spain.

In addition to these volunteer exiles from Scotland fleeing from anticipated persecutions, many political prisoners were being banished and sent to America where they were condemned to servitude. Great cruelty was inflicted on these unfortunates, who were kept below deck, forbidden to hold religious services and deprived of necessaries of life on their voyage across the Atlantic. Their treatment illustrates the general insecurity of life and liberty of the times. A great number of these prisoners died soon after they arrived at Charlestown.

Cardross' claim to equal power with the Governor of Carolina roused intense jealousy. Called before the authorities at Charlestown to answer charges of usurping power in the Province, he forbore to press the point that his authority came from the Proprietors themselves, and the same stand was taken by the Dunlops when with Hamilton and Montgomerie they came to the Governor and Council in Charlestown to ask for aid against Indians and Spaniards. They said that all in the colony were under the same King and Lords Proprietors, and that it was against the interest of either to allow jealousies to prevail when a Spanish invasion was feared. They then gave information about the "sinistrous dealings" of two noted Indians, Wina and Antonio, who were not only "entertaining" a Spanish spy, instigating other tribes to hostilities amongst themselves and against the Scots, but were also in communication with that mysterious person, dramatically called "The Friar."

But, so bitter was the feeling against Cardross and so occupied were the minds of the Council with politics, that the warning fell upon deaf ears. The appeal for arms and ammunition was so indifferently received that five dismounted guns, lying useless at Old Town, were only sent to Cardross when the order was issued by the Lords Proprietors.

Some of the Scots had settled at the mouth of the North Edisto river. In the summer of 1686 the Spaniards came suddenly in three galleys containing a hundred white men, re-inforced by Indians and negroes. They landed at Edisto, sacked the house of Mr. Grimball, the Secretary of the Province, murdered the brother-in-law of Governor Morton, pillaged the houses of both men and carried off three thousand pounds in money and thirteen slaves.

Then, turning upon the feeble Scotch settlement at Port Royal, which could muster but twenty-five able-bodied men, the Spaniards killed some of these, captured and barbarously whipped others and took the remainder into captivity, destroying the settlement. A few of the Scots managed to escape from Stuart Town and made a perilous voyage through the inland passages to Charlestown, where their wretched plight and terrible stories of the fate which had befallen their people served to warn Charlestown of what to expect.

The failure of the attempted settlement at Stuart Town forced military preparedness on this city, and forged an important link in her military history when the settlement which had acted as a buffer between the Spaniards at St. Augustine and the English at Charlestown was destroyed and Carolina was left to face the Spaniards alone.

Immediate action followed. Men were levied and armed. Provisions were made for the defense of the colony. No expense was spared and Governor Morton assessed the inhabitants £500 with which to fit out two vessels and enlist four hundred men, preparatory to an immediate invasion of Spanish territory. For the moment, in the face of the common enemy, all factional contention ceased at Charlestown and party strife was forgotten; but just as preparations were complete and the expedition was ready to sail, James Colleton arrived in Charlestown to be Governor of Carolina in 1686. He had been created a Landgrave, was now made Governor, and began his rule by threatening to hang any of the colonists who persisted in the project to proceed against the Spaniards at St. Augustine.

Cardross had previously returned to his native land and apparently exculpated Governor Morton from blame, placing the responsibility upon members of the Council and particularly upon Secretary Grimball.

Between the period marked by the murder of the Scots and the coming of Colleton a significant episode occurred in the political and commercial history of the town, when an armed vessel came into the Ashley, pretending to have been trading with Spaniards. Robert Quary, Secretary of the Province (and acting Governor) reported to the Proprietors that he had received information that the vessel was piratical, and as such he prohibited it from landing or selling any goods here. Quary slung a quantity of mud at several high officials by his insinuations, but managed, it is said, to make money for himself when he held the vessel for the Proprietors and confiscated the cargo.

By the time that Joseph Morton was made governor for the second time, 1685, Charlestown was fairly well settled, privateers had begun to be quite troublesome. Morton's term was turbulent and political unrest pervaded the colony. Laws suitable to court life in London did not work well in a wilderness. Dissenters looked with disfavor upon the privileges granted to members of the Established Church, who held all the rich salaried positions.

The sober and religious Morton held office only a short time, but during that brief term differences between two parties, already forming in the colony, now became serious and pronounced. One party supported the Proprietors, the other sought to defend the political liberties of the colonists. One party relied upon the Fundamental Constitutions and the Governor's instructions, the other vested its rights in the Charter. In 1682 Carolina was divided into the three Counties of Berkeley, Craven and Colleton. Huguenots, Baptists, Quakers, all came to the Province. Political troubles multiplied with different sects. As new counties were formed voting conditions altered and confusion prevailed. Between 1682 and 1686, or Morton's first and West's last administrations, five governors went in and out. Colleton's coming marked a crisis.

While the colonists burned with indignation at the termination of their efforts to punish the Spaniards, the Proprietors, in an effort to avoid a quarrel with Spain, wrote to Colleton that they were glad that he had stopped the expedition against St. Augustine and that if it had proceeded, Mr. Morton, Colonel Godfrey and others might have answered it with their lives. They justified the Spanish raids, and commenting on the Quary episode, declared that every rational man must have foreseen that the Spaniards believing that pirates were harboring in Charlestown would, assuredly, retaliate.

The colonists replied that the Proprietors seem to have forgotten that the Earl of Craven had written to the Board of Trade in London denying that Carolina harbored pirates and that the attack was made solely because Spain claimed the land upon which Cardross had settled his colony.

Between the upper and nether millstone the bewildered colonists took refuge in the law of self-defense and prepared to defend themselves against the Spaniards. Their chartered rights gave them authority to allow captains (or other officers) to levy, muster and train up all sorts of men of whatsoever condition, or wheresoever born, "and by God's assistance to make war, vanquish, take prisoners and put to death enemies striking at the isolated colony."

When the Proprietors ordered a "civil letter" to be addressed to the Governor of St. Augustine, Colleton gave fresh offense to Carolinians and aroused suspicion as to his loyalty when he entered upon a treaty of commerce with "The Friar", the Spanish agent. The colonists' complaint was that Colleton was acting "contrary to the honor of the English nation, and for a little filthy lucre had buried in silence, atrocities upon Englishmen who wanted not courage to do themselves honorable satisfaction."

When the Spaniards had heard that the Carolinians had set out to avenge their countrymen, they had left their town and castle and fled into the woods to save themselves, but when the expedition against St. Augustine was stopped, the conflict was but postponed for the time being and was renewed during the rupture between England and Spain. But, whereas the first venture might have succeeded, "when the issue finally reached the test of arms, Carolina so far from being victorious presented a spectacle of unpreparedness and precipitated upon herself a long period of strife."

Endless quarrels marked Governor Colleton's term of office. He strove to collect quit rents due the Proprietors, and when he failed he summoned the militia companies and proclaimed martial law in the colony. The action aroused great indignation and the governor was denounced as a tyrant, but as he allowed the law courts to meet as usual and was mild in enforcing military discipline, his act produced few bad results. Colleton said that he feared an invasion by the Spaniards and did not want the militia out of the country and so had brought them together.

Colleton was banished after four years of misrule, and was forbidden to bear or exercise any authority, either military or civil, within the Province.

Charlestown was to experience a new phase of turbulence with the coming of Governor Seth Sothell who had been deposed and banished from Albemarle. He arrived in Charlestown, and himself a refugee from North Carolina became in South Carolina the expeller of others, in 1690.

Colleton's friends, including Colonel Bull, Major Colleton, Paul Grimball and Thomas Smith, opposed Sothell's claims. But as supporters of the Constitution they could not deny that Sothell, who had purchased Lord Clarendon's share, had a right to succeed Colleton. They demanded that before Sothell could assume office he must declare his approval of the Proprietors' instructions as a rule of government.

Colonial Charlestown was posted with placards charging Sothell with treason, and handbills calling upon the people of the city to withhold their obedience to his authority were distributed. The Proprietors had not heard of Sothell's assumption of government and appointed Thomas Smith as Governor, but hearing that Sothell was at Charlestown and had taken authority, wrote that they were sure that he would submit to their instructions for the government, hoped that he was too wise a man to claim power from any other source, and left him in office.

However much of a villain he was, Sothell was a shrewd politician who recognized the value of Protestant votes and tried to bestow political power upon this element of the population. He indemnified officers who carried out orders of Parliament against damage suits and to put an end to malicious gossip he punished persons who "divulged" reports against those in authority and thereby disturbed the peace. But he, too, passed into the discard and retired to North Carolina, where, in 1694, he died stripped of power and possessions. Sir Philip Ludwell, who had married Dame Berkeley and thus become a pseudo Proprietor, became Governor of Carolina. He examined into the crimes, abuses, exactions, trespasses and complaints left over from Sothell's time. Paul Grimball lodged a complaint to collect damage he sustained when suspended from office, Sothell's "creatures" took away the records belonging to his office of the Secretary, and at the same time forcibly entered his room in the Town Marshal's house, opened his box, rifled his goods, and carried off a letter-case full of private documents which had been opened and read in the presence of Captain Quarry, and Mr. Izard. Thomas Smith, called "Englishman and Landgrave," to differentiate him from a person of the same name, became Governor after Sir Philip Ludwell. He founded the numerous Smith family of Charleston, and was said to be a person of "singular merit and serviceable" because of great prudence and industry, but his talents were of no avail in coping with questions of State. He was of the dissenting Church and found the perpetual political struggle a weariness to the flesh. His house on East Bay near Longitude Lane was destroyed by fire after 1861, it is said.

Governor Smith, appealing to the Proprietors for suggestions as to how to quiet the colony, suggested that one of them should come out to see for himself the condition of affairs and bring with him full authority to act in the pacification of the people and the settlement of the affairs of the Province. His appeal was received. It was hoped to induce the third Lord Shaftesbury to go to Carolina, but he was just entering public life in England and arranging his father's affairs. He declined, and Archdale, described as "being in the nature of a Proprietor," having purchased for his son the share held by Lady Berkeley, (widow of fiery Sir William), made a journey to America and, clothed in questionable authority, became Governor at Charlestown. Lady Berkeley's share had been used by Ludwell before, and was later to appear again in Charlestown politics.

Archdale, a Quaker, is described as a "vain, amiable, quick-tempered man, of some cleverness for business, but lacking either the political sagacity or ability of some of his predecessors." He strove to follow instructions that were given to previous governors and, arriving nearly a year after his appointment, spent the first month endeavoring to allay "the heats" of the people and quiet the great confusion in civic affairs. He called an Assembly and appealed to the "serious and rational observation of the people to cease their strife."

Archdale finished his term and "departed" the colony after receiving profuse thanks for his prudent, industrious, indefatigable care and management of the powers which the Lords Proprietors had entrusted to him. But in two matters he was governed by local opinions. He left the political conditions of the Huguenots and the Indian Trade pretty much as he had found them.

Archdale was the first prohibition governor of Charlestown. While he was in office, beer, cider, wine, brandy, rum, punch or any strong drink whatsoever, under the quantity of one gallon at one draught, could be sold only by obtaining a license from the Governor. Archdale put the laws of England concerning the abuses and disorders of taverns in force in Charlestown. The city is indebted to him for a few years of peace. To his numerous accomplishments Archdale added that of a writer and issued in 1708 a "Description of Carolina."

Joseph Blake, his friend, and appointee, succeeded Archdale and fell heir to a great many vexed questions which broke out between the Proprietors and the colonists. A codicil to Thomas Smith's will had given Blake all the baronies, lands, privileges and dignities belonging to Smith's patent as Landgrave. Blake, who was the son of Benjamin, the immigrant who had come out with Axtell and Morton, was a general favorite in the colony. He is remembered for his just dealings with those who were not of the Church of England.

The Huguenots were not the only aliens. Lands were given to Jean François Gignilliat, the first of the Swiss nation to settle in Carolina, and a quantity of land was granted to Seigneur de Wernhaut. Liberty of conscience and full rights of citizenship had been promised to all who should come to Carolina. However, everyone in Carolina was taxed for the support of the Church of England—and country people complained that ministers in the city lived in idle luxury while they toiled for a living. After members of the Congregational Church of Dorchester, Massachusetts, arrived in 1695 and settled on the Ashley River, from whence they removed to Medway, Georgia, sixty years later, no considerable body of settlers came to Carolina.

In 1704, when the colony was subdivided into Parishes, Charlestown and Charlestown Neck constituted the Parish of St. Philip's until the town was divided into two parishes in 1751, when all the land south of the middle of Broad street was formed into the Parish of St. Michael's, and its church was built upon the spot on which the old St. Philip's had stood.

Other religious bodies were established in Charlestown within the first twenty years of her civic life. A historic sketch of the "Old White Meeting", afterwards known as the Circular Church, would cover a period of about two hundred and fifty years and would be interwoven with a history of the First Presbyterian or Scotch Church, which was established in 1731, and might possibly be stretched to include the story of the Second Independent or Congregationalist, afterwards the Unitarian Church, established 1772. All of these churches grew from a church, established or "constituted" by Presbyterians, Congregationalists and a few of the French Protestant refugees, but identified in history as the "Congregationalist Church." Original records were destroyed by a hurricane in 1713, but ancient documents indicate that it was founded at as early a date as St. Philip's, and that one of its pastors was the Rev. Mr. Stobo, said to be an ancestor of President Theodore Roosevelt.

The first building, called "The White Meeting House", was destroyed by fire. The second building, erected in 1729, was reputed to have been used by the British as a hospital during the Revolutionary War. Upon the site a church was erected and dedicated in 1806. Its auditorium became the meeting place of many large and notable gatherings. The cost of the building, with the spire, exceeded a hundred thousand dollars. A portico of six columns surmounted by a pediment formed the western front of the building. It was destroyed by the great fire of 1861. A small brick chapel was then erected on a part of the lot, and there services were held until the present church was built. On account of the numerous fires of unusual severity some of the marble monuments in the churchyard were said to have melted like wax. A few old tombs remain bearing ancient, honorable and distinguished names. The tombstone of Catherine Jour, a Huguenot who came to Charlestown by way of Holland, is found near the church. Some of her descendants possess her "Betrothal Medal", an interesting and unusual family souvenir.

Soloman Legare, founder of a large and distinguished family, worshipped in this church. Among his illustrious descendants is numbered the statesman and writer Honorable Hugh Swinton Legare. Other names there found on old gravestones are Holmes, Simmons, Eveleigh, Perounneau, Mathews, Clelland, Livingston and Vanderhorst. The pastors included Mr. Stobo, Nathan Bassett, Mr. Josiah Smith and a list of others.

After 1731 there were two Presbyterian churches in Charlestown. A disunion of sentiment upon questions of ecclesiastical government caused twelve families to leave the first church and put up another edifice in which they worshipped according to the forms and discipline of the Church of Scotland, under the Rev. Hugh Stewart, of Scotland. Patriarchs of the congregation were James Abercrombie, John Allen, Daniel Crawford, John Bee, John Fraser, James Paine and others. The congregation was much disturbed and scattered during the conflict between England and the colonies. The pastor, Rev. Dr. Hewat, returned to London and Rev. Messrs. Grant, Kennedy, Lorimo and Morrison served.

In 1784 the church was incorporated. Rev. James Graham was its minister till 1788, when he was succeeded by the Rev. James Wilson, from Scotland, whose pastorate was terminated by ill health, after which the Rev. Dr. George Buist, of Edinburgh, came to the church in June. He was succeeded by Dr. Buchan of Edinburgh and in 1812, Rev. Aaron W. Leland, (subsequently a professor of theology at the Theological Seminary of South Carolina) became pastor to the church. During his ministry the tall wooden building adjoining the church to the south was built for a rectory and the present church edifice erected.

David Haig, as chairman of the building committee, advertised in the *City Gazette* of May 3, 1813 for estimates on the proposed church. Rev. John Forrest of Edinburgh succeeded Rev. Arthur Buist. Dr. Wm. S. Plumer served for a brief period, and in 1880 Dr. W. T. Thompson came to the church. This beautiful building was almost completely wrecked by the earthquake of 1886 but is now one of the handsomest auditoriums in the city, and the Rev. Alexander Sprunt, D. D. has been its loved pastor for over thirty years.

One of the characteristics of the churches of Charleston is the feature of mural tablets and in this church there are sixteen. To the right of the front door is one erected to the memory of "Lady Anne Murray" whose remains are in the churchyard. Lady Anne was the third daughter of George, Earl of Cromarty. She was a young noblewoman conspicuous for piety and virtue, for high birth and illustrious descent, and died the 17th day of January, 1768. The body of her husband, George Murray, Esq., Deputy Secretary of South

Carolina, a gentleman of rigid honesty and inflexible integrity, who died on the 24th of September, 1772, is nearby.

The first person buried in the Scotch Presbyterian churchyard was Sarah Witherspoon who, according to family records, came to America with three brothers in 1734. The Baptist people figured largely in the young colony. The present church dates from 1820, although the congregation was among the first to be "organized" in Charleston. The wife of Governor Blake was a member of the Baptist Church but gave liberally to the adornment of the Episcopal Church.

When the English colonists settled Carolina, pirates had visited the territory at their pleasure and had used the harbor of St. George's Bay. Suspicions of governmental connivance with those people and the suspected connection with smugglers attainted the purity of those in authority. The question became a great issue in the controversies which followed the coming of Colleton, continued during Archdale's time and persisted to 1719.

Collector of the King's Customs in America, Randolph wrote that navigation acts were neglected in Charlestown and favor shown to pirates, and not only in Carolina but in all the colonies, and proposed that all the English possessions on this continent should be consolidated and put under his Majesty's immediate control. He said that resistance to navigation laws would end in independence. While his agitation of these matters did not succeed they did cause a reënactment of navigation laws in such a stringent form that the colony finally resisted the rule of the Proprietors.

Randolph also said that "the Bahama Islands, of which Nicholas Trott was governor, was a retreat for pirates and that Charlestown was free for trade in all places", a euphonious way of saying that Charlestown evaded paying her duties to the Lords Proprietors.

Randolph gave the example of a vessel from Jamaica which had been captured by seventy pirates and brought to Charlestown when Archdale was in office. He said that a vast quantity of "Gold from the Red Sea" had been aboard and although the vessel was seized by the Governor for the

Proprietors, as a wreck, and so sold, yet no regard was had for the acts of trade, and the pirates who had been aboard her were "entertained in Charlestown and had liberty to stay or go to any other place as they pleased."

A Court of Admiralty was established in Charlestown. Ex-Governor Joseph Morton was made Judge, ex-Governor Archdale's son-in-law, Thomas Cary, Register, and Jonathan Amory, Speaker of the Commons, became the Advocate and R. Pollinger, the Marshal. The Governor was now required to give bond for a faithful performance of the navigation acts.

Thus far justice had functioned under the efforts of a person who combined the offices of Judge and Sheriff. There had been no prosecuting officer. Charlestown was now presented with Nicholas Trott, ex-Governor of the Bahamas, as an Attorney General, who held in addition the position of Naval Officer and Advocate General of Admiralty. Edward Bohun, an Englishman of learning, entitled by birth to be called a Cavalier, bred a Dissenter, a Justice of the Peace in England and not a lawyer, was commissioned Chief Justice of the Colony of Carolina. The people objected to Trott holding so many offices, and numerous letters now passed continuously between the colonists, the Proprietors and the officers of the Crown. A letter of 1699 tells of the general state of feeling. The Proprietors said that they were sorry that "the sincere love and hearty care they had for their colony should produce no better effect" in Carolina and wondered that the colonists could not see the benefit that would always accrue "to them and their posterity through a judge who did not depend on the will and pleasure of a Governor."

They wrote to Judge Bohun recommending him not to show too great a love for money, "which is not beautiful in any man, much worse becoming a judge," and advised him against showing passion or making complaint and told him to gain the love of the colonists by actions of justice and prudence. Other letters show that their Lordships flourished truism in the faces of these colonial officers who were trying to subdue nature, fight Indians and Spaniards, settle lands, adjust religious and political differences, develop trade and provide revenue to the Proprietors at one and the same time.

Bohun's liberal influence was soon felt in the colony. He assisted Governor Blake in seeing that the colonists secured their rights, saying, "It is hardly to be imagined that men will labour and run great hazards to get an estate if they have not some assurance of being protected by the laws."

Death and disaster soon put a period to all these discussions. A great fire in 1698 nearly consumed the town. Smallpox afflicted the colony. Yellow fever followed and caused the death of at least one hundred and sixty persons, including many members of the Assembly, Receiver-General Ely, Public Treasurer Amory, Edward Rawlins and Chief Justice Bohun, along with many merchants and householders of the city. Even the Reverend Mr. Marshall was taken away by the distemper. As if these afflictions were not enough the city experienced a dreadful hurricane in the autumn of 1699 which threatened to destroy what was left of the town. The tide rose to the second stories of the houses and destruction seemed inevitable.

The superstitious saw in the destruction of the vessel "Rising Sun", whose Captain was James Gibson, a retribution upon him for his cruel conduct toward the poor Scotch prisoners whom he transported to Carolina in 1684. The sole survivors were Reverend Archibald Stobo, who was called to the Pastorate of the White Meeting House, and his wife.

The newly arrived Attorney General, Nicholas Trott, had been spared by the fever, and the greatly diminished inhabitants, finding so many of the Assembly dead and so many political offices vacant, turned to this experienced man for help and direction and thus played into the hands of one who was said at heart to favor the cause of the Crown above the interest of the Proprietors.

Matters mended in the colony, as nature, seeming to repent for having inflicted these punishments upon it, produced such an abundant rice crop that the planters raised more than they could find boats for its export. An enumera-

tion showed nearly 6,000 whites in the Colony. Meetings of
the Assembly were held, and soon the pageant of colonial
life was in full swing again as Landgraves and Governors
and Chief Justices and Admirals, and ministers and officials
and wealthy planters and merchant princes held sway and
pursued their pleasures within the confines of their brick
houses built behind high garden walls. Such had been the
increase since the Province had been divided in 1682 into the
counties of Craven to the north, Colleton to the south, and
Berkeley in the center. Then, population amounted to about
two thousand, five hundred persons, living as far North as
Santee and as far South as New London on the banks of the
Edisto. Now, the Church of England was the State church,
and Charles Town was the seat of government, and official
residence of all officers and dignitaries of the Colony. The
population of the city in 1700, according to McCrady, was
about 3,000 whites composed of 250 families. Carolina was
no longer the home of indigent emigrants struggling for
subsistence.

CHAPTER IV

CHARLESTOWN had five governors between 1696 and
1710; Joseph Blake, James Moore, Nathaniel Johnson, Edward Tynte, and Robert Gibbes. The principal events
during this period were the sending of an expedition against
St. Augustine, and the defense of the colony against a combined attack by the French and Spaniards.

When the liberal Joseph Blake died, James Moore, a
brave, bold, penniless, resourceful son of Roger Moore, who
had appeared in the colony several years before, and had
made a trip across the mountains in 1691 to look for gold,
was made Governor. Twenty-eight Indian tribes in Carolina,
incited, no doubt, by the Spaniards began to be troublesome.
War, which involved France, broke out between Great
Britain and Spain. Known as the War of the Spanish Succession, it was called in Charlestown, "Queen Anne's War."
During this the colony decided to strike Spain by attacking
St. Augustine, and raised an army and equipped vessels at
a cost of £2,000. The expeditionary forces included five hundred Yemassee allies. Colonel Daniel was sent to make a
land attack, while Governor Moore sailed from Port Royal
with four hundred men to attack by sea. The expedition became known to the Spaniards who sent to Havana for rein-
forcements and retreating to their castle, abandoned St.
Augustine. The expedition was an entire failure. The ships
were a total loss and the colony was left with a debt of six
thousand pounds sterling. Moore was heavily censured and
Colonel Daniel was much praised for his share of the enterprise, Mr. Ash dissenting.

Citizens had contended that payment should have been
provided for the first expedition before another one was
started and a heavy tax proposed. Confusion and strife prevailed, some members withdrew from the Assembly and
broke up the quorum. A riot, lasting four or five days, ensued, during which John Ashe was seized and carried on

board a ship owned by Rhett. Landgrave Smith and others were assaulted "and set upon in the open streets." Landgrave Bellinger, a Justice of the Peace, was struck on the head by Captain Rhett, and a woman, who was standing behind the door listening to what did not concern her was thrown down. Indignation arose against the members of the Assembly who, desiring to carry an election law designed to exclude the French from voting and to prevent payment of just claims arising from the expedition against the Spaniards, dared to thwart the desire of the citizens by breaking up the Council. Governor Moore, treating the complainers with contempt, said the matter was one for a Justice of the Peace to settle and passed from the office of Governor.

Sir Nathaniel Johnson, who had been Governor in the West Indies, was appointed Governor by the Proprietors in 1702. His commission arrived in 1703. He remained in office until 1710. Nicholas Trott was made Chief Justice, Ex-Governor Moore, Attorney General, and Job Howes, Surveyor General. Johnson fortified the town and prepared to defend the Province; Moore, hoping to redeem himself, was allowed to go into the territory northwest of St. Augustine to subdue the Indians and Spaniards. He returned victorious after desperate fighting, during which Francis Plowden, Thomas Dale, Captain John Bellinger, and Captain Fox lost their lives. When Moore brought in his captives they included 1300 free Appalachians, a hundred slaves and ten horses laden with provisions and the church plate of the Cacique of an Indian tribe.

In the years following occurred that political and religious episode during which an attempt was made to exclude dissenters from taking part in the government of the colony. Charlestown had become the stronghold of Toryism. The High Churchmen made an attempt to put into effect in Charlestown the obnoxious Church Act requiring all members of the Assembly to conform to the religious worship of the Church of England and to receive the Sacrament in some public church on the Lord's day. At the time Pompion Hill Chapel, on Cooper river, was the only English church outside the city. All who were elected to office had to come to town to fulfill the requirements of the Church Acts. This interfered with business, as well as religious beliefs.

Church buildings and ministers were scarce. The Reverend Mr. Corbin ministered to the Goose Creek settlements. Reverend Edward Marston, who succeeded Mr. Marshall at St. Philips, made a statement about the bold and saucy attempt to force religion into politics. When a commission was appointed to try ecclesiastical cases under civil law, the Society for the Propagation of the Gospel refused to send out ministers to Carolina until the Church Act should be repealed. This was done by the General Assembly, November 30, 1706.

As the Church of England was declared to be the settled and established church of the Province its ministers were paid out of the provincial treasury. Each clergyman received £25 upon arrival and if elected as rector a salary of £50, from arrival. If not subscribed for, churches, rectories and schools were built out of the tax fund. Perquisites included glebes, houses, slaves and fees.

From the earliest period of settlement Carolina fostered education. In those days the strong were expected to provide for the weak and religion and education went hand in hand. The Society for the Propagation of the Gospel in Foreign Parts sent missionaries to preach and teach in Carolina and to set up schools for the teaching of children. Doctor Bray (the Bishop of London's Commissary for Maryland), aided by the Lords Proprietors and wealthy Colonists, in 1703 formed the nucleus of a public library in Charlestown. The Assembly took the library under control, appointed the minister of the Church of England "ex officio" librarian and created an advisory board to aid him. This effort, however, is not to be confused with the library established by the Charlestown Library Society begun in 1743 by some young gentlemen of the town, who, desiring to import a few books and political pamphlets from England, collected funds with which to start the enterprise, and after some delay obtained a charter. *This* Library became the literary center of the town.

Eventually its books numbered six or seven thousand volumes and included books and pamphlets written by Steele, Swift, Johnson and Burke. During the American Revolution the Library's valuable collections of books and philosophical instruments were destroyed by fire.

Under the Proprietary government the subject of education received considerable attention and prior to 1710 the people of South Carolina conceived and attempted the establishment of a free school. Several legacies, all made under the Established Church, were left for the purpose. In 1711 a so-called free school was established with William Guy, assistant to the Rector of St. Philip's, as its head.

Other schools were started in the Colony. Grammar and other "arts and sciences, and useful learning along with the principles of the Christian religion" were taught. Several people gave sums of money to the free school, governed by the Governor and fifteen persons who had power to prescribe rules, elect a master whose religion was according to the Church of England, who should teach Latin and Greek and useful parts of mathematics. John Douglass was made head master at a salary of £100. He was also allowed a house and an usher and a writing master to teach writing, arithmetic and merchant's accounts, the arts of navigation, and surveying.

Schoolmasters who settled in a country parish were appointed by the vestry and received their salaries from the public treasury, and each parish was allowed £12 towards erecting a schoolhouse. The Acts are proofs of the enlightened and liberal spirit of the people who settled and governed Carolina.

The grave of Mr. John Lambert, master, principal and teacher of an early Charlestown school is found in St. Philip's churchyard. The schools of Carolina include those of Charlestown, Beresford Bounty at St. Thomas in 1721, and those established at St. Paul's Parish in 1728, the Dorchester School of 1734 and Childsbury, 1733, so that in 1734 with a population of only 7,333 persons the colony possessed six free schools. To these were, later, added those charitable and educational establishments sponsored by the South Carolina Society in 1737; the Winyah Indigo Society in 1756; the Fellowship Society in 1769, the St. Andrew's; the Beaufort Grammar School and the school between the Broad and Saluda rivers in 1767. A complete roster of the noted educational establishments would include all of these schools and that of the Salem Society, the Bullock Creek, and the Waxaws School at Lancaster, besides private institutions.

The question has been asked, "What has Charlestown done to educate her large slave population and redeem native Africans from ignorance and superstition?" The high type of colored person who lives in this city is the living answer to that question. Efforts made to Christianize slaves began early in the history of Charlestown, when religious instruction was given to the numerous slaves in the colony. The records of the Society of the Propagation of the Gospel state that in the parish of Goose Creek twenty negro slaves came regularly to church and several others were able to speak and read the English language. Among the thousands of negro slaves in the province, many were well disposed toward Christianity and were willing to learn to read in time which they redeemed by extra labor.

The Society says that in 1752 a flourishing negro school was taught in Charlestown by a negro who worked under the inspection and direction of the Society official, and many negroes were taught the Christian culture. It was considered that to be baptized was inconsistent with a state of slavery. To obviate this difficulty, South Carolina passed an Act declaring it lawful for any negro to receive and profess the Christian faith and to be baptized, but that they did not thereby become freemen.

The Rev. Mr. Taylor, in 1713, examined a number of negroes in St. Andrew's Parish, who received instruction through Mrs. Haig and Mrs. Edwards. Rev. Mr. Garden had a schoolhouse for negroes built in Charlestown and for twenty-one years a number of children, varying from thirty to sixty, in number, with sometimes as many as fifteen adults, were instructed there. Other schools were organized and churches erected for the colored population, and their religious instruction became a matter of great consideration with all the Christian denominations.

Many slaves were apprenticed to the useful trades and formed a vast proportion of the mechanics and artisans of the colony. Almost every planter of large means had his own carpenters, masons and blacksmiths. Cabinet makers, butchers, tailors, porters, hotel waiters, sempstresses and laundresses, and pastry cooks, trained nurses and midwives were taken to a great extent from the colored population. Many of these were permitted to hire their own time and thus accumulated sums of money. A few "free persons of color" themselves owned slaves.

Yellow fever broke out in 1706. Five or six deaths a day was not an uncommon thing. Among those who died were ex-Governor Moore and the first missionary to the colony, the Reverend Samuel Thomas (progenitor of the present Bishop Thomas of lower South Carolina). During this year, the Province was divided into ten parishes, and it was proposed to erect a church in each. Charlestown, as usual, was taking its complexion from England, where St. Paul's cornerstone was laid in 1675 and the top stone affixed in 1710 to Sir Christopher Wren's masterpiece. St. Mary of the Strand, and St. Martin's in the Fields were also built in London at this time. St. Michael's Church has been compared to both of these buildings.

If the colony labored under the handicap of a State religion, it certainly experienced the cohesive benefits of an Established Church. A list of colonial parishes and churches with dates of their foundation show St. Philip's established in 1704 as the mother parish, followed by St. James' Parish, Santee, St. Andrew's Parish, Christ Church Parish near Mt. Pleasant, St. James' Goose Creek Parish, St. John's Parish in Berkeley County and St. Thomas' and St. Dennis' Parishes, in 1706. St. Helena's, Beaufort, and Prince George's Georgetown Parish, Winyah were established in 1712; St. John's of John's Island and Prince Frederick's, Pee Dee Parish, were established in 1734; Prince William's Parish, in 1745; St.

ST. JAMES', GOOSE CREEK
Erected about 1704-1707

THE INTERIOR OF ST. PHILIP'S CHURCH.

Michael's in 1751, St. Mark's in 1757, All Saints', Waccamaw and St. Luke's in 1767; St. Matthew's, Orangeburg County and St. David's at Cheraw were established in 1758 and the Church on Edisto Island in 1774.

In South Carolina there are, perhaps, more colonial parishes than in any other state. Of the two church edifices in the United States which show the Royal Arms of England one is in South Carolina near Charleston.

The Parish of St. Philip, Charleston, is coeval with the Province of Carolina, and was territorially defined and limited A. D. 1704. Its first church edifice was built about 1680 to 1690; its second and larger and more substantial church edifice is said in 1723 to have been "a large, regular, and beautiful building exceeding any that are in his Majesty's dominion in America." In 1766 this church was "allowed to be the most elegant religious edifice in British America." The second St. Philip's was built between 1710 and 1723 and was destroyed by fire in 1835, when the present beautiful edifice was erected. In 1835, Mr. J. B. White's picture of the interior of St. Philip's before its destruction was exhibited on April 9th, at Mr. Thayer's Book Store. The corner stone of the present church was laid on the same site in November of the same year, 1835. The first service was held on May 3, 1836. The edifice was consecrated in November by Bishop Bowen. The chimes were broken up and cast into cannon in 1861 and have never been replaced. For many years St. Philip's steeple carried a light to direct mariners to Charleston. When Church street was widened in 1826 the *Gazette* advertised for persons willing to alter the wall of the yard to suit the contour of the street.

This city has been compared to various towns in Europe, but in many ways she duplicates Rochelle, and in the shape of the harbor, in the sea-wall, and in the narrow streets the early Huguenots must have detected a welcome familiarity, which would have been perfect if the towers of St. Michael's and St. Philip's had risen above the skyline in place of La-Laterne and La Grand Horge.

Charleston is a daughter of the sea, from which her safety,

prosperity and health have all come. The sea-feeling penetrates the town through the strange, little streets of the lower town. Through the city there is always a sense of the expectancy of the presence of the sea.

An early plan of the town shows 337 lots and a list of the owners includes names of persons prominent in the city's history, among them Joseph Boone, Andrew Allen, Samuel Eveleigh, Landgrave Smith, Colonel Rhett, all had places on the Bay; others like Mr. Logan and Schenkings and ten or twelve others, had handsome houses. Several had wharves, or bridges in front of their places. Many of these men owned plantations as well as town houses. They lived as English gentlemen were accustomed to live and were served by household servants as numerous as in the homes of many of the nobility. As in Bridgetown so in Charlestown the fashionable owned handsome chaises, fitted with all conveniences for traveling, in addition to trade boats and pleasure boats in which to carry goods or "perform" tours of the river-ways when making social calls. The dress of gentlemen and that of their ladies was fashionable and costly, their behavior was "gentele and polite." In short, Carolina gentry "lived plentifully, were civil, generous, hospitable and very sociable and had everything requisite for pomp and luxury."

Those French Protestants who had come over with René Petit and Jacob Guerard were the forerunners of others who came within the following five years. Carolina was the Promised Land to these people, many of whom were of noble birth but poor in this world's goods. The most tangible record of their sojourn in the city is the quaint Gothic structure at the southeast corner of Church and Queen streets. Many Huguenots passed through Charleston and formed settlements on Cooper river, Goose Creek, St. John's Berkeley, St. Stephens and on Santee. Their churches were maintained as separate places of worship until 1706, after which they gradually merged with those of the Church of England.

Between 1702 and 1720 wars with the Spaniards, the Indians and the Pirates caused such an augmentation of taxes

that during this period they amounted to £215,000. A tax of
ten percent was laid on skins and furs, and a duty imposed
on goods and merchandise imported into and exported out
of the Province. Duties were laid on the importation of
negroes; real and personal property was taxed, and the tax
was apportioned among the merchants and inhabitants of
Charlestown. The Assembly issued bills of credit to the
amount of £33,000. A land bank, established to promote the
rapidly increasing rice culture emitted paper bills to the
amount of £52,000. Depreciation of this paper currency
quickly ensued. The value of produce and exchange rose two
hundred percent in two years. In 1722 the value of this paper
money was fixed at four for one of sterling.

Charity was dispensed by the vestries and wardens of the
several parishes. Church wardens of St. Philip's were empowered to levy a small relief tax for those who required
help in the colony, and an almshouse was in operation at
the time. Charity, while lacking organization, was personal.
Orphans were boarded out among parishoners. Slaves who
might become lunatic while belonging to persons too poor to
care for them were cared for at public expense. The poor
laws of South Carolina, after the Province became a State,
show the same wise and liberal provisions.

A French frigate with four armed sloops appeared against
Charlestown while Sir Nathaniel Johnson was Governor and
the Old Knight hurried down from Silk Hope, summoned
the country companies from the outlying districts, joined
them to his town militia and bravely resisted the invading
forces. Captain Evans, Captain Fenwick and several other
gentlemen of the militia pursued and punished the enemy,
who burnt some houses on James Island and on the opposite
side of the harbor. The French were not allowed to interfere with the flourishing trade. The inhabitants of Charlestown "by wise management and industry" made this colony
of more advantage to the crown than any other of the settlements.

Johnson built his fort at Windmill Point and "barred up
and layed booms across the channel of Ashley river. He cast

up trenches along the White Point and other necessary places" and met the cost of ammunition and small arms out of the public treasury. The tradition that the uncle of Rousseau assisted Governor Johnson in fortifying the town rests upon the fact that in 1730 Gabriel Bernard, Rousseau's uncle was here in the capacity of "Commissioner of Fortifications."

Johnson's friend Colonel William Rhett took charge of the sea forces at Charlestown, and went out with small sailing vessels to attack the French fleet. The withdrawing fleet was pursued by Rhett who captured and brought into the harbor a French warship and ended the first naval attack against the city.

Sir Nathaniel Johnson, appointed by the Proprietors in 1702, was removed by them in 1708, and Colonel Edward Tynte appointed; but he died during the year. Robert Gibbes was elected by Council in 1709. This caused a discreditable broil with Thomas Broughton, who contested the appointment of Gibbes, collected his Berkeley County regiment, marched into town from his plantation at Mulberry, and arrived at Charleston where he found the gates of the city shut, the drawbridge raised and himself and company excluded from the city. Within the walls Broughton sympathizers staged a demonstration, lowered the drawbridge and let the Colonel into the town. Then follows the story of an interesting episode of a proclamation which was read but could not be understood for the noise of rolling drums and a flag torn from its staff and returned at the point of a sword. Gibbes was in the saddle by a questionable election. He never received a salary for his services and so it does not seem that he profited very much by the office which he retained when Broughton and himself reached a compromise. Broughton became Governor in 1735, upon the death of his brother-in-law Johnson, and filled the office with honor.

Though without salary, Gibbes was a good Governor. During his short term the harbor was buoyed, and the Virginians and all other traders were compelled to come to Charlestown to obtain licenses. The inhabitants of the colony were encouraged to build and own ships.

An Act was passed providing for a new brick church in Carolina. (The edifice now standing is the third to bear the name of St. Philip's Church.) It was to be a brick and rough-cast structure, with a seventy-foot nave and thirty-seven foot belfry. It was ready for use by 1732. The church was further enlarged by a portico twelve feet long and twenty-two and one-half feet wide, the entire edifice having a width of sixty-two feet. An outline history of the church has been given elsewhere.

While Governor Gibbes was in office, news came from North Carolina imploring aid against the Tuscarora Indians. Money and men were raised and an expedition put under the command of Colonel John Barnwell, a soldier who early distinguished himself, who was now to gain for himself the name of Tuscarora Jack, when dispatched to the aid of the distressed section.

Barnwell routed the Indians, who renewed the conflict during 1712-13, when James Moore, a son of ex-Governor Moore, succeeded Barnwell in command of troops sent to subdue the Indians. Moore followed the route of Barnwell, came upon and defeated the Tuscaroras at the Tar River, and so completely destroyed their villages that those of the Indians who were not killed pushed their way northward, joined the Iroquois tribe and became in New York a part of the Five Nations, leaving Carolina in peace.

The Honorable Charles Craven, brother to Lord Craven the Palatine, was appointed Governor over Carolina to succeed Gibbes, and it was he who had the law passed fining persons who failed to attend service on Sunday. During his administration the province became involved in two severe contests with the Indians; one on the North with the Tuscaroras, the other on the South with the Yemassees. The colony suffered heavy losses but these tribes were so nearly ruined that they were never afterwards dangerous. Gilmore Simms' novel "The Yemassees" throws a halo of romance around Governor Craven and his adventures that makes his administration the heroic age of the province. (1712-1716.)

In 1715 the Yemassees staged an uprising in this colony

which carried death and destruction to the outlying settlements and almost to Charlestown itself. It began among those colonists who had settled along the river near Edisto river, at Willtown (New London) and on the Combahee and Coosaw rivers and at Port Royal and Beaufort, where there were now people enough to lay out a town. From this point the settlers had penetrated farther to the south and made homes on the Little Wood river, now called by the Indian name of Pocotaligo.

Charlestown's trade with her eight thousand Indians might have called for rum, and the nine hundred hogsheads that were imported for use at home and in the Indian trade may have been considered a small amount for those days, yet, to defenseless people in the colony a day of reckoning had now come. The Yemassees who held the country from Port Royal to the Savannah river had been friendly to the whites but were now armed and excited by the Spaniards of Florida, who considered that war existed between Spain and England. The Indians were induced to make war against the whites who were building upon the Indian hunting-grounds.

In Passion Week of 1715, the traders at Pocotaligo observed a subtle madness kindling among these people, who treacherously welcomed Nairn, the Indian agent, allowing him to sleep in the round house even while they planned to destroy the settlements. Next morning an indiscriminate massacre of the English inhabitants began.

Romance may linger in a story of a white boy who escaped and wandered nine days in the forest before he reached and alarmed a garrison of soldiers, or that of a strong man, Seaman Burroughs, who was a swift runner. He broke through the ranks of the Indians, swam a river, reached Beaufort and saved the inhabitants of that town, from which some escaped in canoes and some reached a ship which happened to be in the harbor, and coming into Charlestown, gave the alarm. The Yemassees and their confederates advanced toward Charlestown, driving planters and their terrified families before them like cattle, toward the capital and safety.

The Indians advancing as far as the Stono river rested there to torture and sacrifice at their leisure their captured planters with their wives and children. There they were met by a force of two hundred and fifty men and forced to retreat down the coast. Craven followed them down to the Combahee river and at daybreak, when a band of five hundred Yemassees tried to rush his position, Craven placed his men behind trees and bided his time until the crack of English rifles mingled with the war whoops and whizzing of Indian arrows, and the Indian leaders fell and the tribes fled.

Another body of riflemen led by Palmer and sixteen men came from town, rushed the Indian fort at Pocotaligo, climbed over the walls, and entering the ditches inside the place, drove out the red men and shot them as they ran.

Insurgent Indians to the north of Charlestown carried their ravages as close as the parish of Goose Creek. The smoke of burning houses and the cries of dying men and women marked their advance down the banks of the Cooper river. There they were checked by Captain Chicken, who forced the Indians to retreat. But in retreating, they sent messengers carrying a "bloody stick" to the other Indian tribes in both Carolinas, inciting them to go on with the war, and ten thousand red warriors collected in response to the sign. Although Governor Craven armed every colonist who could carry a rifle, his field force numbered but twelve thousand men. He now sent to North Carolina and Virginia for additional troops.

This period of history furnishes enough material for a dozen romances that might tell of the Scotch trader, John Fraser, of Mrs. James McPherson, called "Jimmy's Squaw," and of Mrs. Bull, who was captured by the Indians in 1715, or of Mrs. Burrows, who was taken with her baby, carried to St. Augustine, held captive for several years, and finally released. She returned to Charlestown and told the Carolinians that the "Huspah King" who captured her was operating under the Spaniards, who gave him a reward for every dead white man and living negro brought to St. Augustine. In

1716 the Indians being subdued, Carolina faced a domestic revolution. The inhabitants revolted against paying rent for Indian lands. The Council consisted of Thomas Broughton, Richard Beresford, after whom one of our streets and the Beresford Bounty School are called, Samuel Eveleigh, owner of a wharf lot and handsome home on lower Church street, still standing, Charles Hart and Arthur Middleton, the envoy to Virginia, who all struggled valiantly to meet the turbulent political conditions, but with ill success. Governor Craven was allowed to go to England to attend to family matters, and Robert Daniell was appointed Deputy Governor.

Nicholas Trott reappears upon the scene, this time in England, where he had gone after codifying Carolina's laws. There he gained from the Proprietors a grant of power greater than that of the Governor himself. It was ordained that the Governor and four Councillors in assembled session should not have power to pass laws unless Mr. Trott was one of the quorum. The Assembly protested in vain and sent Mr. Joseph Boone and Mr. Richard Beresford to England to argue against this absurd concession made to Mr. Trott. Their instructions concluded, "In case of failure with the Proprietors, apply to a higher power." This meant "Go to the King." The complete story of Trott and his period would embrace much legal history. Trott's career included arrest for sedition, disbarment, a trial, reinstatement, a successful visit to England and a period of lover as well as lawyer, when he married the widow Rhett. Appointed by the Crown, in 1716, Deputy Governor Robert Daniell died in 1718, at the age of seventy-two. "His will, dated May 1, 1718 & proved on the fifth of the same month, makes provision for his widow, Martha, his daughter-in-law, Sarah, and his grandsons, Robert and Marmaduke Daniell." His son is not mentioned. His grave is in St. Philip's churchyard. He was succeeded by Robert Johnson.

Until 1717 there were few houses at Charlestown outside the fortifications. After 1717 no dwelling house, shop, warehouse, stable or barn could be made of wood and all houses in Charlestown must be built of brick or stone. Wooden houses were allowed to stand if they had hearths and chimneys made of brick or stone.

Daniell's records show that Dr. William Crook had invented a preparation for preserving boats from river worms and the planks from rotting; thirty-two white servants were bought by the Governor to be employed in defending the province; rangers were appointed to guard the frontier, garrisons were placed at Port Royal and Savannah Town and an act was passed for payment of five hundred pounds current money unto Mazie, the wife of John C——, late of this province in case she induces the "Huspah King" now at St. Augustine and his people to return and be subject again to this government. Meanwhile England had a new King. Anne had died in 1714. She had been anxious that her half-brother, borne to James II by Mary of Modena, should succeed her on the throne, but fear of the House of Stuart caused the English government to proclaim the son of Sophia, Electress of Hanover, as King. So the Lutheran Prince, George I., a foreigner by birth and speech ascended the English throne in Aug. 1714 and thus introduced a new line of Kings. History of the House of Hanover covers the golden age of Carolina and Charlestown.

While Johnson was Governor, Teach the pirate, known as "Blackbeard," appeared off Charlestown with four vessels, the largest of which mounted forty guns. With four hundred men in his fleet, Teach remained near the town until he captured a vessel commanded by Captain Richards and sent a Mr. Marks to Charlestown to make certain demands of the Governor. Teach threatened to execute certain prominent citizens whom he had taken captive, including Samuel Wragg and his son William, unless the Governor furnished him with medical supplies. Mr. Marks was given two days to go to Charlestown and return. The two days passed and when Mr. Marks and his party had not arrived, Mr. Wragg and the other prisoners were told to prepare for death. Mr. Marks managed to send word that his boat had been overturned in a squall and that after many difficulties he had reached Charlestown, and would soon return. This satisfied

Teach for a few hours, but seeing no boat pulling out from the city he again threatened the prisoners with death.

Tradition has it that Mr. Wragg, hoping to execute a coup, offered to pilot the pirate boat into the harbor, trusting to Governor Johnson and the hundred guns lining the fortifications to effect his salvation in some manner.

Meantime, Charlestown was in a furore. Council was convened. The friends of the captives were both numerous and strong. It was asked, "Will the Governor sacrifice valuable lives rather than allow the pirates to obtain medicine?" The medicines were prepared and sent by Mr. Marks. Teach kept to the letter of his agreement but took their money from his captives and set them, half naked, ashore on James Island, from whence they made their painful way back to the city, glad to have escaped with their lives.

Stede Bonnet, known as the most cruel of pirates, operated near Charlestown at one period. He joined forces with the pirate Blackbeard but the two quarreled and parted company, Bonnet renaming his vessel the Royal James. He secured another crew and spread terror and destruction along the seacoast. He captured two vessels and boldly brought them southward to the Cape Fear River in the Carolina settlements.

Governor Robert Johnson determined to drive the freebooters from the coast and rid the Province of the suspicion that she was indifferent to piratical exploits. Putting two vessels in fighting trim under Captain John Masters, who commanded the Henry, the larger of the two boats, which was fitted with eight guns and a crew of seventy men, and "The Sea Nymph" with a crew of sixty, under command of Captain Fayrer Hall, Colonel William Rhett took charge of the expedition and was preparing to go after Bonnet when Vane, most famous of pirates, was reported to be approaching.

Rhett scoured the neighboring coasts for Vane. Finding no signs of him and believing that danger was past, he did not notify Governor Johnson of his second change of plans

COLONEL WILLIAM RHETT
DESTROYER OF PIRATES, 1718
From an original Pastel, probably by
Henrietta Johnson

COLONEL RHETT'S HOUSE
Built in Rhettsbury: now included in Hasell Street

THE "JACK" AND INSTRUCTIONS FOR ITS USE FURNISHED
SIR FRANCIS NICHOLSON
By Courtesy of Honorable Clarence Lunz
See Page 84

and putting his original idea into execution, sailed for the North Carolina river, where his vessels ran aground.

Bonnet with three boats was at anchor farther up the river. Both Rhett and Bonnet knew that when the tide rose the heaviest combat of their careers would come. At dawn, the pirates, attempting to give Rhett the slip and gain the open sea, came silently down the river, but went aground near Rhett's boats. There they made a "wiff with their bloody flag", waved their hats to the Carolinians and called to them to come aboard and surrender. Though it was almost certain death to man the guns, the Carolinians replied to the pirate taunts and stood ready to fire at the given signal. For five hours the two vessels maintained a continuous and bloody fight.

Fate hung on the turning of the tide. The Carolina boat was the first in motion and sailed straight toward Bonnet's flag ship, the Royal James. The pirate chief stood with drawn pistol ready to shoot any of his men who should refuse to keep up the contest, and swore that rather than surrender he would fire the ship's magazine and send the boat, the crew and himself to Davy Jones' Locker.

His crew, however, preferred to take the chances of a trial in Charlestown and a pardon, threw down their arms and yielded to Rhett. Rhett, ignorant of the identity of his opponent, found "Captain Thomas" to be Stede Bonnet, who was brought to Charlestown and tried.

Judge Trott passed sentence of death on Bonnet, stating that eighteen lives had been lost in this encounter. As there was no jail in the city, the prisoners were placed in the watch house and a military guard set over them. Bonnet was given over to the personal charge of the Provost Marshal, Nathaniel Partridge, and allowed to remain at the latter's house. Two sentinels were placed on guard at sunset and two sailing masters and a boatswain who agreed to turn State's evidence were also carried to the home of Mr. Partridge.

Just as all were to be summoned for trial, another notorious pirate, Moody by name, appeared at the mouth of

Charlestown harbor. Governor Johnson decided to go after this man himself, as Rhett held a fancied grievance against the Governor.

After vexatious delays, four boats, including the pirate ship, Royal James, now owned by the colony, were ready to sail, with three hundred volunteers, when it was discovered that Stede Bonnet, disguised as a woman, and his sailing master had escaped. Hue and cry was raised, a reward of £700 stimulating the search. Bonnet had expected to join the pirate fleet outside the bar but was forced to land on Sullivan's Island, where he remained hidden for several days. Colonel Rhett went after him, crossed sand dunes and myrtle thickets, recaptured the pirate, carried him back to the town, where he was put in prison and finally executed.

It is not known if the pirates who had been hovering in the offing were really intent upon attacking the city, but Johnson, finding them anchored inside the bar, sailed down to the end of James Island, camouflaged his fighting boats as merchantmen and went out to open sea. His plan worked to perfection. As his boats proceeded, and the pirates closed in behind him to demand surrender, Johnson hoisted the King's colors to the masthead, threw open his ports and bringing his guns into play swept the decks of the nearest piratical vessel with a murderous fire. The pirates, taken by surprise, made a bold resistance, but their boats became separated. One was attacked by two of Johnson's smaller vessels in a four-hour fight at close range, during which the Carolinians ran so close to the pirate vessel as to leap on board and capture the crew at point of sword.

Johnson pursued the other ship until the middle of the afternoon, when he opened fire and raked the deck of the enemy so effectually that the black flag was hauled down and the pirates, whose captain was killed in the battle, surrendered. It was found that the slain officer was Richard Worley, who had recently terrorized the northern colonies and ravaged their shipping. When the prize vessels were brought to town and the pirates tried and hung, and the hatches of "The Eagle"—one of the prizes—opened, it was found that she had been captured by the pirates while she was transporting indentured servants to Virginia. Her twice captured prisoners were liberated. Thirty-six were girls.

So the pirates, duly tried and sentenced, were cursed, and cast out without candle, book or bell and hanged, as the quaint wording has it, until their bodies were dead. Then these same bodies were thrust to rot beneath unhallowed soil on White Point Shoal, now filled in to form a part of South Battery, or buried somewhere near Bedon's Alley and Elliott street.

The trial had presented the strange spectacle of a judge said by his enemies to be corrupt and unjust and a prisoner, a decayed gentleman who had taken to the trade of piracy, each quoting scripture to the other.

Carolina, resenting the fact that Virginia had been given Royal assistance in her fight with pirates, while *she* had risen unaided against both Indian and pirate, demanded protection for her commerce, saying that in one year she had supplied 32,000 barrels of tar, 20,643 of pitch and 473 of turpentine for the use of the Royal Navy, and that her Governor was out of pocket a thousand pounds by reason of the expense to which he was put in suppressing the pirates. But instead of helping to defray the expenses of the Indian wars and Pirate expeditions the Proprietors now asked four times as much for land as they had been asking before and claimed that the land of the Yemassees, from which the Indians had been driven by the settlers, must now be bought by the colonists. And, in addition, the Proprietors suddenly declared that they alone must make all laws for the people.

Although the man-of-war, Flambourg, commanded by Hildsley, and the Phoenix, under Captain Pierce, were stationed at Charlestown and cruised along the coast, keeping a lookout for lurking pirates, yet no other effort was made to lift the burden of defending itself from the colony. A drastic change was to be made in the government of Carolina.

In 1719, revolting from the arbitrary claims of the Proprietors, the Carolinians, under the leadership of Alexander Skene, George Logan, and William Blakeway wrote a letter to Governor Johnson, telling him that Charlestown intended to place herself under the protection of the King of England, and asked Johnson to become their governor under the King's authority.

The Crown of England was not to be caught napping. Though she coveted Carolina, she went through certain legal forms before taking over the colony, even though she was petitioned by the majority of the male inhabitants to extend Royal protection to Carolina.

The Proprietors and their descendants had seemed to consider Carolina as a Goose which must lay golden eggs. The Province felt that it was being exploited, and now that its semblance of self-government was to be taken away, it determined to select its own owners.

Impatient of delay, the citizens assembled on December 21st, 1719 and declared themselves direct subjects of the King of England. Men patrolled the streets and with rifles in their hands came together in a "Convention of the People". Flags were flown from the homes of prominent persons and from some of the boats anchored in the harbor. Robert Johnson, last governor under the Proprietors, to whom the office of Governor under the Royal régime was offered, remained true to his trust and threatened to have the Phoenix and Flambourg turn their guns on the town which he held for the Proprietors. But the five hundred men in Charlestown were in command of the walled city and commanded the cannon mounted on the ramparts of the forts looking down the harbor. The will of the people prevailed. The Militia assembled and, with the ceremony of "drum beat" performed at all public places in Charlestown, James Moore was proclaimed "Governor for the King."

Messengers were dispatched to England to inform the King of what had been done, and the citizens anxiously awaited the return of the ambassadors. If all went well and King George accepted the colony, well and good, if he did not they stood to share the common fate of all rebels and lose their heads. But their fears were groundless. Parliament and the King sanctioned what had been done at

Charlestown, and Carolina was "provisionally" ruled by the crown until 1729, when George II purchased the political and property rights of the Lords Proprietors and Charlestown became the capital of a Royal Province under the second George, who was a son of George I and had come to the throne in 1727.

BOOK II

ADMINISTRATION OF ROYAL GOVERNORS, 1719-1776

Chapter V

THE Georgian Era includes the years from 1714 until the Revolution. Immediately after the Colonists took matters into their own hands, local affairs were in confusion. Legitimate authority was still vested in Johnson (whose friends secreted the public records) while Moore was at the head of affairs. The clergy refused to sanction marriages without Johnson's signature. Love might laugh at locksmiths but not at law, and citizens were fearful of the consequences of their part in the action of the colony in throwing off the authority of the Proprietors. If the Crown chose to put a wrong construction upon their motives then the movement might be construed as a revolution and punishable as treason. But England smoothed over the situation by saying that the colony was left defenseless and neglected by the Proprietors, and that the Crown took possession in order to restore peace and promote justice and to retain Carolina which was in danger of being lost (with her valuable trade) to England forever. A lengthy document was drawn up but The London Board of Trade and Plantations was virtually in charge of affairs. Instructions for governing Carolina as a "Royal Province" were sent to Provisional Governor Nicholson, whose experience in Virginia was considered valuable at this time of crisis. Nicholson is described as a proud, vain man. His affairs of the heart comprised such romantic aspects that the ladies of Charlestown looked forward to his coming with great interest. He must have been eccentric, because the historian A. S. Salley, Jr. has recently unearthed records concerning a ceremony during which Governor-in-Chief-Capt.-General-Vice-Admiral Nicholson, is said to have baptized a bear.

The Governor was told to review and revise the laws of the colony, enforce the good ones, annul the bad ones, and submit new ones to the English authorities. The Colonial Constitution followed the British Model. The Governor represented the King, while the Assembly and Council corresponded to the upper and lower houses of Parliament.

The election and usury laws were re-enacted. Liberty of conscience was promised, but the Book of Common Prayer was used on Sundays and Holy Days in the State Churches. The Indian trade was regulated, a duty placed on imported negroes, the slave code was revised to contain clauses placing restraint upon slave owners, demanding humane treatment, sufficient food and clothing and decent shelter for slaves, and the church assumed a constructive attitude toward their religious and moral welfare.

Governor Nicholson, appointed to office in the fall of 1720, did not arrive in Charlestown until May, 1721, and James Moore, acting Governor, had, in the interim, appointed Rhett as "Comptroller of the King's Customs and Receiver General for the Proprietors" to oversee the repairs of Charlestown's fortifications. This caused great discontent. Many persons contended that the Receiver-General for the Proprietors could scarcely be a good Collector of the King's Customs and said that Colonel Rhett was already provided with offices, pointing out that no man could serve three masters, the King, the Colony, and the Proprietors. Nicholson's appearance failed to quiet the political situation. He could brook no opposition. Moore was a martinet and Rhett was intensely individualistic, and the town was treated to public displays of temper.

Nicholson wrote to the Secretary of the Lords Justices in England that Rhett was a proud, haughty, insolent fellow, but as Rhett died soon after history has failed to record his opinion of the Governor: he was bad mannered enough to write to England, "old Rhett is dead of appoplexy. Please send some one to take his place," adding that "his Lordship's interest would have been better served if Rhett had died before he was linked with Mr. Trott." Nicholson did not spare young Rhett in his tirade but Moore's death put an end to the triangular discussion. No one was left to quarrel openly with Nicholson.

The colony seemed to prosper, as trade increased, but finances were suffering. Because of the unstable condition of the Carolina currency, counterfeit bills freely circulated and greatly increased when a great flood caused the planters to lose their crops. The government stepped in, called in the worn bills, reprinted all genuine ones outstanding, issued new bills to the amount of £40,000 and made the crime of counterfeiting punishable by death.

Merchants complained that the colonists had not lost as heavily as they made out, and that the Assembly broke faith when they added to Carolina's bill of credit. The merchants were arrested, put in prison and released only after they each paid a fine of £500. The matter could not be disposed of in this manner.

In less than a year exchange was at a premium, the merchants lost thirty percent of their outstanding debts and there is no telling what might have happened if Mr. Godin, the Charlestown agent, stationed in London, had not secured backing from merchants who traded to Charlestown and thus brought the matter to the attention of the proper authorities.

Nicholson was "instructed" to sink and discharge the bills of credit. Certain members of the Charlestown Council, Middleton, Izard, Bull, Skene, Kinloch, Hart, Schenking and De La-Consiliere, backed up the Charlestown merchants. Nicholson was caught between the upper and nether mill stones, and, weary of fighting, expressed a desire to be allowed to retire and return to England. His request was granted.

His term of office was a time of great progress in Colonial life. He was an ardent member of the Church of England and gave generously to the causes of religion and education, and induced wealthy members of the colony to found such schools and endow such scholarships as the Beresford Bounty. Nicholson tried to control the Indian Trade and put a stop to abuses which occurred when credit was extended to the

Indians. Before this when the savages could not pay, creditors were allowed to seize and sell them into slavery.

Nicholson left Carolina in 1724. From then until 1729 Administration of affairs fell upon Arthur Middleton, oldest Councillor and President of the Council. Sir Francis' abandonment of the government before the King was prepared permanently to establish immediate authority rendered Middleton's position difficult. His office was marked by great political turmoil. Friends of the Proprietors intrigued to overthrow the provisional government. Rhett and Trott, whose overlapping and numerous offices gave him dictatorial powers, based the hopes of the success of their party's endeavor to restore Proprietorial government upon the fact that as one of the Secretaries of state Lord John Carteret was even then administering for the King the affairs of Carolina even while claiming the province as Palatine of the Proprietors. Such were the intricacies of the situation. To continue Middleton's position was further complicated by the old scores left unsettled in the Revolution of 1719, which came to the reckoning, and the situation left over from the recent war between England and Spain. Even though Spain ordered the Governor of Florida to cease molesting the Carolinians and Carolina was instructed to cultivate the friendship with the Spaniards in Florida, yet the truce was only a mockery and the building of Fort King George on the Altamaha by Barnwell of Carolina gave fresh offense.

Middleton's calibre is shown by the fact that between 1727 and 1731, he dissolved the Assembly six times and six times ordered new election of members. The temper of the Assembly is revealed in the fact that a money measure was eight times sent to the Council and rejected eight times.

In social affairs country gentlemen enjoyed the pleasures of the chase, and thus acquired a knowledge of the fields, and woodlands, fire-arms and horses that was to stand them in good stead. The country was too new to need recreation; life itself was entertainment enough, but the schools, the library, the churches, the style of architecture and the permanency of the buildings bear witness to the early culture of the city. The presence in the colony of a native artist is attested by various examples of portraits done in pastel by Henrietta Johnson early in 1700. Her pictures include one of Sir Nathaniel Johnson, as well as members of the Rhett, Wragg, Dubois and other families. Many portraits of colonial worthies, painted by English artists, adorned the walls of the Charleston houses.

The end of Middleton's term was marked by tragic events due to natural causes. During the summer of 1728 Carolina suffered a prolonged drought; cattle and wild beasts perished, the fields and forests dried up. In the fall a hurricane came to complete the disaster. The streets of Charlestown were inundated, the forts demolished, houses and wharves were wrecked and boats were driven up into the town. Many persons were drowned. Yellow fever followed, and planters were afraid to carry their produce into the city, where the dead were so numerous that it was hard to find a sufficient number of persons to attend to the bodies.

In 1729 the King bought the rights of the Proprietors for seventeen thousand five hundred pounds sterling, to be paid free of all deductions; and bought also seven-eighths of the arrears of quit-rents (amounting to over nine thousand pounds) due to the Proprietors from the colonists, and the difficulties of Carolina arising from divided governmental interest were over. John, Lord Cartaret, who by retaining his share of the property and quit rent rights had in 1719, become joint owner with the King, now surrendered his share. The colony was divided into North and South Carolina and a medal struck to commemorate the event. The King appointed governors for both provinces. Charlestown politics flourished under King George II from 1727 to 1760. His reign is called the Golden Age of Carolina.

Robert Johnson, son of Governor Sir Nathaniel, had, in 1719, been asked to take up the government of the Province until the King's pleasure was known. He reaped the reward of loyalty and, in 1731, became a duly appointed Royal Governor and the town gave him a royal welcome. He brought a commission as Lieutenant Governor for his brother-in-law,

Colonel Broughton, upon whom the authority devolved five years later when "Good Governor Johnson" died.

During these years, were made the treaties of peace with the Cherokees at Keowee, in the upper part of the State. Sir Alexander Cummings brought back seven Indian Chiefs who passed through Charlestown on their way to England, to take "Brother George" by the hand and to promise to live at peace with the colonists "as long as the rivers ran and the mountains stood." Carolina was to find that promises, like pie crust, were made to be broken, when France roused the Indians against Georgia and Florida settlements and she, too, became involved.

Meanwhile, as political peace descended, merchants from the interior shipped their produce to the town, following their wares, and enjoying the delights of gay Charlestown. Until 1769 all colonial courts sat in Charlestown. Thus planters, lawyers, citizens, witnesses and all interested in law suits thronged the streets of the town to mingle with great politicians, members of the law-giving bodies and local celebrities. In 1730 the white population was about 15,000.

Charlestown was the ecclesiastical headquarters for colonial Carolina churchmen. Bishop Gibson, of London, under whose jurisdiction Carolina operated in 1725, appointed Mr. Alexander Garden as his commissary (or representative). Garden, a learned and pious man, who came to Carolina in 1719 was made commissary in 1726 and represented the Bishop for thirty-eight years, thirty-four of which he served as Rector of St. Philip's Church. Reverend R. Clarke succeeded him and was followed by the Reverend Robert Smith, A.M., who continued as rector for fifty years and became after the Revolution the first Episcopal Bishop of the Diocese of South Carolina.

The Crown desired to secure citizens from manufacturing towns to ply their trades in Carolina. But manufactures could not flourish while land was obtained on easy terms. It is to be noted that in 1722 machines to make hemp, bright and well cured and to render flax water-rotted in good condition, free from swingle, were invented here. Mellichamp had designed machines for making salt in order to establish fisheries, and several other persons in the colony designed engines which were intended to stimulate local manufacturing. The government gave them a bounty, but their efforts failed. Agriculture and cattle-raising continued to be the chief occupations. From 1720 to 1729, more than forty-five thousand pounds of rice was exported. Charlestown merchants owned seven hundred out of the eight thousand tons of shipping employed in 1723. 1731 marked the end of the first half-century of the city's life on its present site. Despite bad government, pirates, fires, unfavorable seasons and diseases; despite wars with the French, Spaniards and Indians, five handsome churches and several public buildings and splendid fortifications had been built. All of the inhabitants of the city were said by Peter Purry, who desired to found a colony to the southward and therefore issued a glowing account— were rich, either in slaves, furniture, cloth, plate, jewels, or other merchandise. From three to five war vessels defended the trade of Charlestown in 1731. Craftsmen were paid in Carolina money; tailors, shoemakers and smiths received thirty shillings a day and food. Skillful carpenters got thirty, and common workmen, who spoke English, received twenty, while helpers got ten shillings. Currency then stood to sterling as 7 to 1.

It is a curious commentary on the early settlers and upon their descendants that, with cattle enough and to spare, the colonies were importing shoes and leather breeches. They had plenty of clay, but no potters nor potteries. They could grow several kinds of grapes, but they were importing wine from Madeira and putting it away in heated vaults or in the attics of their houses where, sometimes, a stray bottle or two still comes to light.

Purry diffused a delightfully Biblical atmosphere in his description of Carolina. He gives a sort of "India's Coral Strand" turn to the pamphlet when he says that South Carolina is situated in the same degree of heat, fertility and temperature as Barbary, the Isles of Candia, Syria, Persia, and

An East Prospect of CHARLESTOWN, the Metropolis of the Province of SOUTH CAROLINA.

From an Old Print, 1732. By Permission of the City

THE SCOTCH PRESBYTERIAN CHURCH
See Page 58

THE FIRST BAPTIST CHURCH, CHURCH STREET
To the South, a house reputed to have been built before the Revolution
To the North, the D. E. Huger Smith home and the Pre-Revolutionary home of the
Motte family
See Page 191

Mongolistan China, which he comes down to earth long enough to say is in the thirty-third degree latitude.

With all of this high-sounding description Charleston was barely more than a village when compared with European cities. Certain officials, such as a searcher, a naval master, and a harbormaster, were appointed to regulate foreign commerce. 1256 seamen were registered at the Custom House in 1732. Samuel Eveleigh, the leading merchant, who gave sumptuous entertainments to the Indian men, placed four buoys to mark the entrance to the harbor.

The city, although small, boasted of a newspaper, two or three printers, a book-binder, and an engraver, who prepared plates from which the provincial currency was struck. He was also a gunsmith and plied his trade at his own shop on Church street, where his sign "Captain Joseph Massey" appeared over crossed guns.

Because a newspaper was established in the city in this year it is henceforth easy to follow what was going on in the town. Before Thomas Whitmarsh, Eleazer Philips and his son, Eleazer, came to Charleston, set up their presses, issued several pamphlets and published the *South Carolina Gazette*, "word of mouth or placards" had been the favorite method of "putting out the word." After Whitmarsh had been in business a short time he advertised that he would print no advertisement for which money had not been sent. These advertisements show many trades and occupations combined, dealers in foodstuffs, butchers, farmers, fruiterers, confectioners, tobacconists and seedsmen kept each other's goods in as indiscriminate a manner as the law allowed. The first market was held at the corner of Broad and Meeting streets, where a new building was put up in 1730. The Charlestonians believed in combining business and pleasure. There were taverns and public houses, a prominent one being at the northeast corner of Church and Broad streets. The State House was either in the lower part of this building or in an adjoining tenement. Gentlemen frequented other club rooms and coffee-houses on Tradd, Elliott and Bay streets.

Early cabinet-makers used mahogany and other woods to

make tables, chairs, "peer" glasses and sconces. They sold fine scarlet shalloons, striped and plain domestics, colored fustines, mohairs and serges, along with buttons and trimming suitable for furniture that was either to be made or mended.

The mercantile establishments were found near the taverns. Wholesale business was conducted on the Bay close to the wharves. The governors and State officers were townsmen, and included a provost-marshall, deputies, gaugers, measurers, custom officers, constables, and watchmen. Merchants who became weary of attending shop placed money in the hands of traders more venturesome than themselves and when returns justified them in doing so they too purchased slaves and plantations and settled themselves as independent farmers rather than remain socially inferior.

The outlying districts were rapidly taken up by settlers who secured "arrival rights". Many came out as apprentices who hoped to serve their time and in turn become freemen and land-holders. A curious document containing articles of agreement signed by an apprentice shows that he promised not to haunt taverns or plantations and to receive instructions in the trade and mystery of the craft of his masters. The apprentices of Charleston formed themselves into a trade group and at one time owned and operated their own library.

The colony was marked off into twelve townships. Governor Robert Johnson invited settlers to come, each to receive fifty acres of land. This offer brought a few pioneer families who settled Orangeburg County. Salleys, McCords, Russells, Thompsons, came in 1730. McMichaels and others followed. Some Switzers came to settle at Purrysburg, from 1733 to 1735. A company of Scots-Irish came to Charlestown in 1732, went up the coast to Georgetown harbor, there took two small boats, went up the Black river and founded Kingstree. The Welsh settled on Pee Dee in 1736.

Carolina had lost thirty miles of sea-coast when the colony was divided into North and South Carolina. She now gave up a considerable amount of territory lying west of the Savannah river as Georgia was founded by General Oglethorpe.

He brought a load of colonists into Charlestown Harbor in January 1733. Governor Johnson and the city gave them welcome. Private homes were thrown open to the travelers. The Assembly voted supplies and an escort of twenty rangers for the new colony to be planted to the south. Purses were opened. Slaves were loaned and Colonel William Bull went with Oglethorpe to pick out a favorable settlement site. The town of Savannah was soon begun.

Oglethorpe returned to Charlestown and was met by deputation from the Council Chamber and Assembly which had decided to give him ten thousand pounds. A banquet was provided for the General and his officers, whose return courtesy included a dinner and a ball at the Council Chamber. This was attended by the fashionable world and his fashionable wife. Carolina now felt that a buffer had been erected between the Spaniards and Indians and their city. In 1735 a colony of Welsh families settled in a bend of the upper Pee Dee River. Ten years later Highlanders settled in Darlington County and these were followed by a few English families. The Kershaws opened a trading-post at Cheraw. Many men influential in Carolina's history sprang from these outlying settlements and affected the destiny of the colony during the Revolutionary War. The northern part of the colony was settled after the treaties had been signed with the Cherokee Indians. During these years, settlers from the seacoast made their way northward up the Savannah, Edisto, Santee and Pee Dee Rivers. Emigrants now came down into the upper part of the state from Pennsylvania and Virginia, among them the Calhoun, Hampton and Picken families with hundreds of others told about in records of the old 96th District. They all came to Carolina after Braddock's defeat and rendered noble service to the colony. The colony welcomed all worthy emigrants, as she continued to fear slave uprisings such as had occurred at Wiltown on the Pon Pon river.

Governor Johnson died in 1735 and was succeeded by Colonel Broughton, who died two years later. Colonel Bull assumed and held the office of Governor until the 19th of December, 1743, when Governor Glenn, the Scotch Governor, came to the city.

In 1736, a diplomatic squabble over the Indian trade amounted to a border warfare in miniature between Georgia and Carolina. John Hamilton, Charles Pinckney, and Othniel Beal visited Oglethorpe to explain Carolina's stand in the matter. George Ducat and John Ballentine rowed a canoe from Charleston to Savannah with the help of four negroes, in 36 hours.

Charlestown had little place in the picture when Oglethorpe, who had been appointed Commander-in-Chief of the military forces in Carolina and Georgia, decided to invade St. Augustine. Many Charleston men went out as officers but the city did not sponsor the movement. Thus Charlestown's generous gift and warm welcome to Oglethorpe was more than repaid when Georgia bore the brunt of repulsing Spain's attack upon the southern frontier. Carolina delayed to send assistance to Georgia because she paid heed to false, malicious attacks upon Oglethorpe which were later disproved, according to the findings of an English Court Martial.

In 1740, a great fire starting at the west end of the town consumed the lower part of the city. Few buildings survived the flames. Wharves and the goods on them were burnt, great warehouses were burnt, Bastions and the guns on them were destroyed. Great distress was found among the poor, even the well-to-do fared badly, as the fire caused a loss of a quarter of a million pounds. But soon after, the Crown appropriated money to help rebuild and Charlestown rose, phoenix-like, from her ashes. Some wealthy persons were heard to say that "the town had benefitted by the fire which had consumed ugly old houses."

Governor Glenn came to Carolina in 1743 and remained until 1756. He received a royal welcome from the young and growing Capital of the Royal Province, which, though sorely stricken by the recent fire, gladly greeted the first Royal Governor who had come to Carolina in eight years.

Glenn arrived on the man-of-war Tartar and the advent was announced when the great guns of Fort Johnson spoke in salute and were answered from the town. He was met by delegates, brought to a proper landing place and was greeted by Edward Atkins and Charles Pinckney. The Charleston Regiment, standing at attention, was formed into two lines through which Governor Glenn and his escort passed to be greeted by Lieutenant-Governor Bull and the Council. In the Council room Glenn presented his commission and credentials after which the sword of State was taken up; a procession reformed, the assemblage proceeded to Granville's Bastion, where the Governor's commission was read to the town people who received it with cheers and the rolling of drums. Again the cannon spoke and Glenn returned to the Council Chamber where the oath of office was administered to him. Then the new Governor and his friends proceeded to Shepheard's Tavern and spent the rest of the day in feasting and "giving and taking" numerous patriotic toasts, while citizens celebrated by illuminating the town by placing candles in the windows of their houses.

By this period of time, many of the men identified with the Proprietorial Era had died or were dying; Moore and Rhett, Middleton and Trott who had married Rhett's widow (while her son married his daughter) died in 1740. The postscript of the first chapter of Charlestown's history was closed. The church was now functioning under the Bishop of London. Commissary Garden was exercising control over the mental, moral and religious life of the ministers of the Established Church and by 1742 there were twelve missionaries in Carolina supported by the Society for the Propagation of the Gospel.

As Rector of St. Philip's Church, Mr. Garden welcomed John and Charles Wesley, who visited Charlestown several times. Their first visit occurred on July 31, 1736. George Whitfield, their early co-laborer, visited this city in 1739, and, charged with violating canonical laws, was tried in an ecclesiastical court in Charlestown. Mr. Green was Prosecutor, and the newly arrived Andrew Rutledge defended Whitfield, who thereafter used the White Meeting House for services.

Primitive Charlestown being largely destroyed by the fire of 1740 the town felt the need of insurance as adequate protection against the many destructive fires which occurred so often in a city which was lighted by candles. A letter written by a gentleman in London to a friend in Carolina, in 1731 had stated, "According to thy request, I have been at several of the Fire-officers and showed them what thou wrote in relation to their making insurance on houses in Carolina and had for answer that they had divers times proposals of like nature from New York, New England, etc., but that they had never given the least encouragement to any to expect they would comply." The men of Charlestown therefore came together to consider the matter of founding a local company.

Many of the buildings in the lower part of the city were spared during the Revolution because they bore a small leaden disk showing in relief outlines of the Royal Exchange in London, or a design similar to one seen on the bore of an old cannon by the Powder Magazine or one recently found near an old fort and mounted at the residence of Bissell Jenkins, at Riverland Terrace, on the Stono River. These marks were thought to be the sign of Royal ownership and the places bearing them were spared. These disks really implied membership in an insurance society. Volunteer companies extinguished fires in early days. The location of a fire was, after 1752, indicated from St. Michael's steeple by a long pole, the tip of which bore at night a lantern, pointing in the direction of the fire.

Books of subscription to the Friendly Society were opened in 1735, the first day of January, and continued open until the first day of February, next. Articles of agreement were drawn up in December, 1735, and in 1736 were listed the officers elected at a meeting held at Captain William Pinckney's house—they included some of the most prosperous and eminent men of the day, Fenwick, Wragg, Pinckney, Esqrs. Crockat, Peronneau, Manigault and Jacob Motte, Captain Edward Croft, Captain Isaac Holmes, and Mr. John Laurens, were made fire-masters for the coming year.

A letter gives a picture of Charlestown in 1740. The writer

says, "This place is adorned by several stately edifices of
curious architecture, amongst which the Parish Church of St.
Philip's is a standing monument of the nice skill and judgment of ye artifices. The lake sickness carried off ye Pro-
jector who was a Venetian, and several of ye best workmen.
The belfry is a fine piece, consisting of all the fine orders of
architecture. Oppulency and good judgment are conspicuous in all parts of this celebrated Pile. This town is well fortified, along Ashley River and the whole front of the town is
Defended by a double Courtaine Line, consisting of a half
moon and advances and on each end of the town are ye two
Bastions of Broughton and Granville, mounted each with 40
cannons of 12 and 18 pound shott, about a mile from the
town is a large fort called Johnstons, which mounts fifty
cannons of 12 and 18 pounds, shott in 2 tiers an intirely commands ye channel, the house and Lot Brother George sold to
Thomas Kimbol for 400 & 50 pounds, was sold to Mr.
Thompson, Butcher Last week for three thousand and 500
Pounds, and Everybody admires to think my brother was so
hasty to sel it." Unsigned—but ended "Your obedient son."

A few items taken at random from the columns of the
Gazette must serve to round out the outline of what was
going on in Charlestown in the middle of the eighteenth
century. If any of the newspapers of today dared to print
the personal notices that appeared in the *Gazette* and its
successors they would find themselves with a steady number
of libel suits on hand. State notices, elopements, advertisements of wives who had left their husbands, servants, run-
away negroes, absconding Indian slaves and settlements of
estates appeared from day to day. Certain merchants advertised over and over again. Goods were advertised as selling
by inch of candle, lectures were given at early candle light,
and it is said, that unless candles were used lightwood knots
served to furnish lights until whale-oil lamps came into use.
In consequence of this most of the entertainments went on
during the daytime hours. Dinner was eaten in midday and
callers came early in the afternoon and went before nightfall.
An endless shadow of familiar outlines is thrown on the

screen of time. Little shops advertised white and blue negro
cloth, strouds for the Indian trade, oznaburghs, cheque linen,
good blue welsh cotton, fine gulick Hollard linens. Window
glasses and drinking glasses were offered. Barbadoes rum,
Arrack and Rhenish wines were sold. Bread, that was good,
brown and middling, was sold at the left-hand of Elliott's
Bridge, Pewter, Swedish iron, and iron mongery were advertised, felt hats and gold and silver lace hats were offered for
sale. Every now and then somebody would be "departing the
colony" and then Timothy, the stationer, would sell them the
necessary forms for bonds, judgments, bills of sale, powers of
attorney, mortgages for negroes, and articles of apprentice-
ship and indenture. Mr. Timothy also dispensed ink-powder
and slates and advertised some very serious books, "Barclay's
Apology for the Quakers," "Watt's Psalms," and a reprint of
"Bowman's Sermons." He sold music, and carried the score
of the Beggar's Opera, the Village Opera and Robin Hood,
while the drama is represented by a tragedy called, "The
Fatal Extravagant—a short, plain, help for parents and heads
of families to feed their babes with the sincere milk of God's
word, the nature of riches, and the choice flour of mustard
seed in bottles." Thus did drama dispense morality.

Ladies were wearing ribbons and girdles and hair dresses
of various sorts. They used hysteric waters for the megrims,
they wore bone and plain hoop petticoats and boned stays or
jackets. Their feet were shod in silk or calimancoe shoes.

From the fact that surgeons were frequently called in to
make inquests on strangers, the inference was plain that
Charlestown commanded the services of enlightened practi-
tioners. In 1732 the opinions of four eminent surgeons were
asked at one inquest. A further perusal of the stock of books
would show that novels, written by Englishmen, were being
read; romance was represented by "Abelard's letters," history by Lindsey's "Scotland," biography by the "Memoirs
of Queen Anne," agriculture by "Bradley's Botanical Dictionary," and "The art of fallowing land, and kitchen gardens." A Spanish grammar, six volumes of "Musical Mis-
cellany" and "Pitcairns Poemeta" are also listed.

Merchants formed an association to enforce the laws against unlicensed hawkers and peddlers. Others, following the English idea, gathered themselves into clubs or associations. The St. George's Club or Society grew out of the Fort Jolly Volunteers, and General Oglethorpe was the guest of the St. George's at its first anniversary meeting celebrated by a dance, concert, jubilee, and "powder-demonstration."

Until swept away by the Revolutionary War the law of primogeniture and entail held good in the colony and sustained the leadership of the families who helped to settle the colony and develop her resources. Their names are still found in the city and state. The persistence of the old names make for that sense of responsibility and stability in public and private life characteristic of Charleston today. During the two hundred and fifty years of her life the leaders of affairs have come from this set of people, and it gives a precious sense of permanence to civic life. From a constant repetition of certain family names there has come to Charleston a subtle sense of immortality which is the genius and essence of the town. Moreover, the training in managing great estates required, on a small scale, those qualities of wisdom, patience, self-reliance and political insight which Carolina men displayed in dealing with State and National problems. A halo of romance adheres to certain of the family names to this day.

CHAPTER VI

C HARLESTON'S history divides itself into certain logical periods, the first of which was the Proprietary Era, which ended December 21st, 1719. The second period embraces the years following and ends at the beginning of the Revolutionary War. The revolutionary period, however, is itself divided into two sections, one beginning in 1763, and embracing the causes which led up to the actual conflict; the second interests itself in the war itself.

Before passing to a detailed account of the Revolutionary period it is necessary to tell the story of certain persons, their homes and their societies, in order to give a clear account of this city. The years between 1729 and 1775 were marked by the erection of many fine buildings both public and private.

In regard to political history, the second period of Charleston's civic life began with the governors appointed under the King of England, the first of whom was James Moore, the last of whom was Lord William Campbell. Between these persons are Sir Francis Nicholson, Arthur Middleton, Robert Johnson, Thomas Broughton, William Bull, James Glenn, William Henry Lyttleton, William Bull, son of the first William Bull, and Thomas Boone who served from 1761 to 1764.

After this date, beginning in 1764, William Bull, in the capacity of Acting Governor, alternated until 1775 with Lord Charles Greville Montague in holding down the office of Governor; Montague being the appointed Governor and William Bull doing the work and receiving the title of "Acting" Governor. This see-saw concluded at the entrance of Lord William Campbell in 1775.

Charleston's story up until 1732 has been told with numerous details serving to produce the atmosphere of the time and place. After Robert Johnson became the first Royal Governor, in 1729, and served until 1735, Charleston experienced a cessation of incessant political discussions between the lawmakers and the people and settled itself to develop its architecture, its social life and its resources. Leading events from 1735 to 1775, announce themselves logically.

Charlestown betrays her origin in subtle touches. Bristol gave her narrow streets and red brick buildings. St. Michael's place is a copy of the Cathedral closes of Gloucester, Derby and Shrewsbury. Leeds gave open air markets—Norwich gave the idea of a library, museum and botanical garden. It is easy to analyze the social life of Charleston of today and trace the places from which they were transferred. London gave ideas of pomp and ceremony, as well as patterns for many buildings.

Charleston had suffered from fires in 1698, 1699, 1700, 1731 and 1740, yet some of the buildings in the city are quite old and some of the dwelling-houses were constructed previous to the last dates. A quaint brick house on the west side of Church street, adjacent to the Brewton Inn, was built and given by Col. Miles Brewton to his daughter Mrs. Thomas Dale, wife of Dr. Dale, who wrote such interesting accounts of the flora of this section. The Brewtons were great builders and Brewton's Corner comprises this house and the large carriage-house adjacent, but not the house at the corner, which is said to have belonged to a wine merchant. Below the Dale residence, Robert Brewton, brother of Mrs. Dale, built the large three-story brick house now owned by Mr. Arthur Huger and inhabited by Mrs. Charles Kershaw. The large rooms with panelled walls and deeply recessed windows proclaim the house as belonging to the Colonial period.

Wages were fixed by Law in 1740 for the various artisans and their apprentices, classified as Master Workmen, Carpenters, Bricklayers and Plasterers. The excellent work of these men shows in the type of building which they erected from Carolina brick, English brick or cypress and pine wood. The Architects, some of whom came out from England, consulted climatic requirements and planned houses that would be cool in summer. Many of the great houses of town were the summer homes of planters who lived on their great estates during the winter months and came "to the Salt" with their families during the summer.

Church Street was open to the ocean breezes and many fine houses were built in this street below Broad. Several were destroyed in the various fires but today it is possible to identify the Dale house, the Brewton house, and the large house below it as having been built in the middle of the eighteenth century. The large pink house opposite Longitude Lane, now owned and occupied by Mr. D. E. H. Smith and his family, was erected on land once owned by members of the Capers family. The name of the builder is uncertain. It was occupied at an early date by Mr. Jacob Motte, sometime Public Treasurer of the Colony who was buried with great pomp from this establishment in 1770 and interred with other great men in St. Philip's Churchyard. Of his nineteen children ten lived to maturity. His sons were Jacob, who married Rebecca, daughter of Col. Brewton, Isaac and Charles, who were officers in the Revolution. One daughter married Captain Thomas Shubrick, senior, Hannah, married first Thomas Lynch, senior, and secondly General Wm. Moultrie, another married William Drayton, another, Dr. James Irving, another became Mrs. Henry Peronneau, another was Mrs. Dart, and another, Mrs. John Huger. So that if the stones of this house could talk, Charleston History could be transcribed from a personal and inside view-point.

The First Baptist Church had not then been constructed. Tradition says that the house next below the church was built at an early date, and that several of the wooden houses in this neighborhood are very, very old. A quaint brick building with an arch below, looks quite ancient, and the two wooden houses adjacent are of historic interest. When Water street was a creek it flowed through the Vanderhorst lands. After 1740, when Church street was opened down to the Ashley River, houses were built beyond the creek. A bridge connected the town with White Point and Broughton's Battery from which the fashionable promenade of to-day takes its name.

Miss Mary Marshall now owns the house known in history as having been built by George Eveleigh, a prominent merchant whose wharf was on East Bay. The house was once owned by Dr. Pologny, a refugee from St. Domingo. Later it was occupied by Chancognie, official of the French Government stationed here in 1807. Since then the property has passed through various hands until bought by Mr. Maynard Marshall, father of Mrs. Canfield, Mrs. Kittredge and Miss Mary Marshall.

The square brick building with the dormer window, bull's eye light and iron balcony now owned by the Misses Logan and their brother Hampton Logan, was built by George Mathews, son of the emigrant, Anthony, whose large tombstone adorns the yard of the Circular Church. Dr. Skirving bought the place after 1764. To the south is found a three-story, brick, single house, now owned by Mrs. Evelyn Brodie Memminger, widow of the late Judge Withers Memminger. It was built by Thomas Young, who also built a similar house on the other side of his lot, fronting on Meeting street.

This house was occupied by Colonel Isaac Motte, whose great-grandchildren, members of the Mahan Haig family, still own the property. The Church street house was identified for many years with members of the Johnson family. The father William Johnson, an ironmaster and owner of great iron works came South from New York and settled in Charleston. He is called the patriot of the Liberty Tree party. His son Dr. Joseph wrote the traditions of the Revolution, and his other son, Chief Justice William, wrote the Life and Correspondence of General Nathaniel Green. Both the "patriot-urge" and the ability to write, were manifested in Major John Johnson, who was an engineer in the Confederate Service and later Rector of St. Philip's Church. His book "The Defence of Charleston Harbor" is a classic and a standard textbook in military institutions. Charleston's most learned historian and writer, Colonel Edward McCrady sprang from this stock.

West of this house fronting on Meeting Street is the Huger House—pointed out as the residence of the last Royal Governor of Carolina. Built about 1760 it was at one time owned by Mrs. Daniel Blake whose cousin, Sarah Izard, a young lady with a handsome fortune, married Lord Campbell. When Governor Campbell fled from the Colony in 1775 he made his exit by way of the garden of this establishment, down to the banks of Vanderhorst Creek and there took a small row-boat out to the King's ship "Tamar," lying in the stream.

The house passed into the hands of the Morrises and Hugers, who intermarried with the daughters of William Elliott, and has been retained as a family residence by various members of the family, one of the most historic of whom is Francis Kinloch Huger, the friend and would-be rescuer of Lafayette. He failed to liberate Lafayette from Olmutz, but as a Lieutenant Colonel in the United States Army welcomed him to this city in 1825.

Several old and interesting houses are grouped across the street. That of Mr. Henry Ficken was at one period the town house of the Bulls of Ashley river. It was said greatly to resemble the plantation house, which was burned by the owner during the Confederate War rather than allow the Federal Soldiers to set fire to it. Traditions cluster around this and Jenkins M. Robertson's home in Ladson street, once Ladson court. The houses are identified with members of the Bull, Drayton, Blake, Middleton, Brewton, Butler and Guerard families, who were all connected by marriage. During the Revolution one house was occupied by a British pay-master, who gave several brilliant entertainments there.

To the north of the Ficken house is a castle-like structure built by James Simmons, and found at various times in the possession of members of the Gibbes and Brisbane families before being remodeled into its present form by Otis Mills and further improved by the distinguished lawyer and sol-dier General James Conner. He served the South as a soldier during the Confederate War and, later, as a wise counsellor assisted the city and State during and after Reconstruction times.

Below Ladson street several fine houses were constructed just previous to the Revolutionary period. History is positive on the point of the G. W. Williams house, it having been the

THE TOWN HOUSE OF STEPHEN BULL
Residence of H. H. Ficken

BRANFORD-HORRY HOUSE
Showing also Robert Pringle's house and Willis double house

THE MILES BREWTON HOUSE, 1765
Now in Possession of the Frost family
See Page 113

Edwards house when the family of the Revolutionary Patriot were forced to entertain British officers as their unwelcome guests while their father and brother were held prisoners before being deported to Philadelphia. The interesting building called for many years the Charleston Club was built by a descendant of Landgrave Smith, and the tall brick house across the way was the Ladson Home.

Robert Hazlehurst, a prominent merchant, built the large wooden house which is now the home of Dr. A. E. Baker. Another very old house was formerly located on a large lot just north of Dr. Edward Parker's quaint and interesting home, the slate roof of which indicates its approximate age. It passed out of existence and was replaced by a brick house erected by G. W. Williams, Sr., and next North was Manigault house. On the opposite side of Meeting street St. Michael's church owns a quaint brick edifice which bears all the earmarks of age and is found near the handsome new Hannahan house, the McIver, and the Felder houses. At one period previous to the Revolution, St. Michael's had owned the tall three-story brick building now owned by H. V. Salmons and his wife Rosalind Waring, and used it as a rectory.

Robert Pringle's home was another large house built before the Revolution. He was a Scotch merchant who married Jane Allen in 1734, and buried her in 1746; subsequently he married Judith—by whom he had issue. Just west of this place on Tradd street is a strange double house, which has been the home of many persons of note since it housed Chief Justice Wright and his family. It is now owned by the family of the late Major Edward Willis, Quartermaster C. S. A.

The Horry house, built sometime between 1751 and 1767, occupies the northwest corner of Meeting and Broad streets. It is now the home of Judge W. H. Dunkin. The house is built according to the plans typical of colonial Charlestown, with a central hall ending on a stairway leading to the withdrawing room on the second floor front. Downstairs four beautiful rooms are adorned with elaborate carving and decorative panels. The Horry House was constructed for William Branford, whose daughter Ann married Thomas Horry. The house was inherited by their son, Elias, and passed into the possession of the Barbot and Boyd families successively.

Various other fine houses are attributed to this period. No. 128 Tradd street is said to have been Humphrey Sommers' home; and the wooden house on South Battery built after 1768 by Thomas Savage became in time the town house of Colonel William Washington and his famous wife, the patriotic lady who made the Eutaw flag, one of the most cherished possessions of the historic military company the "Washington Light Infantry" of this city whose record is rivaled only by that of the lately disbanded "Light Dragoons."

For many years the City of Charleston centered around the churches of St. Philip's and St. Michael's, but after the fire of 1740 it began to expand. Previous to this time isolated houses had been built in the outlying districts, which would seem to those who have modern methods of getting around to be within a stone's throw of the principal parts of the city. As the town grew to the north and east, Meeting street was opened up as a result of a petition of the inhabitants of the city and of Ansonboro, who stated that should the street that led northward by St. Michael's Church and the Independent and Scotch Meetings (commonly called old Church Street) be opened it would be of great service to those who wished to enter the city or those whose business carried them out by the Quarter House into the outlying settlements. Moreover the muster-fields lay beyond the city, and the street would be both useful and ornamental. The people also asked for a bridge, and after citizens Toomer and Pinckney entered into some sort of agreement about their adjoining lands a substantial bridge was erected which helped the whole Eastern water front to develop. Henry Laurens' brick house was constructed in the neighborhood of Laurens' Green, and Nathaniel Heyward's big wooden house was placed below Laurens' Square. Gadsden's Green, Inspection street, Middle street were all below Boundary street. This section was called Gadsdenborough; it was up in that part of town which was the first subdivision of the city and was called Middlesex by its promoter Christopher Gadsden.

Several of these old houses have recently been destroyed to make way for a railroad yard; this left vacant spots instead of fine residences. As this portion of the town became unfashionable people moved elsewhere, but at that period of time these delicate distinctions had not obtained, and many of the most prominent persons in the city owned and occupied splendid houses east of Meeting street and north of Market street.

Adjacent to the market which was later erected on land left in perpetuity to the city by members of the Pinckney family, stood the Pinckney Mansion justly considered one of the most beautiful structures in Colonial Charleston. It was burned in the fire of 1861 when in the occupancy of a dear old-lady member of the family. Its age is attested by the fact that in 1742 it was leased to Governor Glenn as an official residence when the owner, Chief Justice Charles Pinckney and his second wife, the illustrious Eliza Lucas, went to England with their daughter and their two sons— Charles Cotesworth and Thomas. Both sons became lawyers in England and returned to Charleston to serve the Colony in time of need. Harriott became the second wife of Daniel Horry. The lives of the Pinckney brothers present a curious parallel. Both were lawyers, both married prominent women, both owned large estates, both became Major Generals in the Revolution, both had presidential aspirations; one being defeated in 1796, the other in 1800. Both were of the Federal party. Charles C. Pinckney married Sarah Middleton. Major General Thomas married the widow of John Middleton, a British officer, and as her husband completed, after the Revolution, the handsome establishment on George street now owned by the Water Works. His brother lived close by, and their first cousin, Charles Pinckney, son of their Uncle William, Master in Chancery, was also a distinguished lawyer, and bore the appelation "Constitution Charley." He was a very large landowner who had a handsome house filled with fine possessions. It was on account of his activities for the Federal Constitution that he was nick-named.

The life led by the leisure class is well illustrated by the fact that when Governor Glenn came to Carolina his secretary was a Scotch artist, Alexander Gordon by name, who as "Sandy Gordon" became the model for "The Antiquary" in Scott's novel of that name. Mr. Gordon was popular in the literary, musical and artistic circles of the town, and locally was called "Singing Sandy." His will mentions "pictures, portraiture and effigie by me painted," which he leaves to his friend Hon. Hector Beranger de Beaufain, the Reverend Heyward and to his lawyer son, Alexander Gordon, and to his daughter, Frances Charlotte, who married John Troup.

From the year 1732, when Whitmarsh founded the *South Carolina Gazette*, Charleston had a newspaper in which political subjects were discussed and frequent and bitter letters concerning health, morals and social topics and essays of a purely literary quality appeared and showed the editors of the newspapers to be partisan in politics. It carried Parliamentary Proceedings and Court News, the shipping lists, notices of prominent persons, items of local history, notices of marriages, births and deaths, and advertisements. In marriage notices the bride was generally complimented. As the names of Charleston's gentlewomen were supposed to appear but twice in print, at marriage and at death, some witty person remarked that Charleston ladies longed for both.

Whitmarsh's paper succeeded the *South Carolina Weekly Journal*, established by Eleazer Philips, Jr., who came to this city from New England with his father Eleazer to keep a book and stationery shop while the son set up a printing press. The printer died July 10, 1732 and his grave is in the Circular Church cemetery.

Private parties attempted a parcel post and rural delivery in 1732 and letters and "paquets" were sent beyond the Ashley Ferry, Dorchester, Stono and Pon Pon.

Charleston was not destitute of literature. Her authors include Governors Archdale and Glenn, and John Wesley, who here published his first edition of his church hymns.

Thomas Reese amassed great knowledge and wrote an excellent essay on the influence of religion in society, for which he was made a Doctor of Divinity by Princeton.

Between 1729 and 1763 the Scotch citizens organized the St. Andrew's Club and the Frenchmen formed the Two Bit Club in 1736. It increased its membership, enlarged its subscription, undertook charitable and educational work and became the South Carolina Society, whose aims may be gathered from the golden hand adorning the gable end of the hall on Meeting street. The handsome portico was added after 1800.

The St. George Society was founded in 1733 and the Friendly Society for Insurance Protection came about ten years later. The Masonic Fraternity here established Solomon Lodge in 1736 and a Friendly Society was founded by a number of Germans who had already settled in South Carolina by the year 1766. The society was for mutual benefit and for the aid of fellow-countrymen in the Colony. By the year 1772 the funds had so increased as to warrant the establishment of a permanent charity, and in 1777 a thousand pound loan was made to the State.

The St. Cecelia, a musical society, was organized in 1762. At first it met at different halls, or "long rooms", wherever it suited the managers to hold it and notices appeared in the papers announcing the meetings and asking guests to direct their coachmen to enter and leave certain streets in such a manner as to allow visitors to alight at the entrance of the Hall. Later Josiah Quincy describes one of the meetings, to which he was invited by David Deas, a gentleman to whom he brought a letter of introduction, when coming from Massachusetts. "The Concert House" said he, "is a large elegant building situated down a yard." Mr. Quincy was met by an usher to whom he presented his card, bearing his own and his host's name, after which he was directed to a second waiter, a third finally carried him into the large hall where the concert took place. Quincy saw over two hundred and fifty ladies, heard good music on bass viols and French horns, and listened to Mr. Abercrombie's violin.

In the piping times of peace after 1740 the fortifications

had been allowed to fall into disrepair and streets had been opened through them, but at the time of the Cherokee War the government began the erection of a strong horn work beyond the northern boundary of the city, to be flanked with batteries and redoubts at proper distances and extend from river to river. The war ended while the work was progressing, but parts that were built to extend from present day Meeting across King to St. Philip street, were long known as the Indian Fort and old Draw Gates. A portion of horn work is enclosed in an iron fence on Marion Square. The noted engineer, De Brahms, who was sent from England to repair the fortifications in 1755-56, reported that Charlestown was the richest and most eminent city in the southern part of North America and contained 1,500 houses, on straight, broad and regular streets, and had many fine public buildings which included a State House near the center of Broad St., constructed to contain rooms for the Governor and Council, for the representatives of the people, the secretary's office and a court room. He described St. Michael's as having a steeple 192 feet high, which was seen by vessels at sea before they made any landing. He mentioned that four buildings were "raised" since the year 1752. No expense had been spared to make them solid, convenient and elegant. He said that the city was divided into two parishes and had two churches and six meeting houses and an assembly for Quakers and another for Jews.

A short epitome of the history of the Exchange would constitute an entire chapter of local annals. Details can be gathered from Fraser's "Reminiscences," Johnson's "Traditions," The *Gazette*, the official document of the British and American Armies at the time of the Revolution; records of the Post Office Department and incidents connected with the Confederate War and the tragic era following the Federal occupation of the city. The Revolutionary martyr Hayne was led from his prison beneath this building to die upon the gallows, erected near the present site of St. Paul's Church, Radcliffeboro. The Exchange, which stands on East Bay and Broad streets, has been altered from its first aspect. Then it faced the waterfront; now it looks down Broad street; at one time it had a cupola which served as a watch tower. When advertisements appeared and called for bids for erecting the structure, the Messrs. Horlbeck secured the contract. The worth of their work is shown by the endurance of this building, known as the Old Post Office, now owned by the United States Light House Department and used as headquarters by the Society of the Daughters of the American Revolution.

St. Michael's Church is considered the most interesting monument of Colonial Charlestown. On June 14, 1751 all of the city south of the middle of Broad street was made into the Parish of St. Michael's. In February 1752, the Governor and commissioners laid a corner stone for the Parish church "amidst the applause of a numerous concourse of people." The company then adjourned to Gordon's "genteel house of entertainment" and ended the day in a convivial manner. A bill of £61, 10 shillings was rendered. This included five shillings for broken glasses. . . . Book W. W. (M.C.O.) recording a deed of Conveyance, gives a list of the commissioners appointed to build the new church, when they transferred pew No. 13 to William Stone, who subscribed £225 toward the building of the church. Samuel Prioleau witnessed the deed to which Samuel Cardy subscribes as "Arch." (architect).

Since its opening in 1761 the church has survived the guns of the British artillery and Federal fleet, several cyclones and an earthquake. Her bells have been used to give the alarm of fire and call into use the engine kept in the Church yard; to ring the curfew for the slaves, to chime for patriotic meetings, toll for funerals, peal for weddings and hurry people into the Church when the "parson bell" jangled at eleven o'clock of a Sunday morning. From the Church tower the watchman used to call out "all's well", announce the time and the weather conditions. It has been used as an observation post in all the various wars since its erection.

The Masons held a service in the building before it was completed in February, 1761. Three years later the clock and bells were sent from England, and the organ in 1768. After the Revolution Major Traille seized the bells and shipped them to England from where they were returned by a Mr. Rhyner in 1783. They were sent to Columbia for safe keeping during the Confederate War but two of the bells were stolen and the rest were broken up when that city was destroyed in 1865. Later, the broken fragments were gathered up, sent to England, recast in the original patterns and returned to this city in 1867. When they were re-hung they pealed forth into "Home again, Home again, from a Foreign Shore."

Washington worshipped here in 1791 and sat in the pew still held by descendents of "Intendant" Vanderhorst, then Mayor of Charleston. Lafayette sat here in 1825 and Henry Clay and his valiant adversary Daniel Webster both attended services in St. Michael's, if they did not occupy the State pew.

Before the Revolution, judges and court officers were required by law to wear their scarlet robes and give ear to a long "session sermon" in this building before attempting to administer justice. During the post-Revolutionary period, when numerous patriotic organizations were welding men of the commonwealth together, the church was often filled with officers and men dressed in uniform and wearing badges of the Cincinnati, Palmetto Society, Ancient and Honorable Battalion of Artillery and heroes who had served with Moultrie and Col. William Washington or with his distinguished kinsman at Trenton, Valley Forge, Brandywine, Germantown, and Monmouth.

During the troubles with France in 1798, meetings were held in the church and resulted in the building of Fort Mechanic on East Battery, where the Visanski home replaces the Holmes' house just south of the Alston house, now occupied by Mrs. H. A. M. Smith, and her son, the owner of Middleton Place Gardens.

The church-plate consisted of two large tankards, a chalice, a paten and an alms-basin, given in 1762 by Governor Boone, whose house, or that of his mother, still stands on the northwest corner of Stoll's Alley and East Bay. It was once known as the Roper home, and is now owned and occupied by Mr.

UNDATED PLAN OF THE CITY
It shows Gadsden's Sub-Division, Middlesex. Begun about 1763

INTERIOR OF THE MILES BREWTON HOUSE, COMMONLY KNOWN AS THE PRINCE HOUSE

George Moffett. These pieces were lost in Columbia in 1861-65, with two alms-basins given by George Somers, Mayor of the city in 1816, and Miss Anne McPherson's gift of a christening bowl. One of the tankards was found in a New York pawnshop and returned to the congregation by Hon. Alexander W. Bradford. The cover of the chalice was later sent from Ohio, but at present St. Michael's uses some modern silver given by Mr. Eugene Jervey and the congregation. It has two pieces of ancient church plate belonging to the English Church which has now gone to decay by Ashley River near old Dorchester Settlement. St. Michael's also has in its vault some strange looking old wooden sconces in the form of hands, formerly used to hold lights over the desk from which the "Lessons" for the day, were read.

The gates of St. Michael's churchyard were made by Jusiti, an iron worker whose name is found woven into a grille on the pavement in front of the drug store on Meeting street near Market. Several Charleston gates are attributed to him, including those in the rear of Ashley Hall, those of the Sass house, (once the Arthur Hayne home) on Legare street and possibly the George Edwards house on Legare street.

Although mystery has departed from the trades and the guild has been replaced by the labor-union, yet labor has always been noble since "God was an artisan working away, eager his fingers, covered with clay," and Charleston should extend civic thanks to those sons of Tubal Cain whose work in metal has helped make this a notable place.

In 1761 a terrible typhoon struck the town. It came down Ashley River, fell upon shipping with a sound as of thunder and in three minutes did £200,000 damage to the houses, wharves and boats of the town, and caused the deaths of many persons. The damage extended up into the heart of the city where a Glebe house stood near St. Philips and Beaufain streets of today. The house on Glebe street was built in 1770.

The most beautiful private residence in the city is the house on lower King street which is now called the "Pringle House." It was built by the architect and master-workman Ezra Waite for Miles Brewton who, later, perished at sea with his family. It then passed into the hands of his sister Mrs. Motte, who was living in it at the time of the Revolution. During the British occupation the house was the Headquarters of the commanding officer, whose military family was lodged in a fine residence on the present Legare St., once the Roper house, at that period a short stone's throw from the Brewton house, being at the Western end of the formal garden. Josiah Quincy describes the handsome entertainments given there.

CHAPTER VII

A N OUTLINE, not intended to be historically perfect but given merely as a guide to indicate the position occupied by Charlestown, the place and the people, shows that in 1751 the Legislative branch of government in South Carolina consisted of a Governor, Council and Commons House of Assembly, and was ordinarily styled the General Assembly. The Governor and Council were appointed by the King, or Crown, continuing in office till removed; the Commons House of Assembly was elective, its members chosen by voters of the Province, and were to be residents of the Province, and each Commons House of Assembly was to expire in two years. The Governor had the authority to dissolve the House of Assembly as often as he thought advisable and to issue writs for the election of a new House. The law requiring elections every two years was not strictly carried out, and at times three years or more intervened between elections. And, again, the Governor frequently exercised his power of dissolution. Such was the law until the Revolution, and such it remained until South Carolina adopted a temporary constitution in March 1776, under which the first election for members of the legislative body was held in October.

Plainly Charleston was not an uncivilized outpost of the British empire. She was an important city, with a library, several free, and many paid, schools. She had churches of every denomination. Planters employed tutors for their children on the plantations and wealthy Charlestonians sent their sons to England and the continent to complete their education. As the sons were educated they returned to Carolina, bringing with them a knowledge of, and a taste for, the refinements of cultured life. All the niceties of court life were observed at social functions. The people led easy, gay, showy and hospitable existences, luxuries were easily obtained. Coaches and horses were imported, despite the tax placed upon "Northern" horses and the advertisements of local workmen that they could build as good coaches as could be imported. Tailors, wig-makers, milliners kept provincial Charlestonians dressed, wigged, perfumed and hatted in the latest English styles. The ladies had their fine brocades, laces, jewels and flowers for the hair, while the men had their scarlet topcoats, their rapiers, their military uniforms, and all the accessories demanded by London social life.

Work was plentiful, even though the grand jury of 1742 did present as a grievance the fact that slave labor was competing with white artisans who came here seeking to better themselves. Owners of the slaves replied that those who complained were lazy men who had refused to work for reasonable wages and had held up planters who were seeking to construct plantation boats to get their rice, indigo and products to town ahead of the autumnal gales.

That the culture of Charleston was not a superficial growth is demonstrated by the fact that a hospital for sick sailors and transients was erected here by the vestry of St. Philip's in 1749. A matron, nurses and servants were provided. In 1767 an act was passed and over three thousand pounds were appropriated for the subsistence of invalid soldiers, their widows and orphans, and transient poor. Men do not gather grapes of thorns and when a hospital was operating in 1819 at Hampstead for the benefit of the sick and the poor, it showed that the roots of the old life were bearing good fruit.

Nor were these things the only evidences of culture. When the rich planters came to town and built their summer homes they always surrounded them with fine gardens, laid out in geometrical designs such as Miss Emma Richardson has recently employed in connection with the Thomas Heyward house, where George Washington was lodged in 1791. This entire house has been reclaimed through the efforts of the Society for the Preservation of Historic Dwelling Houses, under leadership of Captain Alston Deas, a loyal son of the State. The society has made it possible for visitors to see the type of house builded here before the Revolution, the material used and the finish obtained by the use of native products. The house of Miles Brewton on King street has needed no restoration, and it also speaks for the class of people who were living in Charleston and carrying on the affairs of the colony. Not only did they have fine houses but they loved flowers. Old Mrs. Scott's lovely garden on East Bay was destroyed during the gale of 1752 and the formal grounds laid out around the Laurens home, by John Watson the English gardener who afterward went into business for himself, were torn up during the Revolution. Robert Squibbs "circulated" plants native to Carolina, and with Watson shipped shrubs from Charleston to be planted in Public Gardens in England.

Charleston was "Well bred, well fed, and well read," and was the bright particular star in the English crown. The first and second Georges were "Nursing Fathers" to this Colony. From the inception of their reigns until the third George ascended the throne Carolina enjoyed an era of unprecedented prosperity. As population increased and commerce prospered, so did the cultural life of the city. The first crude efforts of Anthony Aston, the wandering British Minstrel, to entertain people upon the streets of the town in 1730 have been immortalized in the epilogue to his "Fools Opera" published under the name of "Mat Medley." After that theatrical performances were given in the Council rooms until a regular theatre was built in 1736. The *Gazette* of January 31st announced that the building would be opened on February 12 with the comedy "The Recruiting Officer." As Charleston was a garrison town, this was no doubt a compliment and a drawing card at the same time. This seems to have been a favorite play as the Masons asked for it on the 26th of May, 1737, and the *Gazette* of the 28th said that the house was full and the Masons in the pit joined in singing the choruses. Tickets had been on sale at Mr. Shepheards, where the fraternity is said to have come into existence. Plays were performed at least once a week and included beside the favorite, "The Orphan," "The London Merchant," and various efforts musical and dramatic, interspersed with local offerings. Some of the theatre-minded amateurs of the city took part in these performances and the three theatres in Charleston brought forward those who were not natives, but who later became famous—including the Misses Cheer, Wainwright and Hallam and Messrs. Wools and Wall. Charleston audiences saw the first presentations of "The Orphan of China," "A Woman Keeps a Secret," "The School for Lovers" and "The Oracle."

England was reckoning without her host when she failed to consider the type of people who were maturing in Carolina. Upon the walls of the great houses hung portraits brought over from ancestral homes in England or the pictures owned by members of Huguenot families. Mrs. Catherine de St. Julien's will mentions eighteen paintings and twelve framed engravings. Old wills and inventories frequently carry long lists of books and pictures. Edmond Atkins, the Indian Agent, who married Lady Ann McKenzie, daughter of the Earl of Cromartie, mentions his picture drawn by Mr. Theus; so that beside the portraits painted by Gainsborough, Ramsay and Copley, Charleston was beginning to appreciate the work of her own artists, Theus, Coram, Warwell, Earle and Scarlett. The native American artists of a later date include Washington Allston, Sully, Fraser and a host of lesser lights. After the Revolution, Charlestonians were also painted by Zoffany, West and Romney. Examples of Gilbert Stuart's work are found here, along with many portraits which cannot now be identified. These numerous portraits have preserved for present days the fashions of Colonial Charleston and furnish definite examples of the kind of people who lived here at that date. Mrs. Roger Smith, sister of John Rutledge, continues to look out over the world as she proudly holds her little son, and Mr. and Mrs. Ralph Izard, whose portraits were painted in 1774-75, furnish a correct idea of the fashions of the day and indicate the standards of colonial society.

The Izard house, one of the most substantial and beautiful structures in the city, on Broad street, is known as the Bryan residence. It was built and used before 1757 by the Izard family and at one time was the home of Mrs. John Julius Pringle (a grand-daughter of Ralph Izard). Her second husband was Hon. Joel E. Poinsette, Minister of Mexico, for whom the gorgeous red flower is named.

Pelatia Webster, a visitor to Charlestown, describes the Pre-Revolutionary State House as "a heavy building, a hundred and twenty by forty feet, containing a forty foot council chamber, decorated with many pillars and much carving, rather superb than elegant," also an Assembly room of the same dimensions of plainer work but "convenient enough"— while sundry public offices were kept in small apartments below. Down stairs was a Court House, where the Court of Common Pleas and of the Crown were held in an unfinished building. Webster said, "The streets intersected each other at right angles and were not paved except the footways, which are paved with brick in the principal streets."

The city had stretched northward, the fortifications were in ruins, but no one minded that as England was at peace with all the world and this city had no need for forts and cannons. Plantation folk drove into town down the Broad Path behind handsome horses. The Coach rumbled along fairly well-kept roads. All was merry as a marriage bell, but nevertheless, Charleston was unconsciously preparing for a struggle with the Mother Country.

Members of the different military companies which the Charleston gentlemen formed wore uniforms displaying the scarlet mountings of regiments belonging to the Crown. The Cavalry boasted fine horsemen like the English gentlemen upon whom they patterned themselves, "The Squires" of Carolina were fond of horse-racing, field-sports, and hunting the deer, bear and fox. As early as 1700 the Assembly placed a heavy tax upon all Northern horses when Virginia stock was imported in large quantities. The tax resulted in attempts to rear Carolina horses, stock crossed with Spanish horses imported from Florida. These were handsome, active and hardy, and produced with the English horses colts of great beauty, swiftness and strength. After 1754, the stock was further improved by foreign importations. What was begun as a gentleman's pleasure exercised a tremendous influence upon the history of Carolina during the period of Revolutionary warfare. The Province was prostrate under British rule and the patriots, Marion, Pickens, and Sumter, could never have accomplished its redemption but for the fleet-footed horses of the lowlands used by the followers of these men.

The first race run for a prize took place on the then "neck", opposite the Bowling Green house. The course was called the York, after the English racing ground, in 1734. The next year, a track was laid out about six miles from the town near the Quarter House. In 1754, the New Market course, established by subscription, was laid out about a mile above the town, on the Blake tract which extended between King street road and Broad Path to the marshes of Cooper river, above today's Line street, Upper Childsbury. Meeting street was not yet laid out.

After 1760, races were run at Jacksonborough, Ferguson's Ferry, Beaufort, and Strawberry Ferry near Childsbury. Famous horses were owned by Daniel Ravenel, the two Harlestons, Francis Huger, William Middleton and a Mr. Nightingale from Yorkshire. When Mr. Nightingale's imported horse, "Shadow" raced Mr. William Henry Drayton's Carolina-bred "Adolphus", the latter was defeated in a four mile heat over the New Market course, but "Shadow" was never beaten. Mr. Nightingale then imported "Careless", a celebrated English racer, and Harleston's "Flimnap" was brought to Charleston just prior to the Revolution. When Josiah Quincy was in the city in 1773 he went to the famous races and reported that these were well performed but that Flimnap outran the winner of the last sixteen races. Over £2000 changed hands at this race, and the horse itself was sold for £300, sterling.

The importance of the training received by Charleston men in the campaigns of the French and Indian wars cannot be overestimated. Glenn's treaties made with the Cherokees and Creeks had held good until after the conclusion of the war when an unfortunate incident occurred which plunged Carolina into a bloody war with the Cherokee nation. Glenn had secured land from these Indians and had put up forts at Ninety Six, at Keowee Town on the Savannah river and at

Loudon on the Tennessee river, five hundred miles from Charlestown. These places were garrisoned by colonial soldiers.

The French War was concluded without ever having affected Charleston in any way except that some of the pitiful exiles called Acadians passed through her streets to become absorbed into the rural districts. In 1756, when William Henry Lyttleton became Governor, Cherokee Indians who had been fighting for England were returning from Virginia. They are said to have captured some riderless horses. The owners, forgetting that these men were friends and allies and heedless of the consequences of their act, followed the Indians, shot fourteen of them and made the rest prisoners. The rule whereby old Indians were held accountable for young members of the tribe was invoked. A company of the headmen were coming to interview Lyttleton, who in turn was advancing against the Cherokee nation, which had risen when their young warriors were killed. Lyttleton refused to hear what the headmen had to say and placed these in confinement in Fort George. Little Carpenter secured the release of some of these. In some manner the commander of the fort was decoyed out of the walls and with some of his men surprised and killed. The hostages within the fort were shot. A horrible situation now arose. The settlements of the Calhouns and Hamptons were nearly wiped out. Lyttleton left the country at the expiration of his term as Governor in 1760 and Lieutenant-Governor William Bull the second secured troops from Virginia and North Carolina. The war was pushed by British regulars under Colonel Montgomery, brought to Charleston on transports escorted by the Albany. They were joined by Charleston riflemen under Thomas Middleton and other troops under Laurens, Moultrie, Francis Marion, Isaac Huger and Andrew Pickens, who by fighting with British regulars learned to fight against them and wove the state into a unified whole that was the first step in raising troops in the Revolutionary War. Montgomery was called away and Grant was sent in his place. His overbearing manner led to a duel with Colonel Thomas Middleton, which took place in Charleston.

The Indians carried the fight into Tennessee. There "Little Carpenter" bought and set free his friend Captain John Stuart, the Indian agent whose work carried him as far west as Mobile, and Stuart returned to Charlestown to notify Governor Bull of an intended attack upon Fort Prince George, to which place Bull rushed 2,600 troops in 1761. Peace was made only after the Cherokees had been pitifully punished.

John Stuart's house was built of wood just before the Revolution. Standing at the corner of Tradd and Orange streets, it is now owned by Mr. Walter Pringle. Tales of Reverend Dr. Purcell's life in this house include those of a Ghost, as well as the story of his venturesome daughter who used to scale the old brick wall on the east side of the house, go out to parties, and climb back again. Marion, the Swamp Fox, is also supposed to have gained a broken leg by jumping out of a window in Stuart's house and fleeing around the corner into the present Orange street, which obtained its name from the Orange garden formerly occupying much of this area. The house became Mrs. Stuart's prison during the Revolution, as John Stuart and his family were Royalists. Another large wooden house on the northern end of Orange street was the home of Edward Rutledge, whose brother, Dictator John, lived across the street in the house now owned and occupied by Mr. R. G. Rhett; Mr. F. G. Wagner now owns the Edward Rutledge house. Several other wooden houses of interesting exteriors and historical significance are in narrow Orange street. Particularly so is the double house where Pastor Gilman's grandchildren now reside, the southern portion of which was once used as a home for Confederate widows.

The ship yards of Charleston had been operating since 1740 in turning out rice schooners and plantation boats. By 1769 they were completing about twelve good-sized vessels a year. The ship-builders of the Thames began to lose trade and by the time that the Revolution fairly arrived two-thirds of the American shipping was colony built. Hob-Caw Bill Pritchard was a noted ship-builder of Charleston. England

HENRY LAURENS
See Page 134

BENJAMIN HUGER

STAMP-OFFICE,

Lincoln's-Inn, 1765.

A

T A B L E

Of the Prices of Parchment and Paper for the Service

of *America*.

Parchment.		Paper.	
Skins 18 Inch. by 13, at Four pence		Horn at Seven-pence	
22 —— by 16, at Six-pence		Fools Cap at Nine-pence	
26 —— by 20, at Eight-pence	each.	D° with printed Notices ⎱ at	
28 —— by 23, at Ten-pence		for Indentures ⎰ 1 s.	each Quire.
31 —— by 26, at Thirteen-pence		Folio Poſt at One Shilling	
		Demy——at Two Shillings	
		Medium at Three Shillings	
		Royal——at Four Shillings	
		Super Royal at Six Shillings	

Paper for Printing

News.		Almanacks.	
Double Crown at 14 s. ⎱ each Ream.		Book—Crown Paper at 10 s. 6 d.	
Double Demy at 19 s. ⎰		Book——Fools Cap at 6 s. 6 d.	each Ream.
		Pocket — Folio Poſt at 20 s.	
		Sheet——Demy at 13 s.	

THE OBNOXIOUS STAMP TAX, 1765
Prices of Parchment and Paper

By Kindness of the City

picked a wrong moment to tighten up on the Navigation laws and grant "writs of assistance" which permitted officials to enter any house at any time and search for smuggled goods. These writs were called "Instruments of slavery" and their use was one of the causes of Revolution.

In 1764 The Stamp Act was proposed in Parliament. The next year it was passed. By its provisions business documents were illegal unless written upon stamped paper. The cheapest stamp was a shilling; the prepared paper must be paid for in specie. Law suits were common. Coin was scarce. Violators of the act could be tried without a jury, before a judge whose pay came out of his fines.

Stamps were to be placed on books and newspapers as well. The stamps were made in England and Distributors were appointed to bring them to America. The effect, says E. Benjamin Andrews, was like that of a bomb in a powder magazine. Northern papers came out in mourning. New York made a bonfire and burnt the stamps. Charleston tolled her bells and the flags on the ships in the harbor hung at half mast. The merchants of the city joined the citizens in bitterly resenting this tax. They resolved upon rebellion and having resolved they were not afraid to commit acts of legal treason. They seized a ship which was bringing stamps into the harbor. Lieutenant-Governor Bull seeing the attitude of the people would not allow the stamps to be brought into the city but had them stored at Fort Johnson.

One hundred and fifty men went to James Island, captured the fort, hauled down the British flag and at daylight ran up a blue flag displaying three silver crescents. The officer commanding the sloop which brought the stamps was invited to visit the fort and was shown preparations for its defence; he was told that they were prepared to resist any assault but that if he would sail promptly the stamped paper would be returned. Upon reflection he weighed anchor and vanished. Paper was brought on the ship "Planter's Adventure" from London. During the night a twenty-foot gallows was built in the center of the city and a figure representing a man who sold stamped paper hung upon it. Over the gallows "Liberty and no Stamp Act" was written, and a sign was attached to the figure which read: "Whosoever shall dare pull down these effigies had better have been born with a millstone about his neck and cast into the sea."

The next day these dummies were burned on a green near the present jail. Citizens entered and ransacked several houses in town where they thought paper had been stored. Shortly the courts were unable to transact business as everyone refused to use stamped paper. Finally, the men who were to sell it agreed to hold the paper until word could come from England in reply to the protest made by the colonies. Official protest was carried by Thomas Lynch, Sr., John Rutledge and Gadsden to the Stamp Act Congress held in New York, October 1765.

The Revolutionary period of Charlestown's history began when Joseph Boone, governor between 1761-64, left the province; continued when Lynch and John Rutledge attended the Stamp Act Congress, and lulled when the Stamp Act was repealed. Charlestown erected a marble statue to William Pitt, the statesman and friend of the colonies, and placed portraits of Gadsden, Lynch, and Rutledge in her Legislative halls.

After the repeal of the Stamp Act when William Johnson and his group of Charleston artisans continued to meet under the Liberty Tree in Mr. Mazyck's pasture lot (by the modern Charlotte and Alexander streets) Gadsden said that King George would soon make another attempt to tax the people in the colonies. His prophecy was fulfilled in 1767 when the British Parliament passed the Townshend Acts, laying duties upon glass, paints, colors, and tea. The Liberty Tree Party met, illuminated the tree, fired sky-rockets and named Gadsden as the man they wanted sent to the new legislature. This was shortly dissolved by Governor Montague. A non-importation party was organized under "The Liberty Tree," and, instituting a boycott, appointed a committee to take every step justifiable in its enforcement. A list of the inhabitants of the town was made to find out their sentiments, after which the *Gazette* announced that only twenty-one of the inhabitants of Charlestown (exclusive of the Crown officers) were non-subscribers. The names of these twenty-one were printed on hand-bills and thrown about the city. The names of William H. Drayton and Mr. Wragg were found on the list and Mr. Wragg published a paper expressing his views and courteously expressed his belief that the published list of non-subscribers did not by any means include all who had not signed. Drayton's actions taken later in the cause of the colony spoke louder than any words.

His Excellency Lord Charles Grenville Montague was nominally Governor from 1766 to 1768, but during one of his prolonged absences Hon. William Bull, Lieutenant-Governor, had been for the fifth time called to act as governor and it is supposed that if Bull, who was beloved for his justice and was truly loyal to England while yet a favorite in Charlestown, had been made dictator, war might have been averted.

He was up at his country place when news came that Lord William Campbell, the Governor of Nova Scotia, who was no stranger here, as his wife was a member of the South Carolina family of Izards, had been made Governor of Carolina. Lord William followed Governor Montague.

Governor Montague, who had gone to England for his health and returned in 1771, ordered that British troops be sent to Charlestown to reinforce those left there after the Cherokee War. He asked for quarters for these soldiers and when these were not given voluntarily he quartered them upon private families. The citizens thereupon applied for arms, saying that they needed them for protection against Indians and negroes. Montague had been received with cordiality, he was now detested. He now dissolved the legislature and gave up his office in 1773, after making overtures to prominent Charlestonians, Moultrie among others.

The "London" brought two hundred and fifty-seven chests of tea, which were left to rot in warehouses of the town. In 1774 the ship "Brittania" sailed into port and brought among other things seven chests of tea, subject to duty. Citizens visited the ship and dumped the tea overboard. The *Gazette* called it "an oblation made to Neptune." The act was witnessed by the general committee of observance and was done by the merchants to whom the tea had been sent. After the emptying of the chests a "numerous concourse" of people gave three hearty cheers and "immediately afterward separated, as if nothing had happened." Meanwhile, troops had landed in Boston, a massacre had followed, after which came the Boston Tea Party, the closing of that port, the Battle of Bunker Hill and the burning of Charlestown, Massachusetts. The South Carolina *Gazette* announced on March 1, 1773 that a meeting of the General Assembly would be held a week later. This was the last Commons House of Assembly elected in South Carolina. It remained Commons House of Assembly until dissolved, September 15, 1775. From May, 1774 to March 26, 1776, South Carolina was practically under dual government. The Royal Government was expiring, and the Revolutionary Government forming.

The right Honorable Lord William Campbell, fourth son to the Duke of Argyle and Commander of his Majesty's ship the "Nightingale," who had married Miss Sarah Izard, a young lady "esteemed to have one of the most considerable fortunes in the province", was sent to Carolina to become Royal Governor. On account of his family connections it was supposed that Campbell would be able to reconcile Charleston to the Crown, but the Izards, themselves, were of divided political opinion. Mrs. Campbell was a sister of Ralph Izard, Jr., of Fair Spring, St. George's, Justice of the Peace, member of the Provincial Congress, the Assembly and Continental Convention of Carolina. The St. James branch of the Izards also attained great wealth and prominence in public and social affairs, but remained true to the Crown. Lord Campbell's wife followed her husband's politics and after the Revolution she made her home in England, when her property in Charleston was confiscated and her chaise sold for debt.

Campbell assumed office too late to avert war. When he did arrive the Royal Government had been superseded by that of the Provincial Congress. Mr. Bull was again at his county place but the messenger who came to call him was interrupted by booming guns announcing the actual arrival of Lord Campbell in the harbor. Three years later while participating in an attack on Charlestown, under Sir Peter Parker, he received a wound which proved fatal.

The Governor was received, as usual, by the militia, the place-men and councillors, who numbered in this instance but fifteen persons. He was waited on by private gentlemen and proceeded to the portico of the Exchange, there to read his commission as Governor. The proclamation was received in sullen silence by the assembled citizens.

The house on Meeting street had been secured for his residence, but it was not ready for occupancy, and Miles Brewton, who had married a first cousin of Lady Campbell's, undertook to entertain him and his wife in the interval. An address presented to Lord Campbell was signed by him. He could not sleep after thinking that he had signed the address and subscribed to its terms, and during the night he called up his host and asked him as member of the council of safety to erase the words "and take up arms" from the documents. It is said that the whole matter was dropped rather than allow a word concerning the Governor's conduct to become a subject for public discussion.

BOOK III

THE REVOLUTION, 1776-1783

CHAPTER VIII

AS TIME rolled on the ties with England weakened and realization of the boundless resources of this vast continent strengthened; all things pointed to independence. England seemed to regard the colonies as trading corporations, to be managed in the interest of the commercial classes at home. Conflict was inevitable. Carolina prepared for war when 184 persons from all parts of the colony came together at Charleston, "placed themselves in an attitude of hostility to England", took over the government, called themselves the Provincial or Colonial Congress and appointed W. H. Drayton, Arthur Middleton, C. C. Pinckney, William Gibbes and Edward Weyman members of a secret committee with power to enter arsenals and storehouses and seize British arms and ammunition.

Charleston was a divided city. Friends and families were separated over the words, "Loyalist or Patriot." Mr. Bullman preached a sermon at St. Michael's reflecting upon the unlimited and arbitrary powers of the Secret Council. The Vestry met, acceded to the popular demand that Mr. Bullman must immediately be dismissed and their decision was welcomed by a shout that "shook the pulpit and the Altar." The Colony-State now functioned under a Provincial Congress, which on Sunday, June 4th, attended service at St. Michael's and there received pledges of the lives and fortunes of its members to carry on war. A Council of Safety, empowered to command all soldiers and use all public money, was formed and Carolina set up at Charleston the first independent government in the colonies. Patriotic committees worked together to interpret regulations of the Provincial Congress, call in debts, inspect vessels, deal with threats of slave uprisings and silence foreign incendiaries, some of whom they tarred, feathered and carted through the streets before exiling them to the West Indies. The Council of Safety received a million dollars with which to pay soldiers.

On April 9th, 1776, the House of Assembly is described as the "late House of Assembly"; showing that the period of actual conflict had been entered. Act No. 1128 of the Statutes at Large is signed by John Rutledge, President, James Parson, Speaker of the General Assembly and G. G. Powell, Speaker of the Legislative Council, making death the punishment of those who should counterfeit the certificates issued to support the credit of the colony and satisfy the creditors of the public. Ten days later the same persons signed Act No. 1132, the preamble to which says that a horrid and unnatural war is now carried on by the ministry and Parliament of Great Britain, against the United Colonies of North America in general, and this colony in particular, with a cruel and oppressive design of robbing the colonies and the good people of this colony of their dearest and most valuable rights as freemen, and reducing them to a state of the most abject slavery and oppression. They are using secret agents "to accomplish these impious and unwarrantable designs and create civil dissentions, and animosity, and disorder, confusion and bloodshed among the good people of the colony", inciting them "not only to disturb the peace, safety and good order of the colony, but to take up arms and spill the blood of their fellow citizens, who are only acting in defense of their lives, liberty and properties, against the hands of lawless and despotic power."

The act deemed persons taking up arms against the State, holding communication with the enemy, or supplying them with provisions, or acting with them in any capacity, as being guilty of a felony without benefit of clergy. It was made a felony to assemble or to disturb the peace or raise seditions, and the estates and personal possessions of the offenders were to be confiscated and sold by the sheriffs of the different districts and the money deposited in the treasury. Officers who refused to do their duty were penalized.

The bulk of Carolina's trade, which in 1775 amounted to a hundred and forty thousand barrels of rice and a million pounds of indigo (worth five million dollars), was handled over her wharves besides a large trade in cattle, corn, wheat, lumber, staves, tar and furs. Three thousand wagons brought produce from the up country to this city and took back goods for the Indian Trade or the Scotch and Irish settlers who continued to pour into upper Carolina. By 1775 Charleston had fifteen thousand out of the seventy-five thousand white persons in the Colony, and her share of the hundred thousand African laborers. In this harbor three hundred and fifty sailing ships were frequently counted at one time, besides boats built at one of the five shipyards of the Province.

The so-called "Infant Colony" with headquarters at Charleston was now suddenly grown up, and the land which had beauty, mystery and youth with which to compound romance was to wake from her dream of beauty and face the horrors of war. Meanwhile the thought of rebellion was slow to take hold in the minds of her people. The town was still a dramatically interesting place, the cobblestone streets still echoed to the laughter of colonial beaux and belles, or resounded to the tread of politicians, merchants, lawyers, planters, laborers, each pursuing his usual avocations secure in the thought that England and her favorite Colony could never seriously disagree. The feeling of dependence on England and loyalty to the Mother Country died hard, but it died.

Even after England's oppressive acts and the indignation aroused thereby had fused the divided colonies into a semblance of union, even after delegates had met again and yet again in Congress, the thought of separating from England was a strange one to the people. Delegates to the first Congress of September 1774 had no instructions to seek independence.

As late as the fall of 1775 Congress declared that it had "not raised an army with the ambitious design of separation from Great Britain". But a change took place in six months which made the Declaration of Independence "Possible and even Popular." The country was declared to be not only ripe for independence but "In danger of becoming rotten for lack of it." The colonists believed themselves capable of defending their liberties should the Mother Country persist in her hostile attitude. The Battles of Lexington and Bunker Hill cast the die.

General George Washington assumed command of the American Army on July 2d, and penned the British up in Boston. Finding himself alarmingly short of powder, he asked the colonies to send ammunition from their supplies. Charlestown, hearing that the Indian agent, John Stuart, was shipping powder into Savannah, secured aid from patriotic Georgians, intercepted and seized the vessel, and obtained seven thousand pounds of power. Amounts claimed by Georgia merchants were turned over to them later and five thousand pounds were shipped to General Washington. The first important action in Carolina took place on September 15, 1775 when Colonel Motte led some of Moultrie's soldiers over to Fort Johnson, captured British troops left from the Cherokee wars and took possession of the fort. Governor Campbell proclaimed the dissolution of the Carolina Common House of Assembly, seized the Great Seal, which made all documents legal, and took refuge on board a sloop of war, "Tamar", lying in that part of Charleston harbor called "Rebellion Road", because ships were out of range of the city guns there. Charlestown troops assembled, all forts were manned, Johnson brought the guns to bear on the British boats which lay abreast of the fort. Seeing Moultrie's Liberty Flag flying from Fort Johnson, Campbell sent a messenger to know by what authority the fort was held, and being answered "by authority of the Council of Safety", made a "demonstration of attacking" the fort, but finally withdrew.

Meanwhile Council decided to block Marsh channel by Hog Island with hulls of old boats. A naval force was needed to engage the two British war vessels in case they should interfere with these plans. The "Defense", with Captain Simon Tuft and a force of seventy men, was armed with ten guns and William Henry Drayton, president of the Council of Safety, went aboard as chief in command. The war was on when on Sunday, November 12, 1775, the "Tamar" and "Cherokee" opened fire against the "Defense." Captain Tuft and Hayward's guns at Fort Johnson replied, the old boats were successfully sunk to block the channels, the British withdrew and the bloodless though spirited affair was over. Being Sunday, the South Carolina Congress assembled and asked for Divine aid in the coming struggle.

Before the Declaration of Independence was signed five colonies had adopted Constitutions. Royal government was shattered, anarchy threatened and in the case of South Carolina the Royal Governor fled. By the end of 1776 nearly all of the colonies had established Governments of their own. The general framework of the government of Carolina remained unchanged. Governors were elected, not appointed. The Legislature replaced the Council, with the difference that in neither the upper or lower house were hereditary legislators recognized. All the states had Sunday Laws, and many of them combined to enforce religious tests: in South Carolina only church members voted. Faulty as the first constitutions were they rescued the colonies from anarchy and carried them safely through the Revolution. In the annals of March 26, 1776 the word "State" appeared in place of the word "Colony." One word was to be erased by tears, the other written in blood. The Colonies in 1775 sent a last petition, respectfully worded, employing the word Congress. The appeal was idle. "The root of England's obduracy was in the King personally." The Colonies realized that further supplications were useless. Thomas Paine's pamphlet "Common Sense" was published January, 1776. In June, Richard Henry Lee of Virginia moved that the united Colonies are, and of right ought to be, free, and the document was signed by the President on July 4, yet, not until August 2 had all the representatives affixed their signatures to the Declaration of Independence as written by Thomas Jefferson. Charlestown's bells were ringing on July 4, and announcing Moultrie's Victory when the Continental Congress at Philadelphia was debating the Declaration. Four of Carolina's delegates,

DECLARATION OF INDEPENDENCE

Edward Rutledge ——— South Carolina
Tho: Heyward Jun.
Thomas Lynch Jun.
Arthur Middleton

SIGNATURES OF THE SOUTH CAROLINA SIGNERS OF THE DECLARATION OF INDEPENDENCE

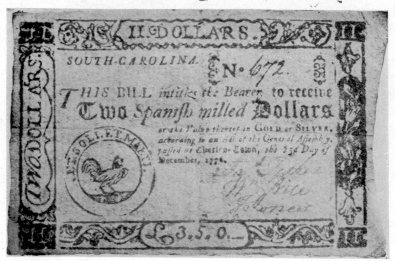

BILL ISSUED ACCORDING TO AN ACT OF DECEMBER, 1776

BILL ISSUED ACCORDING TO AN ACT OF FEBRUARY 8, 1779
Note use of the word "State"

Lynch, Heyward, Rutledge and Middleton voted "aye" on August 5. Charleston celebrated its adoption.

Meanwhile as the Continental Government had no executive power, legislative action was slow. Congress could not enforce obedience from any of the Colonies and, afraid of a standing army, would only authorize short enlistments. Charleston, fearing that reliance could not be placed on the regular organized militia of the State, as it included men of all shades of political opinion, planned a regular force to be officered by gentlemen chosen by ballot and filled by men enlisted for hire—as were the regular armies of Europe. Of the three regiments raised, two were to serve on the coast under Gadsden and Moultrie, and William Thomson was to command the third. At the outbreak of the Revolution the militia consisted of a regiment of horse under Colonel William Moultrie and a regiment from each of the twelve military districts of the Province. The volunteer system came after Charleston fell.

In January, 1775, the first Provincial Congress assembled. It re-assembled, signed an agreement, raised a million dollars, attended service on June 4 and appointed a Committee of Safety. Warships approached the city, and on November 12 the first battle was fought here in the harbor. Under the Government adopted February 1, 1776, dictatorial powers were conferred upon President Drayton, Colonel Pinckney and Thomas Heyward, Jr., and from this time forward the legislature of Charleston proceeded, so it is said, "as if they had never known a King" and the city became a garrison town.

Knowing what to expect after the fight of November 12, 1775, marked the beginning of actual hostilities, Charlestown put her harbor defences in order. A fascine battery was begun near the site of Fort Moultrie and, shortly after, Fort Sullivan, a square enclosure constructed of palmetto logs, designed to have bastions and merlons, was erected and the front finished by June 28th. When the northern half had only reached a height of seven feet and the armament consisted of but thirty-one guns, the fort came into action. Foundations were laid for a second and larger fort in 1796, but it was destroyed by a storm. A third fort was built about 1809, and this is virtually the Fort Moultrie of today.

On February 11, 1776, the Provincial Congress drew up a plan of government and John Rutledge submitted a constitution, adopted March, 1776, making South Carolina an independent state. After this time the Governor was called President and Commander-in-chief of the troops. John Rutledge was elected President; Henry Laurens, Vice President, and William Henry Drayton, Chief Justice.

It may seem unnecessary to dwell upon the attainments, possessions and positions of certain Carolinians, but when it is realized that of the Carolinians admitted to the Middle Temple to study law, all but a few were members of prominent Charleston families, who became leaders in the Revolutionary War, it is readily to be understood that these ardent patriots should become founders of the resulting Commonwealth.

Henry Laurens, son of John Laurens the Huguenot who came to Charleston at an early time and became a merchant, was educated in England, also became a merchant and was probably the most prominent Charlestonian connected with the Revolutionary War. Not only had he been an officer in the Cherokee War of 1761, but he presided over a meeting which the patriots held under the Liberty Tree before the contest started. From 1771 until 1774, he was in England, where his children were at school, and he did what he could to fight the tax which England continued to lay on the colonists. As he embarked for Charleston he sent this message back to the English authorities, "I go resolved still to labor for peace, but determined, in the last event, to stand or fall with my country."

President of the Council of Safety just before the colony became a state, he was Vice President of South Carolina in 1776. Appointed delegate from South Carolina to the Continental Congress in 1777 he succeeded John Hancock, of Massachusetts in the office of President of the Continental

Congress, and during his term three famous measures were discussed. First, the adoption of the Articles of Confederation; second, a treaty with France in order to secure help from that country; and third, the rejection of the overtures towards peace made by the King and Parliament in June, 1778.

To these peace proposals Laurens replied for Congress that Great Britain must acknowledge the independence of the thirteen states and take away her soldiers and warships before Congress would discuss the matter. After which England and America both settled down to the conflict, the last struggle of which was to center chiefly in the South.

Appointed by the United States to ask help from Holland, in 1779, Laurens was captured on the way across the Atlantic by an English ship, taken to London, escorted through the streets, and confined in the tower of London. He was released when he was exchanged for Lord Cornwallis himself, went from London to Paris and was one of the commissioners who signed the treaty of peace. His son, Lieut. Col. John, whose tragic death in the latter part of the Revolution incapacitated his father, negotiated a treaty with France in 1780 and served on Washington's staff. He was a proficient student, an educated gentleman and his accomplishments included those qualities and manners which grace men of the world and were characteristic of well-bred Charlestonians.

Hearing in May, 1776 that Charlestown was to experience a combined land and water attack under Clinton and Parker, materials of war were gleaned and gathered from every possible source. Lead was taken from gutters, house tops and churches, to be run into bullets; impressed vessels were turned into men-of-war; bounties were offered for sailors. Negroes from the plantations were sent to the coast to erect defenses and "the new state looked to the hour of bloody trial close at hand."

On June 28, 1776, at 10:00 o'clock, Fort Moultrie was attacked by Sir Peter Parker, commanding a British fleet of

ten vessels. The bomb vessel, "Thunder", shelled the fort.
The "Actacon", "Solebay", "Bristol" and "Experiment" followed the attack. The "Actacon", nearing the fort, anchored
with spring cables and fired broadside into Fort Moultrie.
Moultrie guns replied only at stated intervals, in an effort to
conserve ammunition. The British, thinking that defence had
ceased, sent up three cheers, but a supply of powder was
sent to the fort which reeled and trembled at each shot received and sent; Moultrie prepared to meet the British behind the crumbling walls of his little fort rather than yield.
Parker was repulsed with a loss of more than two hundred
men. The battle ended at nine o'clock in the evening.

While the British fleet attacked, Colonel Thomson, at the
other end of Sullivan's Island, with his command the third
Carolina regiment was engaging Clinton's forces at Breach
Inlet. Thomson's first service against the king had been in
the upper country. In company with Drayton, William
Tennant, Ely Kershaw and others he had gone to the upper
settlements and later fought there Bloody Bill Cunningham. Now Thomson's special regiment of 50 riflemen, 700
men and two cannon defeated and drove back Clinton's
army of 2,000 men. Had Clinton succeeded in crossing on
June 28, 1776, and marched down the island to the rear of
the fort, Moultrie would not have been able to hold his
position and the credit for whipping a British fleet by an
unfinished land fort would never have been gained for
Carolina.

A monument perpetuating the glory of Colonel Moultrie
and the Second Regiment adorns the central walk at White
Point Gardens. It is surmounted by a bronze figure of Brave
Jasper, whose quiet "Don't let's fight without a flag, boys"
was followed by the brave act of risking his life to rescue
the colors. At the very moment that Edward Rutledge in
Philadelphia was signing the Declaration of Independence,
his brother John was thanking the garrison of Fort Moultrie.

Indians and Loyalists started trouble in the Up-country of
South Carolina on the day that the Battle of Fort Moultrie
was in progress. Colonel Andrew Williamson, in charge of

the defense of the Up-country, then marched through the
Indian settlements and destroyed their crops, and five hundred of the Cherokee warriors fled to Florida. The Indians,
who then begged for peace, were compelled to give up the
land now forming Greenville, Anderson, Oconee and Pickens
counties.

The victory won on June 28, 1776, by Moultrie and Thomson gave security to this State and Georgia for three years,
during which time the campaign was carried on in the northern colonies. The old hostility against Canada broke out and
the great lakes became the scene of conflict. After the surrender of Burgoyne to General Horatio Gates, which disheartened England, cheered America and decided France to
acknowledge the independence of America and send her military aid, little of military importance occurred at the North.
But in 1779 Clinton sent out plundering expeditions along
the coast; Mad Anthony Wayne, who later appeared in
Charleston, attacked and captured Stony Point on the Hud-
son; and off the coast of England Paul Jones lashed the
"Bonhomme Richard" to the "Serapis," which he forced to
surrender after a three hours desperate encounter. Tradition
has it that a prominent Charleston family has either the
original or replica of the John Paul Jones Medal. Tradition
also says that the hero later dropped his last name and was
known simply as John Paul.

The brunt of the war was now to fall on the South. Savannah was captured in December 1778 by the British and
Augusta taken a month later. General Prevost re-established
royal Government in Georgia. The Southern Army under
Benjamin Lincoln assisted by D'Estaing and his French fleet
besieging Savannah, hoping to recapture and hold it for
America, was repulsed on October 9, 1779. Many Charleston men serving with their various commands were killed in
the bloody fighting which took place on the banks and upon
the bluffs of Savannah.

Having established headquarters in Georgia, Prevost now
proceeded to ravage the country between Savannah and
Charleston. Homes were plundered and burned, nameless

atrocities were committed, and Loyalists poured out to Florida and followed the British into Carolina to ravage and burn. Carolina seemed unable to defend herself, although military camps were established at Purrysburg, Black Swamp and Orangeburg. Prevost succeeded in making his way to the gates of the city but was kept out by a clever ruse. In the spring of 1780 Clinton arrived from New York, landed thirty miles below Charleston and marched toward the city. A British fleet under Admiral Marriott Arburthnot took up a position in the harbor and the combined forces besieged the city, to which Benjamin Lincoln had retreated. The Patriot force under Huger that was hastening to the relief to Charleston was intercepted and repulsed at Monk's Corner by Colonel Tarleton.

The Continental Congress of 1774 discountenanced and discouraged all dissipation and extravagance and mentioned horse racing specifically. Carolinians did not take kindly to this prohibition, but the progress of the War put a stop to the sport and dispersed the horses. Clinton lost his cavalry at sea. It became a matter of vital importance to secure remounts, many interesting episodes connected with the British attempt to capture horses hidden in the swamps of Carolina furnish romantic reading. Tarleton now captured four hundred horses near Monck's Corner, but the famous racer Flimnap was conspicuous by his absence.

Charleston, besieged by land and water, was cut off from outside aid. Smallpox and yellow fever came with hot weather, country people would not bring supplies to town. The city was poorly provisioned as for three years Charleston had been sending supplies to the North, trusting to re-provision herself from the West Indies. This trade was now interrupted. March 31st and April 1st had been spent in mounting cannon, throwing traverses, and digging ditches, while the besieging forces moved towards the city. The town had been "summoned" on April 10th and had refused to surrender. The next few days were spent in strengthening fortifications and mounting cannon. To this move the British replied by firing upon the city from nine o'clock Thursday

GIBBES HOUSE, ON THE NECK, NEAR WHICH THE BRITISH ENCAMPED DURING THE REVOLUTION

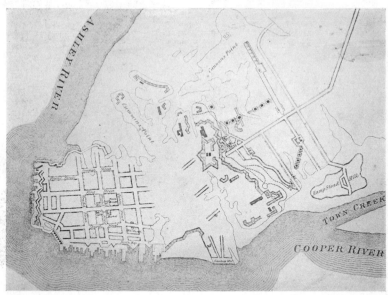

CITY LIMITS, FORTIFICATIONS AND LINES OF DEFENSE, 1780

THE SIEGE OF CHARLESTON BY THE BRITISH
From the Painting by Chappel

night, April 13th, until midnight. Their boats and batteries at Wappoo Creek joined. Houses were struck in the town, many were burned and some women and children killed. There would have been further casualties but the inhabitants took refuge in the cellars of their houses. The effects of a first bombardment had shown the futility of defense and on Friday, April 21, General Lincoln sent a flag to show that he was willing to enter into consideration of terms of capitulation. He contemplated terms allowing his garrison to march out with the usual honors of war and to carry off their arms, ammunition, baggage and such stores as they might be able to transport. Clinton refused to consider these terms, hostilities were renewed. Lord Cornwallis arrived at Mount Pleasant from the North.

Brigadier-General DuPortail arrived in Charleston from Philadelphia and declared Charlestown untenable. The citizens nevertheless refused to allow Lincoln to evacuate and withdraw the Continental troops, saying that if he attempted to leave the citizens to their fate they would cut up his boats, and open the gates of the city.

"Charles Town was completely invested." Moultrie gives an account of the last night before the surrender when the British fire was incessant. The whole night cannon balls were whizzing and shells hissing, ammunition chests and temporary magazines blew up; great guns burst; wounded men were groaning along the lines. "It was a dreadful night. It was our last great effort but it availed us nothing. After this our military ardor was much abated; we began to cool and we cooled gradually and on the 11th day of May we capitulated. On the 12th we marched out and gave up the town."

"About 11 o'clock A. M. on the 12th of May between 1500 and 1600 Continental troops marched out (leaving 500 to 600 sick and wounded in the hospital) and outside the horn work, on the left, piled our arms and the British officers marched our men back to the barracks. The British then asked for our second division and when they were told these were all the Continentals we had, except sick and wounded, they were astonished and said we had made a gallant defense."

Clinton's map, which has been published in one of the Year Books, furnishes a definite and complete picture and record of this section of the country. It shows the outlying islands, the fortifications of Charlestown, the positions of the besieging boats, the headquarters of the British generals and furnishes a complete record of Charlestown on May 12, 1780, when Lincoln surrendered and the victors entered a city which had been almost totally destroyed by fire, devastated by war and depleted by disease. To have remained forty-two days before such a place and been compelled to use all the military tactics of a regular siege before subduing Charlestown, was nothing very glorious for England to have accomplished. Lincoln signed the articles of capitulation and they were counter-signed by Clinton and Arbuthnot. André took charge, arms were stacked by the militia assembled at the Horn Work. The local militia was disbanded, inhabitants signed paroles and all arms were surrendered, when the British threatened to turn the grenadiers loose to search. The weak, infirm, and "disaffected" amounted to twice those who had been on military duty in the city. Friends persuaded President Rutledge to leave the city before its surrender, so that a semblance of civil government was left in a state in which the militia was depleted, the paper money valueless, and no actual government functioned to authorize a renewal of the fight or provide men and material for a conflict. South Carolina was prostrate; the City was helpless. The British centralized their efforts: using Charlestown as a base they overran the State.

In the city, houses were considered spoils of war to be plundered by the soldiers. Fires became unusually prevalent and Balfour replaced the old system of announcing conflagrations by a new method of ringing bells in place of shouting, beating drums, or firing guns, as such noises were too common in war times.

The State House was commercially used. 82 Church Street was the rendezvous for general business. Forage yards were established at Gadsden's Wharf and Cummings' Point. Charlestonians who wished to regain property entered claims at 51 Queen Street. The base of supplies was the Commissary General's at 3 Queen Street. The Barrack Master, Mayor, Billet Office and Regimental stores were in Bedon's Alley. Other offices were established in King Street, where Lord Rawdon made himself comfortable in the home of Mrs. Rebecca Motte, who was required to remain as unwilling hostess in her own home (the Miles Brewton house). Mrs. Motte placed her three pretty daughters in the upper rooms under the care of faithful slaves. The house was considered the handsomest in the city and still carries the marks of the British occupation. Rawdon's official family was lodged in the house on Legare Street now called the Roper house, as the Brewton Garden extended across to the residence. Rawdon is said to have had a keen eye for a beautiful woman, for which reason he is said to have frequently been flattered by the Tory, and insulted by the Whig ladies. Troops were quartered at private residences, and several of the ladies who neither could, nor would, stand the familiarities of the common soldiers were forced to vacate their homes rather than witness the soldiers and their demi-rep companions drinking and revelling. Mrs. Izard was turned out of her home with a dying child in her arms for remonstrating over such scenes.

Mrs. Heyward, whose home on Church street sheltered Washington in 1791, was nursing her dying sister, and refused to illuminate in honor of the British. She was attacked by the low element of the town, her ears assailed with vile language and her house defiled with filth. Others who ventured to remonstrate against these oppressions were punished by having soldiers quartered in their best rooms while they were sent to the garrets, and two sisters who refused to obey these orders were thrown into the dungeon under the Exchange. The sting of these proceedings was that they were inflicted by men who but a short time before had been friends and countrymen—now their overtures of friendship were considered worse than their insults.

Ladies "bidden" to the balls and festivities soon found that

an invitation was but a veiled command, and the refusal to
attend brought both subtle and open retaliation from the
British. So policy compelled the Patriot women to accept
British civilities. Patriotic women frequently turned these
parties to good account by learning British military movements and sending word of them to the Patriot troops.

Mrs. Sabina Elliott, the wife of William Elliott, whose
winter residence was at Accabee and summer home at Johnson's Fort, had a daughter Ann, called "the beautiful rebel"
because her coquettish bonnet was decorated with thirteen
small plumes to proclaim her patriotic sentiments.

The "Beautiful Rebel" married the eldest son of Lewis
Morris of Morrisania, led a brilliant social life and numbered
Kusciusko, the Polish patriot, among her numerous admirers
and correspondents. She died in New York in 1848 in her
eighty-sixth year.

Botta, the Italian historian, pays tribute to the Charlestown
women, calling them heroic beings who gloried and exulted
in the name of "Rebel", and who, instead of frequenting
public resorts of gaiety and amusement, visited the ships and
other places where their husbands, brothers, sons and friends
were held prisoners and sought to animate and sustain them
by every womanly art.

Official despatches during the Siege mentioned the houses
of the widow Pinckney, Mrs. Elfe, Thomas Shubrick on the
Green, Colonel Skirving, near the Governor's, Mr. Ferguson,
Daniel Horry, and Thomas Fuller as having been shelled by
the British.

This "Widow Pinckney" was none other than Eliza Lucas
Pinckney, who, for all her learning and energy and weaving
of silken robes, which she wore at Court, had proven an
obedient daughter, a reverential wife, a good mother, and
was now showing herself an ardent patriot although her
training had been that of a loyalist. She neither gave advice
to her sons nor attempted to influence them in politics, and
because both sons were officers in the American army and she
had made their cause her own, the British destroyed, burnt
and stole almost all of the Pinckney property.

In contrast to the Patriots, the Tory ladies enjoyed the many parties given by officers of the British Garrison. Tradition tells of three beautiful Harvey sisters of wild, passionate tempers and rich, exuberant beauty. One of them, Moll, is described as having dark, Cleopatra-like eyes and long black hair; as being intellectual, subtle, keen and quick at repartee, and a divine dancer. Her most famous flirtation was with Prince William (later William IV) then a Lieutenant in the Royal Navy and stationed in Charlestown. Miss Harvey, whose proud spirit would be content only with a public espousal, rejected his proposal of a secret marriage.

Mary Roupelle, another Royalist beauty of "Tory Row", was as haughty as a queen, and Pauline Phelps, called "The Phelps" by her British admirers, an heiress in her own right, who came of a respectable family, was rushed up to Goose Creek parsonage to become, willy nilly, the bride of "Mad Archy Campbell."

Mistress Cornelia Rivington was another leader in the élite of Tory circles. The widow was fair and forty and if not herself fat, her purse was so. Her evening parties at her Broad street home and morning "levees" were gay occasions where stout Majors and other British officers met to mingle with Charlestown Royalists. It was at Mrs. Rivington's house, no doubt, that British bantlings and witlings called the Patriot women who were meeting at Mrs. Richard Singleton's home in Church street "Tragedy Queens."

Mrs. Singleton's House was the meeting-place for Whig ladies who met to sew, provide comforts for prisoners and take counsel together. The Gadsden, Savage, Parsons, Rutledge, Edwards, Horry, Pinckney, Elliott, Ferguson, Huger, DeSaussure, Gourdin and Pettigru ladies met "to consult the future, review their conditions and consider their resources."

Mrs. Daniel Hall, as staunch a Rebel as ever lived, was noted and feared among the British officers for her keen wit and sharp tongue. She lived to the venerable age of eighty-nine and once remarked to Bishop Bowen that she intended to live to be a hundred. Telling her grandchildren of a dinner she attended against the advice of her husband, who warned her that no American officers would be there and that she would hear unpleasant things, she said, a toast was given by a young Tory lady, "To the blood that flowed at Guilford Court House." Mrs. Hall said she took the toast and responded, "Thank God, the blood of the British washed away that of the Americans." But, she said, "I tell you, children, I had to leave them then."

Colonel Cruden, who occupied the mansion house of General Pinckney, gave a magnificent entertainment to which the town was invited. The gardens were draped in lights and at the end of every avenue the illumination was reflected from pyramidal lusters of steel bayonets, burnished muskets and sabres, grouped in stars and crescents. Bowls of punch furnished liquid refreshment and a large enameled vase belonging to the Pinckneys held several gallons of the potent fluid. Large cups of filagreed china served the individual guests.

At this party Mary Roupell was leaning against an open window when the heavy sash fell upon her wrist and caused her to swoon with pain. Mr. Stock, a local beau, anxious to revive her, seized the mammoth bowl of punch and threw its contents over her face, whereupon Major Barry, a British wit, wrote an epigram which began:

> "When fair Roupelle lay fainting in her pain,
> 'Oh, what', cry all, 'will bring her to again?'
> 'What! What!' says Stock, 'but punch, a draught divine,
> 'Twill ease her pain; it always conquered mine!' "

Another noted Tory entertainment was given by Biddulph, the British postmaster, who occupied a house in Ladson street, then a court, the whole of which was brilliantly lighted. Every room in the house was filled with the select of the garrison and all of the distinguished ladies of the city, who attended without regard to politics.

As neither fear nor favor moved the Patriots in the city to accept their terms, the British now banished additional men and redoubled their insults to women. Reluctantly the Patriots took "Protection" rather than abandon their wives and children to starvation and perhaps a fate worse than death. Military Government was established by the British Police Board. Conditions were intolerable, and people gave up their homes and their few possessions and went into voluntary exile rather than submit to the outrages of the British soldiers.

The State, itself, had escaped surrender when neither the person nor the power of her governor fell into the hands of the British. Rutledge and some of his Council had left town before the capitulation by the advice of General Lincoln. By the articles of capitulation officers were to be exchanged and citizens under parole were to be left unmolested in person and property, but after Cornwallis succeeded Clinton these articles were disregarded.

Finally only the sick and wounded men were left in the city. Many of the Continental officers had been captured and were still prisoners. Patriots had been put in dungeons under the Exchange and were now either aboard prison ships or had been deported to Florida or exiled to Philadelphia.

The British claimed that when Lieutenant Governor Gadsden signed the surrender the whole state had capitulated and that any man in arms was a rebel and traitor and would be treated as such.

Using this as a pretext, the British visited the country, searched for arms and supplies and made Domiciliary visits upon homes and plantations, where they hoped to surprise and arrest the Patriots who ventured home to visit their families. By advice of the Patriot leaders many women in the country "took protection," raised provisions on the plantations and kept up communication with the men in camp, which was a great service; as by this time, the British were patrolling the roads, intercepting all communications, and impressing all men and horses that passed upon the road. Even official permits were disregarded. If the horse was a fine animal it was confiscated.

The forlorn condition of the state and city can hardly be imagined, much less described. But while the State was prostrate and persecuted, Sumter, Marion, Hampton, Pickens, Postell and Harden, employing tactics learned from Indian warfare, were harrying the British who were being guided toward the central spot, Charlestown, like deer on a deer-drive. The British, accustomed to fighting in regular formation, were bewildered by the Patriot tactics. It was now that Low Country horses, bred for fleetness and used in the Charlestown races of former days, played important part, when the Swamp Fox Marion and his men, mounted on steeds that had been sired by famous pace-makers, were able to appear, attack unexpectedly and get away again at a smart pace.

The General Assembly had been in session and had adjourned when Charlestown was first surrendered, but before so doing had placed all power in the hands of John Rutledge. An election was due in November, 1780, but with the Patriots exiled or in prison, it was impossible. Affairs had gone from bad to worse. The state was almost entirely in British possession and it would have been difficult to have found a place in which to hold an election or at which the Assembly might convene, even if it had been possible to find persons capable of serving.

Meanwhile the Patriot bands pursued their guerrilla warfare unaided, but none the less effectively, and presently an American army, headed by DeKalb, came down from the North to aid the South. Congress interfered, and placed General Gates, the conqueror at Saratoga, in command, with the disastrous result that, when, on August 15, Cornwallis met and defeated Gates at Camden, the whole country was left at his mercy and the whole sea-coast in the power of the British.

At the battle of Camden, Major Thomas Pinckney's leg was shattered. It was saved from amputation by the attention of English Surgeons. It has been said that the British pursued this policy of kindness in an effort to induce prominent American officers to enlist in His Majesty's service. Pinckney's leg was saved, and he, returning toward Charlestown, stopped at Mrs. Motte's place on the Congaree River, where sometime later, according to relatives, Mrs. Motte loaned arrows tipped with fire to the Americans to destroy her own home in an effort to dislodge the British then in possession.

Carolinians who had been granted paroles by the British found that they had been tricked and were required to take up arms against their own people. Many broke their paroles, feeling that England had violated her part of the contract.

General Williamson, the American turncoat so well described by Simms in his novel "Katherine Walton" was a thorn in the side of loyal Americans. Hayne, who had given his parole, pursued Williamson, and Mad Archy Campbell pursued Hayne. Hayne, who had first broken his parole to visit his dying wife, was captured and condemned to die as a traitor and not as a spy, and was sent to the gallows by Rawdon, despite the pleas of friends and foes alike. In the Pringle house, Hayne's little motherless children went on their knees to Rawdon and asked for the life of their father. *The Royal Gazette*, Aug. 8, 1781, says, "Mr. Isaac Hayne, who, since the capitulation of Charlestown, had taken protection, and acknowledged himself a subject of His Majesty's Government having not withstanding been taken in arms, and at the head of a Rebel Regiment of Militia was therefore, on Saturday morning, last, executed as a traitor."

In 1780 the defeat of General Gates by Cornwallis was balanced by the American victory at King's Mountain and the recapture of Camden for America by Colonel William Washington on December 4th, while the Patriots Marion, Sumter and Pickens continued to harass the British. At Cowpens, Morgan put one-fourth of Cornwallis' Army to rout and compensated for the defeat sustained by Greene at Guilford Court-House. By the end of 1781 the Patriots had almost entirely recaptured the State, and after the Battle at Eutaw Springs the British retreated to Charlestown and the war was virtually ended in South Carolina. Meanwhile, Cornwallis was blocked in by the French fleet in the Chesapeake Bay and besieged near Yorktown by the combined armies of Washington and Rochambeau. On October 19th he was forced to surrender and the war was virtually at an end.

Charlestown was evacuated by the British according to

terms arranged by Greene and Leslie—Greene, at Dorchester, Leslie at Middleton Place. After thirty-one months of oppression and misery Charlestown people saw, on a bright winter morning, their oppressors march to Gadsden's wharf, there to embark on the three hundred ships, arranged in a semi-circle around the harbor.

The British departed with 5,333 slaves, the bells and books of St. Michael's, thousands of dollars in gold and the possessions of many Tory families. It is said that in addition to the soldiers 3,794 whites moved under the British flag.

Greene's attitude toward the patriot leaders has never been rightly understood. Marion and Hampton had helped him win the decisive battle of Eutaw Springs on September 8, 1781 and were still in the neighborhood of Charlestown. They should have been called to share in the victorious entry of the American Army into the city.

Out of a hundred and thirty-seven battles and skirmishes fought in Carolina, the State had carried on one hundred and three unaided. Carolina had dared more, suffered more and achieved more than any of the other states, and it was a great blow to the pride of the patriots that their ragged warriors were ignored by Nathaniel Greene when he repossessed Charlestown.

So reluctant were the British to leave, and so keen the Americans to get back to the city, that the British officers complained that General Wayne was pressing them sorely.

The American Army came down the Broad Path, through the city gates, and halted on the South side of Board nearly opposite Church Street and there formed into military array, before being dismissed. The Governor was escorted into the city by General Greene, two hundred cavalrymen, the State Council, and troops of citizens, soldiers, and officers.

Balconies and windows were crowded with aged men and women and children who for three years had wept with apprehension and sorrow for the absence and loss of their dear ones, but who now welcomed the returning patriots with "God bless you, gentlemen, and welcome home!" Moultrie, the soldier, says "The patriots went forward with martial music and flying colors to play the last joyful act in the drama of their country's deliverance, to proclaim liberty to the captive, to recall the smile on the cheek of sorrow and to make the heart of the widow leap with joy."

Of the city termed "The stainless maid of the ocean" Hayne, the poet, has said she stood that day

"Pallid yet proud—half sad, half joyous hearted, as one who hears far off, the roll of thunder clouds departed—and upon whose brow war had left furrows hot and gory yet she stood with calm exultant smile, her dark eyes flushed with glory."

BOOK IV

FROM THE REVOLUTION TO THE CONFEDERATE WAR, 1783-1861

CHAPTER IX

THE British marched out, the Americans marched in. Charlestown was left to her own devices. The Volunteer Patriot troops, feeling that they had done all that could be expected of them, dispersed and retired to their homes to salvage what had been left by the British. Carolina was a free state, but her agriculture was destroyed, her commerce stagnant, her Government disrupted and her people penniless. The State gave its creditors indents, interest upon which was to be paid by other special indents, the money for which was to be raised by taxes. Several hundred thousand dollars was furnished and circulated by this method. A hundred thousand dollars was issued in bills of credit in 1785. This was lent, at 7 per cent interest, in small amounts on mortgages or deposits of plate. The merchants came forward in a body and agreed to take these bills at their face value. No second issue was made and the depreciation was so small that when The South Carolina Bank was formed it not only redeemed the paper on deposit but made repayment in specie on its own bills.

The city was incorporated in 1783 under the name of Charleston. Amendments were made in 1784, and Richard Hutson became the first Mayor, or Intendant. A handsome marble tablet in the City Hall tells of his life and services. One of the problems with which Governor Guerard had to contend was the fact that Congress had no money with which to pay General Greene's unemployed Continental troops encamped on James Island, and there arose a conflict of authority between himself, who objected to the troops foraging for their own supplies, and Greene, who in his endeavor to preserve discipline, assumed all but arbitrary authority.

Intendant Hutson was having troubles of his own. His hands were full with controlling those who were Tories at heart and putting down mobs of turbulent spirits, many of whom were no doubt soldiers who were forced to sell their pay indents for a pittance. Everyone was dreadfully poor, there was no money in the State: the Continental currency had "fallen asleep" in the hands of its last possessors. But life went on. Necessaries were divided by those who had with those who had not. Somehow, the task was accomplished.

Richard Hutson took no part in the wrangle between Governor Guerard and General Greene. He was too wise a lawyer. Richard Hutson, John Rutledge, and John Matthews had been called to the bench and were the first three Chancellors of the State.

Certain names appear and re-appear constantly in the story of Charleston. Mrs. Pinckney wittily divided Charleston into the Mobility and the Nobility, and in the controversy between the State and Military Government several prominent persons, many of whom were hereditary members of the Society of the Cincinnati then being formed, sided with Greene. The ordinary people regarded the Society as of English origin and an effort to perpetuate the English caste system. Unfortunately, a rift was produced in the civic consciousness. It bore direct fruit in a divided community and emerged again and again in different questions. Floods of passionate oratory were loosened on the various sides, but the old order triumphed and the same groups of men who had led the fight for freedom and guided the policies of the State during the war now controlled the first formative years of the young Republic. The same names continue to appear at the head of important movements in national, state, and city affairs.

Slowly the town got on its feet. It had been all but destroyed by a fire of Tory origin in 1778, since which time it had been ravaged by war and inhabited by the enemy. Churches were closed, theatres silent, but the voice of the

Press prevailed. Through the newspapers, merchants were called together. These agreed to accept the paper money at its face value. Hidden treasures were unearthed, family possessions sold, and slowly specie payment was resumed. The Pine Barren Acts, for paying debts on installments, were passed.

The City Government functioned under Commissioners who not only policed and lighted the city, but filled in the waste places, repaired the wharves, took down wrecked buildings, widened and lengthened the town, passed sanitary measures relating to the beef, fish, and vegetable markets, made regulations for ringing curfew, regulating the slaves, had St. Michael's clock repaired, arranged for patrols, fire masters, marine patrols, and harbor regulations and markings.

Because a Democracy was in process of evolving, although the surface flowed smoothly, yet a hidden bitterness was felt in the civic consciousness. So the General Assembly enacted laws concerned with establishing circuit courts and jury lists, vesting certain tax rights in Congress and regulating Admiralty sales, preventing suits for recovery of debts under certain conditions, procuring recruits and preventing desertion, purchasing an estate for the use of the Honorable Major General Greene, regulating the militia, *and disposing of certain estates.*

The preamble to Act No. 1268, for banishing certain persons and disposing of their estates, recites in miniature the horrors of the Revolution, and announces that whipping, hangings, banishing and putting to death in cold blood of Loyal Carolinians had proceeded under the direct authority of Clinton, Rawdon, and Rugely. The Statutes at Large furnish a list of Carolinians whose estates were considered as falling within the line of those who favored British rule. The Charleston *Gazette* of November, 1779 and January 11, 1780, September 21, 1780, and July 11, 1781, all furnish lists of South Carolinians who "took protection, who withdrew from the State to join the enemies thereof, those who addressed petitions welcoming Clinton (there were 166 names on this

MAIN BUILDING OF THE COLLEGE OF CHARLESTON
By kindness of Professor De la Torre
See Page 162

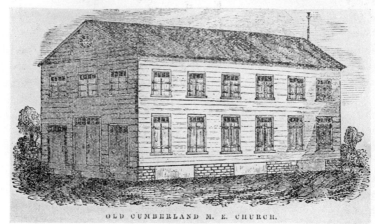

OLD CUMBERLAND M. E. CHURCH.

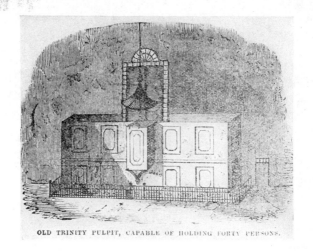

OLD TRINITY PULPIT, CAPABLE OF HOLDING FORTY PERSONS.

From Year Books. By kindness of the City

list) and lists of petitioners for protection." A list of those whose estates were confiscated by the Jacksonboro Assembly is found in the Royal *Gazette* of March 20, 1782.

Historians Garden, Gibbes, Drayton, Ramsay and McCrady furnish lists of patriotic Charlestonians who were confined aboard the prison ship "Torbay", but a more complete list is said to be filed at Washington, D. C.

Guerard was Governor from 1782 to 1785. During his term all persons who had negroes or other effects that were not their own property were required to make an account of these under penalty of law.

In 1787 the legislature was wrangling about releasing poor Mr. Bull, the erstwhile Deputy Governor who had been such a favorite in the colony but who had remained true to the Crown, from the "pains and penalties of the Confiscation and Banishment Act." They finally decided to allow him to return, minus his civic rights, to his native land. His petition stated that "he only wished to come and lay his aged bones in that land where he first drew breath."

The deep resentment felt against those who had not been in sympathy with the American cause is illustrated by an incident that happened when it became known that the Reverend Thomas Coke, Doctor of civil law of Oxford University and Presbyter of the Church of England, would open the new Methodist Church in Cumberland street on March 11, 1787. A letter appeared in the papers stating that John Wesley was no friend to America and, asking if Dr. Coke who was his successor, had taken the Abjuration Oath. Dr. Coke pledged his honor as a Christian gentleman that he was a real and genuine friend of the American Revolution.

When Bishop Asbury attended the conference in Charleston in 1791, Reverend William Hammett, an Irish Methodist preacher who had come to Charleston from the West Indies, was a visitor whose brilliant oratory captured the people, who clamored for him to receive an appointment. Bishop Asbury had already made his appointments and in consequence refused. About one half of the congregation seceded and followed Mr. Hammett, who organized the Primitive Methodist Church, which thrived and prospered until his death in 1813. The church occupied the late site of Trinity on Hasell street. After his death, his friend and successor Mr. Brazier sold the property to the Reverend Mr. Frost, rector of St. Philip's Church, and an extraordinary litigious complication ensued between Trinity Church congregation and the Episcopalians, resulting in victory for the Methodists.

Until its recent destruction Trinity Church, at the corner of Hasell street and Maiden Lane, was the oldest house of worship in this city belonging to the Methodist Church. Cumberland Church, the first structure, was destroyed in the fire of 1861. Trinity was burnt in 1838, but rebuilt and dedicated in 1839. It was again damaged in 1861 and was not put in thorough repair until 1869. It was recently pulled down when the congregation bought Westminster Presbyterian Church on Meeting street. Westminster moved up-town and built a fine place of worship on Rutledge Ave., near Hampton Park. Bethel Church, on the corner of Pitt and Calhoun, is now the oldest Methodist-Episcopal Church in the city. It is a very beautiful building and the large stained glass windows which adorn the chancel of the church are memorials to Bishop William Capers, who died on January 26, 1855, and Bishop William M. Wightman, who died February 15, 1882. Bishop William Capers' son became the Episcopal Bishop of South Carolina many years later. He is known as the fighting Bishop on account of the part he played in the Confederate War. His son is now the Episcopal Bishop of one of the western states. His daughter married Dr. William Henry Johnson, a descendant of the Patriot of Revolutionary days.

When the Revolution came to an end many of the churches in Carolina had been burnt or destroyed and the worshipers scattered. Everything pertaining to England was cordially disliked and many members of the "Church of England" severed their connection with it on account of the hated name. Many others, however, remained loyal to the form of worship as prescribed by the Church of England, and in 1785 Reverend Robert Smith, Rector of St. Philip's, called a meeting of the

Episcopal churches of this State, saying that he had received a letter from Rev. Dr. William Smith of Maryland, informing him of a meeting held in New York City in 1784 for the purpose of organizing the "Protestant Episcopal Church in the United States."

A greater contrast between Colonial Carolina and the mature city of 1783 can scarcely be imagined. The old Baronial estates had been divided when the law of entail lapsed. Men unused to labor were learning in the hard school of experience how to sow and reap. Through Agricultural and Hunting clubs and similar organizations, the older generation gave of their knowledge to the younger, and soon the country around the city was again producing rice, indigo, naval stores and supplies. As the hinterland improved, the city flourished. The Chamber of Commerce began to function, under the presidency of Commodore Gillon; foreign boats again put into the harbor; a branch of the National Bank was established in the city in 1792 and others followed soon after. A high pitch of prosperity was quickly reached. Between there is comparatively little on record of the social life of the city. Many of the beautiful women and handsome men were dead and gone. The beautiful Miss Golightly, the toast of the town of 1767, had attended a ball, put on her straw hat, slipped through a French window, joined her romantic lover, Mr. Huger, passed through the garden, become his bride, and had soon died. He had taken another wife, whose son became the friend of Lafayette, and now he too had died, being killed just outside of the Charleston lines. Twelve marriages had taken place among the élite in 1768. The grooms were wealthy rice planters, the wives the belles of Charleston. Tradition tells of twelve carved beds ordered out from England: carved rice stalks formed the columns and sheaves of rice formed the capitals. These and other beautiful things had been destroyed by the British but the rice plantations endured.

The great flooded fields on Santee, Combahee, Edisto and Winyah still remained. The Pinckneys, Rutledges, Morrises, still planted; among others was Daniel Horry, whose second wife, Harriet Pinckney, had given him a son, Daniel. This son later married the niece of Lafayette, changed his name to Charles Pinckney Lucas Horry and lived in France. She also bore a daughter Harriott, who became the wife of Frederick, son of Dictator John Rutledge, and to whom had passed "Hampton," the plantation which had been such a refuge for patriotic women during the war of the Revolution.

To gain an adequate idea of how rapidly prosperity came after the State issued its bills of credit to the amount of a half-million dollars, it is only necessary to glance through the papers after it was realized that specie payment was to be resumed. Charles Barrel proposed to coin and pay into the State treasury copper and silver coins valued at ten and twenty thousand pounds respectively, to be exchanged within fifteen months for South Carolina paper money, and as if by a pre-arranged signal, things began to happen. Stages were run North and South, places were "taken" in it "At the Tavern." The Middletons, Heywards, Manigaults, Lowndes, Draytons, and Hugers began coming every summer "to the Salt," as they had been used to doing at this season. They deserted their plantation homes and with their coming Charleston resumed fully the social life that had been interrupted.

Rice planting received great stimulation from the machines invented by Lucas to clean and prepare the grain for market. Jonathan Lucas was an Englishman who sailed to America and landed near the mouth of the Santee river, when a storm wrecked the boat upon which he was a passenger. A local planter befriended him, and he in turn, struck with the labor required to thresh the rice, applied his mind, produced a machine which brought fame and fortune to himself and his future family and put the rice crop back on a paying basis. Pinckney Alston, Horry, Laurens, and others pressed him for mills. At first, power was supplied by fresh water reservoirs and salt water ponds, but in 1817 Mr. Lucas built a steam mill on the Ashley river at the foot of Mill street, and Lucas and Norton built the second mill operated by steam

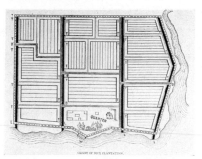

CHART OF RICE PLANTATION

RICE FIELDS. TRUNK GATE IRRIGATION DITCH

RICE MILL, ASHLEY RIVER, WEST AND CALHOUN STREETS
Operated by Machinery designed by Jonathan Lucas

THE SWORD GATES ON LEGARE STREET
See Page 262

near Gadsden's wharf on the Cooper river. Mr. Lucas' son Jonathan Lucas, Jr. moved to England in 1822, having received flattering offers from English officials, and the third Jonathan Lucas was left in Carolina to carry on the work that had been started by his grandfather and father. Hopsawee is the name of the Lucas' plantation on Santee, but members of the family have built several fine houses in the city which they still call home. Rice was soon rivalled and eventually displaced by cotton, after Eli Whitney invented the cotton gin.

Monetary affairs were not settled by any means, however smoothly life seemed to progress, and in 1787 the Legislature regulated theatrical representations because they thought that too much money badly needed for necessities was being spent on amusements.

Benjamin Walters at 192 King street, opposite "Inspection", advertised for tobacco, indigo, skins, beeswax, tallow, etc. where the highest prices were paid and goods were sold on low terms and "when issued the new paper medium will be received as silver or gold."

The Jockey Club met at the New Market Race Course on January 5, 1786. Mr. Drayton introduced a bill into the Legislature to allow houses to be erected outside the "curtain" line on East Bay and the street to be widened. Certain wharves were set aside for naval stores to avoid fires. Lands on Trott, Quince and Hasell streets were sold after a fire had broken out at Michael and Sarrazin's distillery on Trott's Point.

The City began to stretch herself; waters of creeks were "estopped" from entering certain streets. Water Street was filled up; many acres were thus added to the city. Subdivisions began to emerge. Several lots at "Romney" on Meeting street about a mile from the lines were sold at auction, the inducement being that "entrance to the city will shortly be made through Meeting street and these lots will increase in value." Quite in the modern vein, lots in Mazychboro, laid out on streets which were to be 56 feet wide, were advertised, "where the Liberty Tree formerly stood, adjoining Boundary street." Some land in Ansonboro, in front of General Gadsden's dwelling house, facing Front street, was offered for sale. Louisburg was a subdivision just above the lines near Boundary (Calhoun) Street. In order to escape taxes, the proprietors of a theatrical venture there erected a large theatre called Harmony Hall. It opened July 11, 1786. In the evenings, varied theatrical, oratorical and musical affairs went on, attended by all the fashionables. But in the mornings or afternoons the younger beaux of the town went to Harmony Hall to learn fencing and dancing, while the belles drank tea in a newly opened establishment nearby or visited the Botanic Gardens owned by the Watsons, or promenaded languidly down to the pier at the end of South Bay to enjoy a cup of tea, while their escorts called for other refreshments. Mr. Lafar and Mr. Goodwin, of the Theatre, opened an academy to teach the minuet, allemand, cotillion, hornpipe, and country dances to members of the younger set.

Lands of the Cherokee Indians were thrown open for occupation. Commissioners of "forfeited estates" offered many pieces of property for sale and significantly enough the papers show many advertisements of persons "departing the Province." Commissioners Josiah Smith and Edward Lightwood informed those who had bought public lands near Lyttleton and Broughton's Bastions that if they did not settle for these they would be dealt with "as the law directed." Three lots situated on the highest point of Darrell's Fort, each measuring thirty-two feet on the new sixty foot street, East Bay, were sold, and the City Treasurer advertised that the whole center cellar under the Exchange was for rent.

Details of several Post-Revolutionary duels were spread in the columns of the papers, many of which produced a vast array of legal talent on both sides when gentlemen of ability and integrity prosecuted and defended. Dr. Ladd, a poet as well as a kind-hearted physician, lost his life as the result of a duel. Tradition tells of a Sunday morning duel held in Philadelphia street behind St. Philip's Church, when General Moultrie "pinked" his man, wiped his sword, made a bow, walked around the corner and attended divine service.

Some of the literary quality found even in the advertisements in the papers is due no doubt to the presence of Peter Frenneau in the town. He was the editor of one of the papers, and with his brother, Philip, a bold venturesome fellow with a flair for writing popular verse, operated a trading boat out from this city to the West Indies. John Miller, another Editor, was popularly supposed to be the editor of the celebrated "Junius Letters."

It is said that "Dictator" John Rutledge was a man of varied attainments. William Henry Drayton left a manuscript history of the American Revolution in three volumes. Christopher Gadsden understood Latin, Greek, French, Hebrew and the Oriental languages and such was the temper and spirit of the man that when imprisoned at St. Augustine by the British, instead of idly repining he devoted himself to study and came out much more learned than when he entered.

After the Revolution there were a number of learned and scientific men in Charleston. David Ramsay, who married Miss Laurens, introduced vaccination into Charleston in 1806, four years after its discovery by Jenner. (Nathaniel Ramsay, who was the first subject, lived until 1882, when he died near Columbia.) Besides this David wrote a Universal History, a History of the Revolution, and one of the State.

Dr. William Bull was the first native South Carolina physician and Dr. Lionel Chalmers practiced medicine here from 1737 to 1777 and published several books, while the Rev. Richard Clark, rector of St. Philip's experimented in electricity and corresponded with Benjamin Franklin upon the subject. Dr. Alexander Garden, an early Carolina botanist became vice-president of the Royal Society of England. The naturalists, Walter, Catesby and Michaux made gardens and wrote of Charleston. When Justice Pinckney made Eliza Lucas his second wife he took her to Belmont, a plantation about two miles above the city. Here she made friends with the great botanist, Garden, and under his direction planted a fine avenue of oaks. She became interested in raising oak timber for Carolina boats, as she had been interested in silk and indigo. Mrs. Pinckney came to town and lived in the East Bay house and planted a fine garden; her neighbor Mrs.

Logan wrote a book for gardeners. It is said that when Chief Justice Charles was leaving for England he took his seven year old son to walk throughout the town, pointed out interesting and historic places to him and showed him the large caravans of up-country wagons then flocking into the city. 3,000 a year came into the city. Mr. Pinckney did not live to see the revolution in transportation which occurred when wagons gave way to trains. He returned from England in 1758 and died soon after, of yellow fever.

When the State had thrown off royal authority, it had adopted in 1776 a provisional constitution, under which the civil powers operated as far as they could be operated at all. After the close of the Revolution it became necessary to form a permanent constitution. This was accomplished in a constitutional convention held in 1790, when a constitution was established that remained in force with but few modifications until the end of the Confederate War. Under this, progress was marked and steady—the upper districts were settled, county-seats established, judicial circuits formed and judges and chancellors alternated with each other in different circuits. Appeals were heard by a full Appellate Bench in Charleston or in Columbia.

C. C. Pinckney, Charles Pinckney, John Rutledge, Henry Laurens and Pierce Butler represented Carolina at the Federal Convention in Philadelphia, when George Washington was president of the body, the purpose of which was to weld the independent states into a republic. Charles Pinckney, then under thirty years old, presented a plan to the convention similar to that finally adopted. Debates ran through months. Rutledge and Pinckney, who spoke often, had a large share in the work of preparing the constitution of the United States which was completed by the convention in September, 1787 and presented to a State Convention, meeting in Charleston, May 12, 1788. The Rutledges, William Moultrie and Colonel William Washington favored the adoption of the Constitution. Its ratification was opposed by Rawlins Lowndes, Thomas Sumter and Aedamus Burke, that brilliant, absent-minded Irish Judge who once hastily snatched his landlady's black petticoat from its hanging place behind a door and bore it off to the court room. Trying to put it on as his judicial robe he is said to have muttered an oath to the effect that he had on "the Van Rhyn's petticoat."

General William Moultrie was elected Governor in 1787 and served for two years. After this year the most important events center around Charleston's social, religious and human phases, rather than around politics. This is true because in this year the State decided to lay out a new site for a capital city, nearer to the center of the State. Four square miles of land near Friday's Ferry on the Congaree were bought from Thomas and James Taylor. Public buildings were begun the same year, but the State House was not completed until 1790, nor did the General Assembly meet there until that year. When the scepter departed this city three visible links of the past went with it—the seal of the State, the Mace and the Chippendale chair said by William G. Preston, the donor, to be the quasi throne on which the later colonial governors sat when presiding in Charleston in the old State House. The Mace, a handsome symbol of authority costing ninety guineas, has often been called Cromwell's bauble. It was used in the Provincial House of Assembly to open all legislative meetings. It was carried off by the British, offered for sale in the Bahama Islands, made its devious way to the vaults of the Bank of the United States in Philadelphia, where it was located by Hon. Langdon Cheves, then President of the institution. He secured the relic and returned it to the State. It now rests in front of the desk of the Speaker in the legislature of South Carolina at Columbia.

Before the Revolution a school which had been conducted by Rev. Dr. Robert Smith had given an education in the classics to young men from all over the colony who came to be educated in Charleston. Plans were made in 1770 to enlarge this school. Lieut.-Governor William Bull sponsored the movement and an endowment fund was started, but it was not until 1785 that the institution received its charter and resumed operation in the brick barracks which are now incorporated in a portion of the college buildings. The first commencement occurred in 1786 in the presence of "a numerous and elegant assemblage of ladies and gentlemen."

Governor and General Moultrie was President of the Board of Trustees of the College of Charleston. Two signers of the Declaration of Independence served on its board. Dr. Smith wore his University gown and Oxford trencher-cap when he presided at this first commencement. If a list of the graduates of this institution were annotated to contain biographical sketches of all who had received diplomas from that day down to this, when the city has taken it over, it would be found to give an outline history of the nation, state and city. Its graduates have served America in every capacity, and served her well.

The high quality of intellect and education possessed by Charlestonians in general is attested by the numerous brilliant essays which continuously appeared under various non-de-plumes in the newspapers of the day, particularly as Charleston men began to make themselves felt in National politics. As late as 1812 no less a person than Governor Joseph Alston was thus appearing under the pen name of "A Mountaineer", and Mr. Noah was publishing his political satires "Oriental Correspondence" signed "Muly Malack." In 1783 Mr. John Miller established a circulating library to supply the scarcity of books caused by the destruction of private libraries. The Library Society, instituted in 1748, which had lost its valuable collection in the Revolution, now reopened in the State House building, with the newly organized Medical Society, whose "museum" was transferred to the Literary and Philosophical Society in 1815, and formed the nucleus of the present Museum located on Rutledge Avenue.

Owing to the changed form of Government many organizations which had previously existed were now reorganized and incorporated under the laws of the State of South Carolina. Among others thus conforming to the altered constitution were the St. Cecelia Society, the St. Andrew's, the South Carolina, the Fellowship Society and the German Friendly. All became active again, as did the Protestant Episcopal Society for the Relief of Widows and Orphans of the clergy, which had been organized in 1762. After the Revolution the church shared in the general independence at the sacrifice of the help she had been receiving from England. When a definite program for the Episcopal Church was adopted it was found that only fifteen parishes out of the twenty-five that had been created in colonial days remained. Many of the colonial churches had been destroyed. The parish system soon gave way to counties. The church had been a gathering place and rallying point for all civic, educational and religious movements. Today no such conditions obtain. The only one of the numerous societies evolved from war-time association which has survived is the hereditary society, the Cincinnati. Even the "Bats", or Battalion of Ancient Artillery, has ceased to exist, as has the Palmetto and the Friendly Hibernian. The Friendly Brothers of Ireland, formed in 1786 with Pierce Butler as President, James Lynah, Vice-President, Daniel O'Hara, Treasurer, Samuel Corbett, Secretary and Bartholomew Carroll and George Archibald, Stewards, has been absorbed into other societies.

Wise men were striving to upbuild the town and open trade-routes. The Congaree boat "Five Sisters" made a "quick trip" of five weeks up and down to Friday's Ferry. Engineers began to figure upon canals which would shorten the route: Santee river was surveyed, a canal to connect the Santee and Cooper rivers was projected and eventually dug. Other companies sought to join the Ashley and the Edisto, but their schemes came to naught. Roads were laid out to communities beyond the new capital, and lands of the Cherokee Indians were thrown open for occupation. Travelers in stage-coaches made speedy trips to Georgetown. By starting at five o'clock in the morning from Haddrell's point on Mondays and Fridays, they arrived at Georgetown the evening of the same day, said the schedules.

In 1789 Thomas Pinckney came into the office of Governor in the old regal style, with a procession through the streets, an official affair at the State House, a blowing of trumpets and a proclamation from the balcony by a page.

People began to enjoy life again. Among other providers James Scot conducted a Tea, Wine and Grocery Shop in Elliott street and sold appetizing goods. His shelves fairly groaned with their supplies of Hyson, Souchong, Bohea and Green teas, coffee and chocolate, loaf and Muscarollo sugar. He carried pepper, allspice, nutmeg, mace, cinnamon, cloves and all other spices needed by the housekeeper of the time who catered to palates that demanded high and hot ingredients common to hot countries. The rest of his goods are rehearsed for the benefit of those who would shop by proxy from this establishment of 1789. Scot had all of the regular wines with a few others, such as Old Hock, Tent, Muscat and Frontignac and Malaga. He had all the brandies, as well as gin and Burgundy. His pickled goods comprised walnuts, capers, girkins, mushrooms, French beans and red cabbage. His preserves included all the fruits of the earth and tamarinds in addition; he had Burlington hams, cured with saltpeter, and dried figs and prunes. His syrup list was extensive, covering lemon, orange, DeCapillaire, Orgeat, Charpentier, along with cordials called cherry brandy, cinnamon water, annissette, guignolet and ratafia. His perfumes were positively Oriental in name, as Marechall, Sultanne, Pompador, Sans-Parcillo and Chypre. His hair tonics and pomades were strictly a-la-mode and in addition to all these things, Scot's list gives a fair idea of the kinds of glassware used by the bon ton of Charleston. He advertised decanters, mugs, tumblers, rummers, green ware, tureens, dishes, plates, bowls; and in addition to all else he had castile, white and turpentine soap, spermaceti and tallow candles, sweet oil, vinegar, lime juice, wine-bitters, corks, currant jelly, blacking-balls and biscuits in "kegs."

In 1789 the Grand Jury presented in its list of grievances the then ruinous condition of St. Michael's Church. Nevertheless the law makers met there in February and adjourned to the city tavern where they were informed by his honor, the Intendant, that they might, if it was agreeable to them, sit in the Exchange. They adjourned to the City Hall and one of the things they did was to appoint a committee to repair the State House. Public thanks were extended to one and all who helped to save the valuable records of the city in the recent "alarming fire."

Some time in April the vestry and church-wardens of St. Michael's published a notice saying that they had in hand a considerable sum of money and are determined to begin the repairs as soon as *May Be*; they are ready to contract with any master workman, with carpenters, plumbers and painters who wish to undertake the repairs. Robert Dewar and George Bampfield signed for the church-wardens.

On April 10th, Robert Joor and Mr. Bampfield joined with John Cooper Folker and Edward Trescott from St. Philip's in calling an election for members of the State Convention. The election was to be held at St. Michael's and was to proceed from ten in the morning until five in the afternoon on Friday and Saturday the eleventh and twelfth, and all persons entitled to vote were invited to take notice of these facts. Returns were published on April 17th. The work which the convention accomplished is celebrated in history, and the ratification of the Federal constitution was duly marked in this city by public ceremonies beginning at five in the morning with bell-ringing and rounds from the fort and ending in the wee small hours of the night. The "business commenced" (says the newspaper of Thursday, May 29th, 1789). Tuesday (the 27th), the day appointed for the celebration of the ratification, came in at dawn with the sound of bell and gun. At eleven, citizens paraded to Roper's Wharf. They were adorned with the ensignia of the different societies to which they belonged. The procession then moved with "great regularity" to Federal Green, where dinner was prepared for a vast number. At night the vessels in the harbor were decorated with lights from the top-gallant-mast to the deck. Captain John Hamilton was marshal of the parade, which was headed by battalions of artillery followed in regular order by gentlemen planters, gardeners, inspectors of rice, indigo and tobacco, with a hogshead of tobacco drawn by horses. Then came butchers with decorated tools, bakers, brewers, distillers, No. 8 were the blacksmiths, No. 9 the whitesmiths; then came the cutlers.

The fire-engine makers were headed by Duncan and Murdock; architects led by Ems and Hope were followed by groups of carpenters, bricklayers, painters and glaziers, while the coach-painters paraded by themselves, as did the coopers, coach-makers, wheelwrights and turners.

William Axon led the cabinet-makers, of which there were a large and interesting group in Charleston, including Elfe, the master workman whose account-book reposes in the files of the Charleston Library and furnishes proof that much furniture attributed to England was made here. Tanners, curriers and skinners, each had a division to themselves, demonstrating that furs were still a considerable item of commerce.

The parade wended its way in seventy-nine separate groups, headed by the soldiers and ending with the Secretary of State (who bore the Constitution) and all State officials. Judges in robes immediately preceded these, with sheriffs and all court officers, clergymen of all denominations followed by physicians and surgeons under Dr. John Budd, these followed by the vinters. Members of the Bench and Bar were far up the line, mingling, fully robed, with the Judges of Chancery.

Between the tanners and vinters were groups Nos. 26 to 64 consecutively; these included stocking weavers, boot makers, saddlers and harness makers, hatters, tailors and habit makers—peruke makers and hair dressers. Enow Reeves headed the goldsmiths and Coram and Abernathie the engravers. William Lee led the watchmakers who were followed by workers in other metals, copper and gunsmiths and brass founders, tallow chandlers and soap boilers were followed by a group of printers with a stand and compositors and press men at work.

Then came the pilots and their commissioners, and the harbor master, the ship Federalist was represented by Captain Cochran, his mates and crew. A group of masters and sailors from different boats filed past, carters and draymen

had their representatives. Daniel DeSaussure led the commissioners of the Marine Hospital, Consuls of the different
nations were followed by groups of merchants, factors, vendue
masters, who were followed, in turn, by the ship carpenters
and all those in any way connected with boat building.

Rope makers whose waists were encircled with hemp,
showed that the old trade still persisted and was practiced in
some of the Rope Walks. The only one of which can be found
in Charleston leads from Meeting street to the rear of the
house where George Washington lodged on Church street.
Along this little passage several old gardens formed passage-
ways to Tradd street. Other Rope Walks used to be up near
Line street and adjacent to places on the Bay.

After all of those in any way connected with boats had
filed past and been followed by carvers and guilders, under
John Parkinson, then came tinmen, tobacconists, umbrella
makers, glass grinders and rubbers, diamond cutters, polish-
ers and silverers, headed by Edward Weyman. McLeish led
the makers of mathematical instruments and John Speisseger
those who made musical instruments.

Ben Bridge led the "Limmers," then came stationers, and
book binders, schoolmasters and their pupils. The 64th dis-
tinct trade to be represented in this procession was the sugar
refiners, then the vinters formed the connecting link with
the doctors, and the procession ended with the State officials,
as before stated.

Every trade was well represented in this living presenta-
tion of the resources and artisans of the city. Soon after this
Mrs. Ramage started a cotton factory on James Island, in
February, 1789. Ten years later commissioners of the Orphan
House published a request for contributions for a manufacturing establishment which was to be started in connection
with the orphanage. At a performance, given in October,
1799, at the institution some of the little children were
dressed in the stuff that they had woven. Just as the little
children of the Orphan House sing, so they sang that day
while Mr. E. C. Hart played the organ and the collection
was taken up.

Twenty-five years after the formation of the National Constitution, out of the thirty-nine members of the convention who signed the instrument twenty-three were dead. Among the survivors were C. C. Pinckney, Charles Pinckney and Pierce Butler, all of Charleston.

MAJOR GENERAL C. C. PINCKNEY
By Courtesy of News and Courier Publishing Co., Special Editions

ST. MARY'S ROMAN CATHOLIC CHURCH
See Page 175

CHAPTER X

THE far-reaching effects of association on the destiny of people and places is shown in the friendship of the Pinckneys and Rutledges with President Washington. Thomas Pinckney was sent as Minister to England, where, as some one has wittily said, "the treaty of peace had only put a semicolon to War." Pinckney as special Minister to Spain negotiated the treaty of San Ildefonso and his brother Charles Cotesworth Pinckney was sent on a mission to the French in 1797. John Rutledge was made an Associate Justice of the Supreme Court, and after John Jay's resignation became Chief Justice. Rutledge, a man of large frame, great muscularity, inexhaustible energy, keen wits, had an almost preternaturally active intellect; his thoughts were clear, rapid and forceful. He died in 1800, leaving six sons and two daughters. His wife, Elizabeth Grimke, had pre-deceased him in 1792. The Dictator is buried in St. Michael's churchyard. Washington visited this city in 1791.

The President's visit may have had a political significance but at all events he journeyed overland toward Charleston, visited the Pinckney homes, stopped at Georgetown, planted a tree at Hampton and arrived opposite to the city on May 2. He was met by Hon. John Bee Holmes, General Charles C. Pinckney and Edward Rutledge, Esq. A barge, rowed by the captains of twelve American vessels then in port and commanded by Captain Cochran, furnished passage for the presidential party. An escorting flotilla was formed of boatloads of ladies and gentlemen and two bands of music.

As Washington approached the town a salute of artillery was fired. The President's barge came to rest at Prioleau's wharf to be welcomed by Governor Charles Pinckney, Lieutenant-Governor Isaac Holmes, Intendant Arnoldus Vanderhorst and other city officials and members of the Cincinnati Society. After a brief speech of welcome, Washington was conducted to the Exchange through streets gay with flower-decked arches. He spoke from the steps of the building, greeted the citizens and was officially introduced to members of his escort. The procession was then reversed to place the President in the forefront, his suite followed, then came Mr. Vanderhorst, and wardens bearing new black wands, the Recorder, City Treasurer, the Clerk, Marshal, and the Sheriff, who bore the mace, and the procession moved to Major Heyward's house in Church street, then occupied by Mrs. Jamieson, from whom it had been hired for the use of the President. A housekeeper and retinue of servants had been installed: a "proper" stock of liquors, groceries and provisions laid in, his horses were provided with stables and hay, corn and oats. The chimes of St. Michael's rang out over the city to welcome the President. He was lavishly entertained by the Pinckneys during his visit.

The President spent a week in Charleston, during which balls, dinners, breakfasts and other entertainment were given for his pleasure, and every attention that hospitality, public and private, could devise was showered upon him. He attended church at St. Michael's. At a splendid public concert and ball, held at the Exchange, the ladies wore, interwoven in their hair, bandeaus with Washington's portrait and the words "Long live the President" painted on them. In due time, the President took his departure after "exchanging parting compliments with Mayor Vanderhorst" and proceeded southward to visit other cities. In the City Hall hangs a portrait of General Washington painted by Trumbull and a marble bust sculptured by the famous Italian artist, Guiseppi Geracchi, bequeathed by Mrs. Elizabeth Middleton Heyward to the Carolina Art Association is housed in the Gibbes Art Gallery.

Although it is nowhere recorded, Washington probably made a tour of the city during his stay and visited not only those colonial dwellings which had been left untouched by fire, flood and unravaged by war, but others, erected a few years after the conflict and those in process of construction. No doubt he saw the old Roupell house, at Tradd and Friend streets, near the home of Colonel Stuart, as Roupell and John

HOUSE WHERE WASHINGTON WAS LODGED DURING HIS STAY IN CHARLESTON, 1791

Cabbage Row to Extreme Right

STEPS OF ST. PHILIPS' OLD PARSONAGE, GLOBE STREET
See Page 45

Stuart were Loyalists and their homes were called "Tory Row." Roupell was at one time Postmaster in the city; Miss Polly Roupell was a Tory belle. When she grew older and poorer her taste for society survived. Although obliged to part with her horses, she kept the carriage and when she attended receptions at the home of Mr. Henry Deas, at his large brick house, now the Buist home, she would arrive in a carriage drawn by her footman and butler, from which she was handed with great ceremony by her host. At an appointed hour her servants would reappear and draw her a a distance of a hundred feet to her home, where she triumphantly emerged, perfectly satisfied.

Henry Deas, long the presiding officer of the Senate of South Carolina, was one of the ten children of John Deas, of Thoroughgood, Goose Creek, of whom the current saying ran that he had "nine sons and each had a sister." So that some persons really supposed that there were eighteen children in the family.

Laurens and Gadsden Squares occupied eastern portions of the city, just within the city limits near Laurens street. Advertisements in the *Gazette* announced the sale of houses in that neighborhood as being near the residences of the Legares and Linings, and one of the houses was said to be occupied by General Moultrie in Anson street. The Anson house known as the Bishop Wightman home facing Laurens street, is thought to have been the old Legare home. North of Laurens street handsome houses were erected after 1800 by Theodore Gailliard and members of the Ball and Robertson families. In this neighborhood is a house built for Mrs. Middleton, a daughter of Jacob and Rebecca Motte who married John Middleton of Lee's Legion in 1783. He died the following year, leaving his wife and infant son. She became the wife of Major General Thomas Pinckney in 1797. The house passed to John Middleton, Jr., and after his death to Mrs. Juliet Georgiana Elliott, née Gibbes, widow of Barnard Elliott. It is now the office of the Charleston Water Company.

Several fine houses erected after the Revolution are attributed to the Manigault family, who seem to have been great builders. Elizabeth Wragg married Peter Manigault, and her sons, Joseph and Gabriel, both built handsome houses between 1790 and 1800. The Joseph Manigault house stands at the intersection of Meeting and John streets and is now being restored to its former grace and beauty by the recently organized Society for the Preservation of Old Dwellings, which now also possesses the Heyward House on Church street, where the President lodged in 1791.

Dr. Gabriel Manigault, who had studied architecture in Europe, planned his brother Joseph's home as well as his own establishment, which stood on the corner of Meeting and George streets. Another Manigault house, of later date, is found on Gibbes street. The two Manigault sisters became respectively Mrs. Nathaniel Heyward and Mrs. Thomas Middleton.

Harmony Hall evolved into a place of general entertainment and lasted as such well into the first quarter of the next century. The City Theatre was later opened on Broad street, in 1794, where New and Broad streets come together, on a little triangular plot of ground, near Savage's Green, used as a parade and military ground. Other amusements were advertised to occur at Sollee's Long Room or in the Great Room in Tradd street, or at Mrs. McCrady's on the Bay where wonderful feats of horsemanship were shown. "Benefits" were quite ordinary and certain productions were frequently "given by request." After 1812 a riding circus was opened on a lot on Broad street, near Friend street, now Legare.

The year following President Washington's visit to the city "Citizen" Genet from France stopped over in Charleston on his way to Philadelphia, where he was to serve as the French Minister at the American capital. Despite President Washington's Proclamation of Neutrality, Genet thought he could persuade Americans to embark in the French cause. The French Revolution produced great excitement among the French element in Charleston, and when Genet arrived flags of the two nations waved together. Citizens wore tri-colored cockades, and shouted "Vive la Republique Francaise," and sang "Ça ira," and the Marsellaise.

THE OLD PLANTERS' HOTEL, 1785-1800

MIDDLETON-PINCKNEY HOUSE, GEORGE STREET, 1795
Now the office of the Municipal Water Company

See Page 107

HOLMES HOUSE, EAST BATTERY
On the site of the Fort Mechanic House

Genet commissioned and fitted out vessels at Charleston and projected hostile expeditions against the Spanish colonies of Florida and Louisiana, and brought Boutelle, who had acquired great wealth by his captures, to the city. Privateersmen swaggered through the city streets with long sabres at their sides. A recruiting office was opened, and on the anniversary of the destruction of the Bastile a great civic pageant was held in the city. St. Michael's bells were rung and a salute was fired by the artillery. On these occasions even the Governor, Chief Justices, Judges, and Chancellors attended the parades.

Minister Genet was properly "recalled" to France through the efforts of Washington. The excitement subsided and the recruiting office was closed by order of Governor Moultrie: a Jacobin Club was left in Charleston, but was suppressed in 1794, shortly after the *Gazette* announced a meeting of the Society of Sans Culottes.

After 1794 the town supported a French theater which gave three performances a week. It opened with a grand military and patriotic representation of the attack on Fort Moultrie, and on July 4th gave a similar performance concerning American Independence. During 1793 the capital of St. Domingo had been burnt during the slave insurrections. Refugees who came to Charleston were received with open arms and cared for until they could support themselves by becoming teachers of art, music, or sewing.

Perhaps the most fascinating story connected with Charleston's theatrical life grew out of the French Theatre. It concerns itself with Mr. Thomas, the French refugee from St. Domingo, whose daughter Cornelia was befriended by a Charleston lady whose house stood on Broad street. This lady secured music-teachers for the little girl but Cornelia's father, fearing that she would forsake the Catholic religion, took her away and, eventually she married the comedian Burke in Augusta in the Fall of 1812. As his widow, she married Joseph Jefferson, Sr., and their son Joseph became the famous American character-actor.

Another interesting person was Mrs. Tubbs, who before

her second marriage was the widow Arnold. Her daughter became the mother of Edgar Allan Poe, who was stationed on Sullivan's Island in 1827 as a soldier.

Broad Street Theatre plays an important part in Charleston's social life when the Sullys came to this city. The senior Sully had many children. Lawrence Sully studied art and painted miniatures; Charlotte became the wife of Mr. Chambers the comedian, the ceremony being performed by Rev. Dr. Purcell of St. Michael's. Romantic Elizabeth eloped with Middleton Smith, a member of the family of Landgrave Smith. Harriet wed with Dr. Porcher. Matthew and Chester fade somewhat out of the social picture, but in 1794 Julia Sully married M. Belzons, a French painter of miniatures. Thomas became the celebrated portrait-painter, and Jane married Mr. J. B. LeRoy of Charleston. The papers of 1812 announce a "Comedy in 5 Acts," called "Town and Country," at the Theatre, for the benefit of the orphan children of Mr. Sully. Ground and lofty tumbling, some dances and a skit called "Rosina" or "Love in a Cottage," were performed.

By 1797 many of the best musicians were appearing in the two theaters of the town and distinguished actors were giving performances here; among them Elizabeth Kemble, a younger sister of Mrs. Siddons. Pierce Butler's love affair with Fanny Kemble ended with a tragic marriage in the middle of the next century. The papers carry "kicks" about tall hats, ticket-scalpers and star performances all in the most modern manner, and discussions of the morality vs. immorality of the drama and its effect upon the young people of this town.

Yellow fever raged among the foreign population in 1795: refugees from San Domingo lived with a few Spanish and Portuguese in the obscure streets in the down-town section. But another class were included among the refugees and the house which had been headquarters for Admiral Arbuthnot was occupied by some of the distinguished members who arrived at Charleston in 1793.

On June 19, 1786, a fire had started on the south side of

Broad near East Bay and swept the block to Church street. Those houses that were slated or tiled escaped, the others were burnt. Robertson's grocery store was pulled down to check the flames. Now, ten years later, in 1796, another large fire began in Lodge Alley and swept the lower portion of the town. The Hand-in-Hand Fire Company had been organized in 1784, but fires went merrily on.

Between 1796 and 1797 an epidemic of clubs made their appearance according to the newspapers of the day—The Ugly Club, The Three Pace Club, for duels, The Kolf Baan Club, with Andrew Vos as treasurer, and the Golf Club, with James Gardner, for President, William Blacklock, Vice-President, and William Mulligan, as Secretary and Treasurer. The latter club's members dined every other Saturday at the club-house on Harleston's Green.

Charleston was building churches at this period. St. Mary's Church on Hasell street, the first Roman Catholic Church erected in South Carolina, was constructed at this time. Its walls and cemetery carry memorials to the early members of the faith. The site has been occupied since 1789, although the present structure is the third to be used. The original wooden structure was replaced by a brick building destroyed by fire in 1838, rebuilt the same year, and opened for worship in 1840.

The congregation was composed of Irish people and a few exiles from the French Revolution, augmented by an influx of settlers who fled from St. Domingo to escape the horrors of a slave insurrection. These became so closely associated with the Church that St. Mary's has often been called "The Little French Church." In the yard are tombs recording the deaths of prominent residents. Particularly noticeable is that of the family of the Count de Grasse, who commanded the French fleet in the war for American independence. It bears a coronet displayed over a shield with the de Grasse coat-of-arms. Other coats-of-arms are displayed on other stones in this ancient graveyard.

The Rt. Rev. Dr. England, first Bishop of the Roman Catholic Diocese, was a brilliant scholar, a noted orator and faithful bishop, loved and honored for hurrying to the sick and dying and visiting those who sorrowed. Through many years of terrible epidemics his unflinching spirit knew no rest until his work was finished. He died April 11, 1842.

Soon after he arrived from Ireland he bought the Vauxhall Gardens at the corner of Broad and Friend streets and established a temporary cathedral in an old building which stood there. His successor, Bishop Reynolds, at a cost of one hundred thousand dollars, built the brownstone Cathedral of St. Finbar that was destroyed by fire in 1861. After this the parishioners worshipped in a plain brick church, built by Bishop Lynch, until the present Cathedral was erected.

St. Patrick's Church was established in 1837 by the Rt. Rev. Dr. England. For three or four years previously a small dwelling-house was used as a place of worship. Interments were made in the cemetery adjoining the church as early as 1834. In 1837 the corner stone of a wooden church was laid, and now a handsome brick edifice adorns the northeast corner of St. Philip and Warren streets.

Opposite St. Mary's Church on Hasell street is found the Synagogue of the Jews, built in 1795, one of the most beautiful structures in the city. Its architecture is not fully appreciated as few persons see the front view of the edifice. Beth Elohim of Charleston was practically an offshoot of the old Spanish and Portuguese Jewish community of London. The Portuguese Jews in Charleston were already in a minority, but until 1850 the ritual followed that of the Portuguese communities as practiced in London and Amsterdam.

As early as 1740 there had been several Jewish families in Charleston, and in 1750 they were sufficient in numbers to have a house of worship. This was located in Union, now State street, near Queen. The Rev. Dr. Moses Cohen was the first pastor who ministered to the congregation of "Beth Elohim." In 1757 the congregation moved to a building on King street, near Hasell street, and there remained until 1789, when they again removed to a building in Hasell street near the present site of the handsome Synagogue, purchased in 1795 from the heirs of Nicholas Trott. Among names of the congregation are found Cohen, de Costa, Tobias, Pementa, Olivera, Mordecai, Shefftall, Levi, Lazarus, Cardoza, Ottolengui, Myers, Noah, Rosa, Moise, Hart, and others who are interred in the burial grounds on Coming street.

Until the year 1791 St. Philip's and St. Michael's churches had been under joint incorporation. Upon becoming separate corporations, they divided the glebe-lands and other mutual possessions and became separate entities.

In 1796, Charles Pinckney, Governor, was succeeded by Edward Rutledge, and he was succeeded by John Drayton. Yellow fever appeared in Charleston in 1798 and a great fire broke out in the town. The dramatic story of how a slave negro climbed to the spire of St. Philip's church and plucked from there a burning brand and saved the church has been told in verse. He received the precious gift of freedom for his heroic act.

In 1797, Marshall, Guerry and Pinckney (of South Carolina) were sent to France on the "X.Y.Z." mission which failed to accomplish anything but aroused deep feeling against France. Mr. Izard, who was in that country, gave to Talleyrand, who was to visit America, letters of introduction to his father in Charleston, but whether or not the letters were ever presented or if Talleyrand came to Charleston is not definitely known. Pinckney's famous "Millions for Defence" reply to the French proposal has become a fixed American principle. It is engraved upon his tablet on the South wall of St. Michael's Church.

The friction between France and England and the resulting embargo stimulated American ship-building, and the government invited bids for the construction of a limited number of ships for which money guarantees had to be raised by those bidding. Charleston held a meeting at St. Michael's, raised $100,000 and put in her bid on August 11, 1798. She raised her quota, and offered it as a loan to the President with which to secure a vessel of war of not less than 550 tons, to carry twenty-four guns on main deck, of not less calibre than nine-pounders. Thus the frigate "John Adams" was financed and built in Charleston. The *Daily*

Advertiser says "The Frigate John Adams does credit to Mr.
Paul Pritchard." The papers state that she was officered by
presidential appointees and manned by a corp of marines.

John Adams was elected President in 1798. Through the
activities of the Federal party the alien laws gave Congress
power to expel aliens from the land and to require fourteen
years of residence before an alien could become a citizen.
Under the sedition laws, criticism of the government was
punishable by fine or imprisonment. The refusal of Kentucky
and Virginia to subscribe announced the first agitation of
"States rights."

In 1789 a society for the relief of the disabled Ministers of
the Independent or Congregational Churches had begun to
function and the Mechanics had set about forming themselves into an Organization and to assist worthy young men
to secure a trade education. The Hibernian Society, which is
possibly an out-growth and combination of several other
societies formed by the Sons of Erin, came into existence at
Corbett's Thatched Cabin, which stood somewhere between
Broad and Queen streets on the East side of Meeting. John
White, Andrew Cunningham and George Thompson served
on the building-committee when the present handsome hall
was erected. James McLeish made and gave to the society the
harp in front of the building and the scroll-work over the
entrance gate, in 1841. A portion of the Giant's Causeway,
from Ireland, decorates the vestibule of this edifice, in the
upper portion of which the St. Cecelia Balls were held and
the suppers down stairs. The President of the St. Cecelia
always escorted the Bride of the Season to this repast.

It is quite possible that some of the St. Cecelia set patronized Madame Sauvage who "flattered" herself in her advertisements that she merited confidence by her punctuality
in filling orders left with her for working human hair up into
rings, "bracelates" and lockets—a fashion which has lately
returned to style, after working around the cycle of a century.
Mrs. Fell on Broad street was importing fashionable millin-
ery and attire—chip straw hats and bonnets, satin coats, blond
lace, feathers, flowers, gold and silver fringe, silk handker-

chiefs lined with fur, tippets and muffs, silk and cotton girdles, black and white veils, beaver and cotton gloves and morocco slippers were brought over aboard the "Two Friends", from London and sold in her shop, while other ships were fetching in round and cocked hats and silver shoe- and knee-buckles for the men.

It is also quite probable that at the St. Cecelia suppers some of the good things brought across the water were eaten and others consumed in another way. The gentlemen were drinking "four year old St. Lucas wine, imported in casks," disposed of by James Blair at a private sale in his vendue store Northeast of the Exchange. Others were importing and selling puncheons of Granada rum, butts of stout and porter, Lisbon and Calcavello wines, Maderia, Claret, Port Champaigne and Tokay. Bordeaux Brandy or Antigua Rum well proofed and flavored sold for notes payable in specie in ninety days *if* well endorsed. New England rum came by the mail-packet to Alexander Fraser's wharf. Others also advertised Northward rum, Malaga wine, Leghorn brandy, Holland gin and Philadelphia beer. It is to be presumed that the ladies quenched their thirst with spruce beer brewed by Mrs. Hunt in Elliott St. or with the orange shrub so often met with in the advertisements along with lists of Teneriffe wines, West Indian rum, sweetmeats from the Windward Islands, oranges, paupaus, limes, guava jelly, citron, orgeat and sometimes "Ladies sweetmeats." Boats fetched Muscadova sugar, coffee from Lisbon and Liverpool. Salt was coming from St. Ubes, Lymington and Turks Island when an enterprising Mr. Niroth erected some salt-works on the eastern end of Sullivan's Island.

The town was spreading out in several directions. A favorite way of raising money with which to enlarge the city was to set up lotteries, which were sedately carried forward under duly appointed city commissioners. East Bay was thus enlarged and commissioners advertised for a quantity of pinewood with which to carry out the project. A walk was to be run down to South Battery. The lottery must have appealed to Mr. Corbett of the Thatched Cabin. He bought some tickets, which were stolen out of his desk along with an insurance-policy and a title-deed. He offered a reward for their return. It is interesting to note that not only did the city indulge in civic lotteries but that individuals, among them Thomas Washington, used this method of raising money. It was also utilized by the Presbyterians when they decided to build Flinn's church in the year 1812, or thereabouts.

Lots were advertised on Lamboll and South bay. Mary Warham sold her father's house on Gibbes street, which was named for him, and sold at the same time all the wonderful possessions which he had accumulated in it. Lots on Savage's Green were sold as on a street recently cut through from Tradd to the upper end of Board adjoining the theater. In the great storm of 1800 Mr. Ravenel's new house "In the upper end of Broad street" was said to have been injured by bricks which fell from the theater chimneys.

In 1799 "Cross" advertised that they were "Dying and Scouring at their place of business in Dutch Town Beresford Street," and the present Clifford street went by the name of Dutch Church alley for many years. In 1799, William Savage's Estate advertised his lands on South Bay, 86 x 200 feet, bounded east by Corbet and west by Mr. Ash. Charleston was growing toward the west, and lots on Harleston's Green were sold for a lumber-yard, as they lay beside a creek upon which Mr. Wyatt had his mill.

The schooner "Betsey" from Virginia had already landed in September, 1788, a quantity of free-stone, part of which was intended for the repair of the State House. March, 1789, the commissioners were ready to treat with anyone who had an acre or an acre-and-a-half in or near to the city suitable for the erection of a tobacco warehouse and convenient for transportation in boats or drays to the "shipping"—which serves to establish the age of the buildings on Marion Square used for years as a military college and now called the Old Citadel.

Governor Edward Rutledge found it necessary in 1799 to quarantine against Philadelphia where yellow fever was

THE CLARKSON HOUSE, MONTAGUE STREET, ABOUT 1800

THE ADGER SMYTHE HOUSE, LEGARE STREET
Now the Salmons' home. Built by George Edwards

EAST BATTERY FROM THE SITE OF GRANVILLE'S BASTION

raging. Boats were required to stop at Fort Johnson, be over-hauled and secure a permit before entering the inner harbor. Regulations were published, September 30, 1799. An interesting and quaint notice appeared in August to say that Mr. Lewis Moret had for sale at his place of business, 121 Broad street, a concoction which he distilled there, the famous vinegar of the four thieves, said from Marseilles to be a counter-poison against the bad air, the plague and the yellow fever. Sometimes the fever is called stranger's fever. Marine intelligence states the names of boats bringing numerous emigrants to this colony during this year: 340 came in one boat but unfortunately they are not listed.

The city was alarmed by a daring series of robberies just about this time and the citizens were warned to take all precautions against these hardy rogues, one of whom was captured in Savannah and sentenced to be hanged. He had already been whipped and "sentenced" to the wheelbarrow, but he was a cheerful rogue who said that those who attended his hanging would learn some new dancing steps at his marriage to the "Widow Wood." Vigilance committees composed of private citizens were formed and it was publicly regretted that the police could not be formed into a small horseguard in order to patrol the streets. Small wonder that the street committees tried to get bigger and better lights for the growing city. One interesting item concerning these robberies tells of a trunk which was rifled of its contents, and a little black bag that had in it thirty dollars in species, a half eagle, a whole and a half guinea, several whole and half French crowns, an African dollar, a Dutch guilder, several Prussian and Swedish pieces and some English money over a hundred years old.

Don Diego Morphy, Consul of his Catholic Majesty of Spain for the Southern States gave public notice, on June 28, 1799, "to the merchants and others, trading from these states to any of the Spanish ports, that all goods of the growth or manufacture of Great Britain, were most strictly prohibited in His Majesty's domain." Dealers were warned to be particularly careful to have property certified under oath that it was the growth or manufacture of a neutral, friendly power. Vessels must be furnished with passports similar to the Mediterranean passports—otherwise they would be involved in difficulties and the boats would be liable to confiscation. The passports for Charleston traders had to be signed in the city and the ports most strictly guarded were Havana and La Guaira. Mr. Morphy kindly furnished a list of prohibited articles. That this notice was not taken "lying down" is indicated by numerous auctions of vessels and their cargoes that were taken as prizes by English ships on this station. Some merchants, wishing to avoid trouble, only imported articles which were allowed to go to the Spanish ports—the advertisements diplomatically word their wares as well calculated for the West Indian markets and entitled to a drawback or bounty. A straw which showed which way the wind was blowing is an advertisement signed by Thomas Shubrick who wanted negro carpenters and axemen to cut live-oak timbers on Bull's Island, also a person qualified to superintend the cutting of the frames of two, seventy-four gun, ships on the same island.

The end of the century brought a threat of war, for which Charleston prepared by repairing Castle Pinckney, subscribing for the frigate "John Adams", and erecting Fort Mechanic. A dreadful fire, the death of General Marion, and the death of Washington at Mt. Vernon close the record.

Chapter XI

IN 1800 the population of the State was 345,591, of which number 196,255 were white persons. John, the son of Chief Justice William Henry Drayton, a graduate of the English law courts and a noted writer, was governor. His successor, James B. Richardson, son of the Revolutionary General, was the first executive not a Charlestonian. Hamilton, Pinckney, Drayton and Henry Middleton subsequently governed the State. Her financial condition was so flourishing that the Legislature subscribed $300,000 to the State Bank, established and endowed the South Carolina College at Columbia and provided for the establishment of free schools throughout the State. Charleston erected two handsome public buildings, the County Court House and the State House of stone brought from Virginia, sometime during the latter part of the century just past, and in 1800 altered the Exchange.

On September 28, 1805, the Governor announced "the death of a distinguished patriot and soldier, the late Major General William Moultrie," and invited "all officers of the State to unite with him in a token of respect to the memory of this meritorious veteran and Revolutionary hero."

The war between England and France, causing the embargo acts, gravely affected the commerce of Charleston as many of her merchants owned and operated vessels. In Timothy and Mason's *Gazette*, Crafts, Morris, Haslett, Hazelhurst, Ellison, Corrie and Schepeler, Mure and Boyd, Campbell, Harvey and Company, Coffin, Cracker, Hichborn and Wright, Turner, Teasdale, Watson, Gardner and Company, advertise vessels up for London, Liverpool and other English and American ports in 1797.

McKenzie, Hooper, Winthrop, Webb and Lamo, Banks & Company, John Love and the David McCredie Company were in the importing and grocery trade, while Trezevant, Skrine, Travers, Robertson, Colcock and Patterson; Jacobs and Conyers, Jacob DeLeon, Joseph Parks, Cohen, Potter, Cripps, Denoon, Campbell and Company, North and Vesey were all in the auction and brokerage business.

From December, 1807, foreign trade was almost entirely cut off. Agricultural productions accumulating in the hands of the planters became well-nigh unsalable: money ceased to circulate among the people and business came to a standstill. To relieve this distress, the Legislature chartered the Bank of the State.

Jean Lafitte, the pirate of the Gulf, came from France and with his brother Pierre, appeared at New Orleans and engaged in smuggling and piracy, after establishing headquarters on the Island of Grand Terre in 1809. Although the British made tempting offers to him Lafitte joined the forces of General Jackson, for which they received the reward of being pardoned for their previous piracy and from 1817 to 1821 Lafitte occupied Galveston, nominally as Mexican governor. Lafitte was in Charleston during the War of 1812. The United States was apparently on peaceful terms with the nations of Europe. Bonaparte was in exile on rockbound Saint Helena from 1815. Nicholas Girod, Mayor of New Orleans had for friends the Lafitte brothers. All were great admirers of Napoleon. Securing the support of a few Frenchmen in New Orleans and Charleston, a boat called the Seraphine was built at Charleston with which to rescue the exiled emperor.

This vessel was constructed under the inspection of Lallemande the younger; and under command of Dominick Yon. Captain Dominique, the creole, trained his crew to obey orders in silence, but the death of Napoleon put an end to the plans for his escape. In 1817 Gregor McGregor was gathering in Charleston a band of lawless recruits preparing to proceed against Amelia Island, a Spanish possession at the mouth of St. Mary's river in Florida. He proclaimed that he and his followers were commissioned officers of the insurgent South American countries, then revolting against Spain and proclaimed a blockade of St. Augustine, where Spain still retained garrisons with one at Pensacola. Aury, another notorious adventurer carried on the work of free-booting and slave smuggling, under cover of favoring the South American patriots. Lafitte was operating alone at Galveston. Monroe disclaiming these irregulars, sent vessels to suppress them and wishing to send an investigating committee to South America, roused a hornet's nest by inserting a $30,000 expense item. Loundes of Charleston withdrew the item until further information was secured. But in 1810, owing to the war between France and England, English weavers were starving and out of employment, and no cotton could be sent across. The marine notices of the papers carried lists after lists of American vessels captured and destroyed by the French fleets. The *Times*, of June 23, 1812, furnished a list of twenty-three vessels captured, part of the American fleet bound to Spain and Portugal which sailed immediately before the embargo was declared. Threats of war with *Spain* began to circulate, recruiting offices were opened. The Forts were repaired. Samuel Champlain advertised for six hundred palmetto logs at Fort Moultrie. Bids for boats to be constructed were called for. The papers of August 5 announced that "the beautiful Privateer schooner 'Saucy Jack' will be launched at seven tomorrow morning from Pritchard's and Knox wharf." She was of seventy tons burden, was pierced for sixteen guns and was commanded by Captain Thomas H. Jervey. Her complement of one hundred and fifty men wore ribbons on their hats bearing the motto "Success to the Saucy Jack." Someone tried to destroy the boat because on August 10 appeared the notice, "The enemy in our camp—$300 reward for the atrocious villains who spiked the guns belonging to the Saucy Jack."

When war with *England* finally materialized, Joseph Alston, D. E. Huger, Blythe, Pringle, Cross and Barr, were put in charge of military defences of the State. This was in the nature of a triumph for Joseph Alston to whom a letter had been addressed in the *City Gazette*, June 8, 1812, from the officers of the Upper Battalion, 26th Regiment who refused to serve under Alston until two questions were disposed of.

The full affair is thrashed out in the papers of June 25 and elsewhere—Alston's reply and the answer of the officers. The August 29th *Times* announced that, "The question of the rank of Brigadier General Alston was decided in his favor as to his rank as Captain and Major." The whole affair is sad when taken in connection with the newspaper notice of July 11: "Died on 30th ult. at the residence of Colonel William Alston, Aaron Burr Alston, only child of General Alston and grandson of the late Vice-president Burr in the eleventh year of his age." General Joseph Alston became Governor of the State in December, but the honor must have been a barren one with his only son dead. Tragedy dogged his footsteps, for when his wife, the beautiful Theodosia Burr, left Charleston aboard a sailing ship to visit her father she was never heard from again. Tradition has it that Theodosia Burr Alston was captured during this war in an effort at retaliation against Governor Alston. Her fate is unknown.

The failure to check British aggressions resulted in the growth of a resolute war party in the south and west, led by Clay, Calhoun, Crawford, Grundy, Cheves and Lowndes, who succeeded in so forcing President Madison's hand that in June 1812 he declared war against England. The election of Democratic Madison again marked the defeat of Federalist C. C. Pinckney.

The news that War was declared was contained in a letter from Honorable John Gaillard of South Carolina who, for a few brief hours, was once President of the United States of America. It was dated Washington, June 19. Upon its arrival in Charleston a thousand copies were struck off and distributed about the city. The Proclamation of War was formally made by beat of drum at 12 o'clock June 26th, 1812 by Nathaniel Greene Cleary, Sheriff of the District. The citizens celebrated freely. On July 4th, when from dawn to noon salutes were fired in town and repeated by the Castle and the forts in the harbor, Brigadier General Jacob Read headed a parade. The troops were reviewed by the Governor, his suite and Major General Thomas Pinckney (who had charge of the Southern Coast Defences). After the parade they marched to New East Bay, fired a few salutes and were dismissed. The Revolutionary and the Cincinnati Societies and The Seventy-Sixth Association then met at the Exchange, and marched jointly to St. Michael's to listen to an address by William Crafts, Jr., and The Seventy-Sixth Association marched to St. Philip's where the Declaration of Independence was read and the Honorable William Johnson delivered an address. At Fort Moultrie Lieutenant Hayne of the Volunteer Cadet Infantry delivered an address recalling Jasper and McDaniel to his troops. The First Battalion had a display of fireworks in the Orphan House Yard: the Second Battalion at Fort Mechanic.

In the evening the Seventy-Sixth Association assembled at the Concert Hall, which was decorated with a large collection of portraits of heroes and statesmen of the Revolution, crowned with laurel and palmetto leaves.

It was not until 1812 that the Reverend Theodore Dehon, rector of St. Michael's, was elected Bishop. He was consecrated October 12 of that year and exercised his office until 1817, when he died at the early age of forty-one. Under Bishop Dehon the Episcopal Church in South Carolina entered upon a new phase of its life. The first address to the clergy and laity in convention assembled was made by him; he was the first to administer the rite of confirmation; he was also the first to make regular episcopal visitations and to consecrate churches in the diocese.

The increasing prosperity of the Episcopalians made a new church necessary. A third congregation was then collected in the then vacant French Huguenot Church, and, in 1810 under the care of Rev. Dr. Percy, arrangements were made for building a brick edifice with rough cast exterior, in the suburbs of the city. The new church was known as St. Paul's.

The style of architecture of St. Paul's, Radcliffeboro, is modern, with a Gothic tower, a handsome portico, composed of four Doric columns, supporting an angular pediment which adorns the Coming street entrance. The floor level is five feet from the ground, and on each side of the chancel is a vestry room thirteen feet square. The building was erected through the generosity of individuals and was completed in 1815, through the exertions of Dr. Percy, the rector, Major Charles Lining and Messrs. Brisbane, Ball, Parker and Lucas.

Papers of September 1812 announced that a Charleston citizen (Lieutenant Shubrick) an officer of the Frigate "Constitution," who was present at the late action with the "Guerriere", passed through Charleston with dispatches from Captain Hull to the Secretary of the Navy. [Captain Isaac Hull after a severe engagement lasting forty minutes captured the English Frigate "Guerriere"—49 guns, 302 men. The "Constitution" had but 44 guns.]

The papers were full of calls for volunteers to enlist against the British boats just outside of the harbor. From certain notices it would seem that the city already had The Federalist Artillery, The Republican Artillery, The Uniform Company, the 28th Regiment South Carolina Militia, the Independent Greens, and the Washington Rangers. The Cadet Infantry was called to assemble at "Sally Seymours." Two hundred men under Captain Strobel and Moorhead were sent over to Sullivan's Island as part of the State quota of the U. S. A. Infantry. Further troops from the up-country were to camp at Haddrell's Point. The entire force was to form part of the 3rd Regiment of the South Carolina line under Colonel John Rutledge.

The Commissary Department advertised from its office in the rear of 6 Coates Row that separate proposals would be received for anyone wishing to furnish or make articles of army clothing for a regiment of infantry. The list includes leather caps with bands, tassels, capped plates, pompons, cockades and eagles, nine hundred and fifty coats and vests for privates, fifty coats and woolen overalls for sergeants, twenty-two coats for musicians. Bids were asked for linen, overalls, shirts, shoes, socks, stockings, black cloth galleans, blankets, watch coats, horse-hide knapsacks; canteens, ten drums, ten fifes, a hundred and thirty camp kettles, mess-pans and some twenty-five axes with slings.

In 1813 the British plundered Deweese Island. During the same year Captain Diron, commanding the privateer "Decatur" of Charleston, engaged the British Schooner "Dominicia" and shortly after the "Decatur" captured an English Ship, "London Trader", and brought her with her valuable cargo to Charleston. In 1814 engagements took place between the Schooner "Alligator" commanded by Master Basset of Charleston and an English frigate near Coles Island, Stono Inlet. Suits in admirality were now advertised.

Mr. Lawrence Kearney captured the tender and launch of the British ship "Hebrus" at North Edisto, under circumstances of great danger. Several guns and forty prisoners were taken at the same time. A few days later, Mr. Kearney also captured the tender belonging to the British vessel "Severn" in which there were forty men. Many other small engagements along the coast of South Carolina were announced in the marine news of the day. Peace was declared December 24, 1814. At the same time Governor Alston's term expired. During it the Bank of the State had been established in this city, and the boundary line between North and South Carolina determined by actual survey. This second war with England had lasted two years, Carolina suffered but little from its effects, except that her trade was curtailed: the European markets being closed to her, she became more dependent upon the North for her supplies.

The City was still extending northward and one of the subdivisions was at the Botanic Garden—lots 57 & 58, land belonging to the Medical Society, lying on Meeting Street Road one mile from town. A little later all sorts of shrubs are advertised for sale there.

Amusements included North's lecture on Astronomy and novel exhibition at Vauxhall Garden, of an apparatus entirely new. "The moon to turn red and green and dance with any of the stars, every evening until 10 o'clock, when the sky is clear, from three days after the change to two days after the full."

There is a long notice about John H. Sargent having been imprisoned for rent which he says he does not yet think he owed. He signs himself and then says "Heretofore Editor and Proprietor of 'Strength of the People' at the Old Orphan House in Ellery Street opposite Church Street." This is followed by a notice that he is candidate for office on the Union Ticket.

Before the Revolution dependent children had been cared for by Parish authorities or bound out as apprentices. Now the City took over their support, care and education and the present Orphan House is the result of various movements. As soon as dependents were listed and cared for, a new Jail was built, hospitals for soldiers, sailors and transient poor were opened and a work- and sugar-house provided for punishment of laborers.

After the ratification of peace in the spring of 1815 Charleston raised her head. Cotton was found to pay the planter better than tobacco. The tobacco warehouses were discontinued. The weed was taxed to death and "restricted" into its grave. The increased production of cotton developed into a lucrative business centered in Upper King Street. The chief retail shops were situated near the wharves and shipping offices occupied Broad, Elliott and Tradd streets. Anything from a yard of ribbon to a plantation outfit could be bought there. The section beyond Calhoun street was scarcely settled and was given over to hucksters, peddlers and tavern-keepers.

Freights were hauled from the up-country in wagons and when cotton commenced to come in in large quantity it was either bought direct from the wagons or goods were bartered for it, and then the cotton was sold at an advanced price to the shippers on the Bay.

The wagon yards were located in Upper King street. The papers frequently announced such items as, "Arrived in forty days from Richmond, Virginia, two wagons consigned to Simpson Morris and others." Also, "Freight wanted for the above wagons for Richmond, Baltimore and Philadelphia. Apply to David Mock at Steele's Wagon Yard."

After this second war for independence the great possibilities of the cotton trade from Charleston to Europe and

ST. JOHN'S LUTHERAN CHURCH AND UNITARIAN CHURCH
ARCHDALE STREET

OLD BETHEL METHODIST EPISCOPAL CHURCH

BETHEL METHODIST EPISCOPAL CHURCH

to the New England Mills brought outside capital to the city and new citizens who became factors and commission-merchants on "The Bay." Such men were not only agents of the cotton planters to sell their cotton and buy their plantation supplies, but by advancing money to the planters, taking a lien on the crop and themselves furnishing supplies, the factors became operators on an extensive scale.

Several fine houses were built in Charleston in the early 1800s. Perhaps the finest example that has been preserved was completed in 1811 for Nathaniel Russell on Meeting street, just below the Scotch Presbyterian Church. Architectural details of the house have been repeatedly described along with the life history of the persons into whose possession it passed at different periods.

Mr. Radcliffe's house on the northwest corner of George and Meeting Streets, built about 1806, lived in till 1821 by his widow, was sold in 1824 to Judge Mitchell King. As the King mansion it was the center of Charleston's literary life. The rising young pamphleteers of the city, the lawyers serving their novitiate, the young literary lights delighted to assemble here and discuss questions of the day and hour with Judge King and his brilliant, witty wife, who was a writer of note and once bested Thackeray in a verbal encounter. The house has stood forlorn and neglected since its desertion for a larger building by the High School that formerly met here for many years. After Mr. Virgil Dibble had ceased to be the head of the school principal "Billy" Whitehead shared popularity with teacher "Billy" Schaffer.

Stephen Elliott, accomplished scholar and naturalist born in Beaufort, Yale graduate, founded the Literary and Philosophical Society of Charleston in 1815, where lectures on botany were given. His writings include "The Botany of South Carolina and Georgia." Elliott became editor, in conjunction with Hugh S. Legare, of the *Southern Review*, to which he contributed many able papers. Among the curators of the society were found men distinguished in social and literary circles.

The corner stone of the Baptist Church laid early in the

century by Dr. Furman was the beginning of the present edifice standing today on Church street. The Lutheran Church also redoubled its efforts under Dr. Buchman. The Unitarian church was erected in 1817 and remodeled in 1852. The Old Bethel Methodist Episcopal Church was built in 1852.

Audubon married a daughter of Dr. John Bachman, Pastor from 1815 to 1870, of St. John's Lutheran Church, erected in 1756, burnt in 1812 and rebuilt in 1812 when Wesner contracted for the wood and Horlbeck for the brick work. The iron fence was made later and is thought to be the work of Tebo. A separate entrance and gallery seats for slaves were placed in St. John's when it was rebuilt.

On March 28, 1818, there was born in his grandfather's house in the Fitzsimmons' residence, now 54 Hasell street, Wade Hampton, who in after years was to become the foremost citizen of the State. No blowing of celestial trumpets announced the birth of the man who was destined 58 years later to redeem his State from radical rule.

Monroe, imitator of Washington, follower of Jefferson, originator of the famous doctrine and ex-Secretary of War under Madison, was inaugurated President of the United States in 1817 and served two terms famous for the aftermath of the Spanish Revolution, the Seminole War and its strange political consequences, Calhoun's appointment as Secretary of War, the National Road and Lafayette's visit.

Soon after his inauguration, President James Monroe visited the Southern States to inspect the coast defenses and to acquaint himself with the people. He came overland as Washington had done, arrived in Charleston on Monday, April 26th, 1819, and remained for a week, having been a visitor at the mansion of Jacob Bond I'On, in Christ Church Parish, in company with Mr. Calhoun, Secretary of War, his lady and family, Major General Thomas Pinckney, Mr. Gouveneur his private secretary and Lieutenant Monroe, his nephew. Upon leaving, the party was escorted by Captain Toomer's Cavalry to Gordon and Spring's (since Clement's) Ferry, and embarked on an elegant barge manned by twenty-

HALL OF THE ST. ANDREW'S SOCIETY. ERECTED 1814, BURNT 1861
House at Right was the Dictator Rutledge home. Now remodelled it is the R. G. Rhett home

"THE FIRE-PROOF BUILDING," CHALMERS AND MEETING STREETS. DESIGNED BY ROBERT MILLS

Showing Statue of William Pitt in Washington Square Park

See Page 104

one members of the Marine Society and steered by their president Captain Thomas H. Jervey.

After his arrival, the President dined with the Governor, met the members of Council and, in the afternoon, greeted citizens and heads of the charitable organizations. During his stay the President was exceedingly busy. On Wednesday he visited the Library and other interesting places, dined with the Society of the Cincinnati and wound up the day at the theatre. Thursday was spent visiting the forts in the morning and viewing fireworks at the Orphan-House, in the evening. He breakfasted at the villa of J. R. Poinsette, inspected the defences, enjoyed a dinner given in his honor by the different societies, went to a St. Cecelia concert and ball, attended services at St. Philip's Church on Sunday morning and the first Presbyterian in the evening, sat for his portrait to S. F. B. Morse and bade the city adieu on Monday morning. When the St. Andrew's Society had been reorganized after the Revolution, permission was given it to hold lands and erect thereon a school house. Their Hall was erected on Broad Street in 1815, and on St. Andrew's day of that year the Society for the first time dined in their new building. The Hall was used as a meeting place of the St. Cecelia Club, the South Carolina Jockey Club and for patriotic, social and cultural meetings. Agassiz and many eminent scientists made its walls resound with learning. The hall was loaned to the city in 1819 as a temporary home for President James Monroe, and in 1825 Lafayette was there sheltered, while a guest of the city. This building was destroyed in 1861. The Society has in its possession the Secession gavel and the table and chairs that were used at the Hall when the Ordinance of Secession was passed on December 20, 1860. These are now in the Society's Room in The South Carolina Hall.

Questions of water-supply, paving, drainage and sanitation were agitated. Cisterns were then the source of water supply and in July 1818 a contract for building a cistern at the eastern end of the City Hall, capable of holding 101,015 gallons, was called for. Wells and pumps supplied the wants of ordinary people and frequently notices were published about pump-handles being stolen and thereby increasing fire-risks. Attempts to bore an artesian well had been made before 1820 but resulted in failure. In 1840 operations were begun at Wentworth and Meeting streets under Captain Bowman, U. S. E. Corps. City Council bore the cost of two wells which amounted to $150,000. The city now enjoys a supply of pure water, piped from the Edisto river, held in the Goose Creek reservoir and after being filtered distributed to the city.

The Market was divided into the beef market, described as an oblong brick edifice, with a conical roof surmounted by a cupola, crowned with a cock, under which the commissioners of the market met and once a year devoured an Epicurean repast, from which descent was made into the vegetable department where the vegetables were excellent. With the iodine content found in fish, oysters and vegetables there is no finer market in the world today.

A writer visiting the early market described the negro women as, "silent as the gingerbread which they sold." Two or three dollars in a pocket book and a servant with a market-basket furnished a cheerful occupation for a cool summer morning in the passage from Meeting street to Cooper River.

Robert Mills designed the City's system of drainage and some of her handsomest buildings. He was the son of William Mills who came to Charleston from Dundee, Scotland, in 1772 and married Ann Taylor. Robert was born two months before the surrender of Cornwallis, and he is a great-grandson of Governor Thomas Smith. As a writer Mills left his "Atlas" and "Statistics of South Carolina" as his literary monument, and as builder, The Fire Proof Building on the southeast corner of Meeting and Chalmers streets. Mr. Mills was State Architect when the first railroad was constructed in South Carolina. He designed the Washington Monument in the National Capital.

The Apprentices' Library Society, designed for the use of apprentices, minors and others willing to avail themselves of the opportunities of reading, was established in 1824. The

SITE OF THE OLD MARKET. THE PRESENT BUILDING ERECTED 1841
It Contains a Museum of Confederate Relics

FRASER'S MINIATURE OF LA FAYETTE
Painted for the City on the occasion of La Fayette's Visit, March, 1825

fire of 1861 destroyed their building. In June 1870 an appeal for its reorganization was made.

Adam Hidgson of Liverpool, was a visitor to Charleston in 1824. He found that the best society consisted of a few old patrician families, who formed a select circle into which the newcomer, unless distinguished by great personal merit, found it difficult to gain admission. "Many of the old gentlemen", said he, "were educated in the English colleges. Manners were of 'the old school,' the young ladies delicate, refined, intelligent, yet frank and affable to those who are formally introduced to them by their fathers and brothers. They went early into company, were generally married before they were twenty years of age and had retired from the vortex of society before the fashionable part of English women would formally have entered it." Another traveler, Capt. Basil Hall, wrote a book on Charleston.

LaFayette made a tour in 1825 and visited this city. Forty-eight years before, he had landed near Georgetown, had been brought to Charlestown by Major Huger, and from Charlestown had gone to Philadelphia, tendered his services to the Continental Congress and been made an officer in the American Army. Now he returned and found among his old friends, Col. Francis Kinloch Huger, who had endeavored to secure his freedom in 1797. LaFayette spent four days in the city, each one of which was marked by fetes and processions in his honor. He was lodged in the St. Andrew's Hall which was fitted out as a residence for the time being.

General Pinckney took part in the demonstration in honor of LaFayette and that was probably his last public service. The two brothers appeared in public, together, at the welcome of LaFayette to Charleston, who appeared in an open carriage, drawn by four handsome grays, and escorted by the civil and military bodies, the patriotic societies, including the Cincinnati, while the school children and citizens, all wearing a broad blue ribbon stamped with the words, "Welcome, LaFayette" lined the side walks.

When the carriage bearing LaFayette, his son, Col. Francis

Huger, and the Mayor of Charleston, reached the corner of George and Meeting streets the music and shouting so excited the horses that a more quiet team had to be substituted. Learning that the two General Pinckneys were immediately behind him, the Marquis took advantage of the halt to salute his old companions in arms. The brothers rose from their carriage, and there, in the broad daylight, and in the presence of ten thousand spectators, LaFayette with French enthusiasm embraced his comrades and kissed their cheeks in true French style.

HOUSE KNOWN AS THE LADSON HOUSE, LOWER MEETING STREET

HOUSE OF GOVERNOR WILLIAM AIKEN, "BUILDER OF
RAILROADS"
S. E. corner Ann and King Streets
See Page 266

AIKEN-RHETT HOUSE, AIKEN ROW, JUDITH STREET
See Page 266

ONE of the great periodical depressions in trade and finance occurred in 1825. The banks shut down, private loans became impossible, the cotton factors who had made large advances in supplies to the planters were caught between the upper and nether millstones and many leading firms went down in the crash. Many merchant princes of the day became financially involved by the capture and condemnation of their ships by the French. John Geyer, who owned a range of stores and a row of wharves and whose home was the scene of such elegant hospitality that "Who dines with Geyer?" was a current question of the day, lost many ships, among them the "Ruby," "Rising Sun" and the "Rainbow." Charleston trade was now almost altogether in the hands of an outside element.

By 1827 the city's trade (that had been upset by the War of 1812 and the subsequent tariff), had improved, but in 1827 Alexander Black of Charleston and his associates petitioned the South Carolina legislature for a charter to organize a railroad company that would help the city by increasing her overland facilities. The South Carolina Canal and Railroad Company was formally organized at the Charleston City Hall on May 12, 1828. An effort to build a road to the west resulted in the construction of a 130 mile stretch between Charleston and Hamburg, completed in 1833, forming the longest continuous railroad then existing, owned by the stock company which had organized in 1828. Branches of the road were later built to Columbia, S. C.

While the performances of George Stephenson's "Rocket" had been astonishing Europe there had gone into service a little steam locomotive called the "Best Friend of Charleston," constructed in the United States and brought to Charleston.

The population of the city was 30,289, of whom 12,828 were whites in 1830, when James Hamilton, Jr., of Charleston, a lawyer, ex-mayor of Charleston, successor of Lowndes as representative from Charleston in Congress, was made Governor of South Carolina. An ardent opponent of the tariff laws, he urged their veto by the sovereign interposition of the State. This period was distinguished by the debate in Congress involving the interpretation of the Constitution, which was the beginning of the great States' Rights controversy waged in Congress for thirty years and which was one of the causes of the War Between the States.

The Constitution bore within itself the seeds of two great parties. Great unrest had been felt in the South after the passage of the Tariff Act of 1787. The North was a section of manufacturing, the South a region of agriculture. To dispel the fear of centralized Federal power, Hamilton, Jay and Madison wrote and circulated through newspapers a series of essays known as "The Federalist" and Charleston's press was crowded with political communications bearing on these subjects.

The more distinguished local literateurs of Charlestown, Crafts, Harby, Percival, Gilman, Cardoza, White, Timrod the elder, the father of the poet, and many others appeared in the papers after 1820 under fictitious names. Charleston had always made her newspapers the battleground of local politics and in the great Nullification movement the press rushed to the support of the politicians.

Though unrecognized, the movement to "bring the mills to the cotton" had begun. William Gregg, whose handsome home on Calhoun street is now the residence of Mr. Anderson, was the pioneer worker in building the cotton mills in South Carolina. In his mills in Horse Creek Valley he was the first advocate of welfare-work among cotton mill operatives.

In December, 1832, R. Y. Hayne became Governor of the State. The political situation showed a state of affairs in which he had everything to fear and nothing to hope. In these troublesome times, amid the haranguing of the newspapers, amid the speeches and processions, were Nullifyers and Unionists, who although they continued to meet in social life, were politically at each others' throats.

The merchants of Charleston were obliged to pay a tariff on all coarse woolens and cotton cloth (which went by the name of honisburgs or plantation cloth), on iron, salt and much that was needed to sustain her immense population of slaves and their families, including medicines, tools and crude looms used in homespun weaving. Thus, when the manufacturing interests began to govern the country, the politicians of Charleston led her merchants and planters into their protest during the Great Nullification period.

The Union candidate for representative announced, in 1830, in the *Courier* was Daniel E. Huger with James L. Petigru for Senator. Yet, when theories were discarded and foes were to be faced these sons of Charleston sided with the city and the State.

Judge Petigru's remark on the morning after the passage of the Ordinance of Secession was typical of the attitude of the men of Charleston. "Well, Petigru", said an acquaintance, "the State is going to hell!"; to which the answer was given, "Yes, and I'm going with it."

The split in political parties hung upon the interpretation of the term, "States' Rights," and there were even two factions of the States' Rights' party. Colonel Preston, aided by Rhett, Smith, Elliott and others, equally enthusiastic and able, were known to their friends as "Free Trade and States' Rights." Their enemies dubbed them "Fire-Eaters." Against these men the "Union States' Rights" party, called by their enemies "Submissionists" and popularly known as "Unionists", were headed by Poinsett, Middleton, Richardson, Pringle, Grimke, Drayton, Johnson, Elliott, Memminger, Huger, Petigru, Legare and King.

Politics entered every phase of life, even that of the family. The ladies began to inform themselves on these matters and "petticoat politics" flourished in social circles.

Then began the golden age of the pamphleteer, when the agitation of the questions of the day through numerous private pamphlets gave additional life to political discussion.

Leisure had come with prosperity and with it literature. Older and younger groups followed the fashion, holding debates with arguments and speeches, more or less logical, declamatory and rhetorical and always political.

The crisis that occurred in the time of Van Buren produced a state of general bankruptcy in which Charleston shared.

The *News & Courier* of April 30th, 1835 gives an account of White's painting of St. Philip's Church done from memory by this distinguished Charleston artist. A letter of about the same date furnishes a description of the fire of that year and gives a weird description of ghostly sounds and moans which proceeded from the organ when heated air rushed through the pipes of the instrument. Colonial silver, which had been given to the church was saved. They include a chalice, paten, and a large alms plate. Some pieces given by the British Government had the Royal Arms of England engraved on them. One tankard, a chalice, a paten, and a large alms plate were "the gift of Col. Wm. Rhett to the Church of St. Philip, Charles-Town, South Carolina." One large paten has I.F.R. engraved on it. Many beautiful mural tablets are found on the walls of "The Westminster of the South" and many illustrious men are buried in the churchyards.

After difficulties over the Spanish claims in this country had been adjusted and Florida had been ceded to the United States, many slaves fled to that territory and took refuge among the Seminole Indians. Efforts to recover these and move the Indians to western reservations had resulted in the Seminole War, during which the wife of Osceola was classed as a slave, and seized. For this act Osceola butchered Taylor, was captured, brought to Fort Moultrie and in 1837 died there, where his grave is made. The yard of a Lutheran church on Society street contains a monument bearing the names of a few of the Charleston men who fell in this war, and the *Courier* for September 25, 1837 contains a notice concerning a portrait of Osceola, exhibited by Charles H. Lanneau, said to be the work of Fischer.

The tragic wreck of the steamer "Pulaski" occurred during February, 1838, and plunged the city into gloom. The newspapers were filled with heartrending accounts of the tragedy, and in the endeavor to identify victims listed personal belongings taken from the bodies.

The Nullification Convention met in Columbia, continued in session one short week, passed an ordinance nullifying the recent act of Congress to increase the tariff, ordering that no duties should be paid after the first of February of the next year and defying the government to collect duties.

The triumphant Nullifiers rejoiced and called the Unionists base submissionists. These replied that the Nullifiers might die for their rights but that the government would never allow itself to be bullied by one small state. President Jackson met the situation by issuing a proclamation denouncing the ordinance and commanding obedience to the Federal law, and stated that the State would be "rescued by force" if the duties were not paid. Governor Hayne's counter-proclamation asserted the sovereignty of the state and declared that South Carolina was prepared to resist oppressive measures even at the cost of life.

The country came to the brink of strife. The state spent large sums of money for arms and raised and drilled companies of militia, but blood-shed was averted when a compromise measure was introduced into Congress which satisfied Mr. Calhoun and the representatives of South Carolina.

Charleston men had intervened. Mr. Poinsett, an intimate friend of Jackson's, had pointed out to him that nothing was to be gained by forcing the issue. Jackson's terrible temper had manifested itself but was held in check by the influence of such men as Judge Huger and Colonel Drayton.

Relations between the State and the Federal Government were harmonized, though it was felt that the reunion was but temporary and that Jackson's oath "to make blue cockades as scarce as blue roses in South Carolina" held a threat against the State. Armed vessels were sent to Charleston to enforce the revenue laws, but the city, with inimitable social grace, engulfed the troops and the navy and tactfully made their presence an occasion for social gaiety. No city of the Nation boasted of more beautiful possessions. The mahogany sideboards of the affluent shone with silver: fine oil paintings and miniatures, the work of Fraser or Allston, decorated the walls of the houses.

At this period Sullivan's Island was the summer home of many prominent citizens, including the Pinckneys, Hugers, DeSaussures, Behrings, Williams, and others. It was a time when the wealthy planters of the sea islands, who had waxed rich on long stapled cotton, traded with the cod-fish aristocracy of New England. The New England Society in this city was composed of Northerners who had moved here, become leading business men, taken over the factorage business, and formed themselves into an organization which ranked with the best social clubs in the city. If the cod-fish aristocracy was well versed in history, literature, philosophy and politics, members of the bacon and rice aristocracy were equally so. A witty person said that the difference between the looks of a Charleston and a Boston man was that the latter looked as if he thought he knew everything and the former everything worth while for a gentleman to know. Charlestonians and Bostonians discussed the matter with great spirit over the banqueting tables of the New England or the South Carolina Society.

Fashionable babies, who made their debut into society at their christenings, were always baptized at home in the presence of close friends of the family. Invitations were sent out, cake and wine served, and if the baby were a boy the fond father celebrated the event with a dinner-party given in honor of the new heir. Cake was sent to the absent relations just as wedding-cake was distributed. A person of great importance at the baptismal ceremony was the negro mammy. It is said that sometimes the mammy took such a prominent part as to be in danger of being baptized instead of the babe which she held in her arms. Funerals were formal functions, to which written invitations were issued. Friends of the family, wearing long crepe veils and streamers from their hats, were the chief mourners. It has been said that a person's social position could accurately be gauged by the funerals at which he mourned.

In 1832-33, the exciting political issue of nullification had culminated in several bloodless riots, in one of which the office of the *City Gazette*, an anti-nullification paper, came very near being wrecked.

The "intended insurrection" of a portion of the slave population in 1822, had demonstrated the necessity of, and led to the establishment of, a strongly built arsenal in Charleston, for the storage and proper care of a large supply of arms and ammunition, subsequently named in legislative acts "the Citadel." The excited agitations of nullification times led to the further enlargement of the State's guard at the Citadel in 1832, and the establishment of an Arsenal with a guard at Columbia in 1833. The citadel survived here.

Nullification excitement having been allayed by the "Compromise Act of Congress", the Honorable John Peter Richardson, Governor of the State, in 1841 urged the plan of substituting for the guards of enlisted men a corps of young men, who, while performing the service of guards, should be educated also. Hence "The Citadel" of 1931 commanded by General Summerall.

A peculiar social feature of Charleston's social, literary, and political life grew out of meetings held at various houses of leading citizens at which congregated leading writers and speakers. Like French salons these affairs brought together men who were eager to discuss affairs with leaders of opposing factions. Groups were held together by similar political sympathies. Such a group was wont to assemble at the home of General Hayne in Ladson's Court, where of an evening might be found together Stephen Elliott in deep conversation with the learned and fluent lawyer Thomas S. Grimke and the eloquent Hugh Swinton Legare, or the equally eloquent Robert Y. Hayne, in company with J. N. Cardozo of the press.

Richard Yeadon, a bold and brilliant writer, now appeared in the newspaper world, aligned himself with Lee, Petigru and Huger in upholding the Constitution against Nullification, but declared that there is no power, direct or indirect, in Congress to interfere with institutions of the South. One of his political adversaries, Stuart, the editor of the *Mercury*, had many amusing and witty tilts with Yeadon, which increased the subscription list of both papers. Mr. Yeadon was out of the city, and filled the columns of his paper with detailed accounts of his doings. A poem appeared in the *Mercury* that set the city in a roar of laughter and all but caused a duel between Yeadon and Stuart.

A new theatre was built in 1837. The main floor was for a stage and accommodation of visitors. The front was designed as a handsome Ionic portico of four columns, elevated on a flight of stone steps. The theatre was lighted by a chandelier suspended from the center of the ceiling.

In 1846, a company for making gas began operations in the city. This company amalgamated in 1849 with another gas company, whose "holder" was once hit during the Civil War by a Federal Shell. In 1893 the unexploded shell was found in the pit.

When William Henry Harrison was elected President, Charleston, the city of aristocrats, held herself aloof from the log-cabin, hard-cider-drinking Whigs who supported Harrison. Harrison died within a month after he became President, and Tyler came into office. He not only quarreled with the Whigs but vetoed their measures. John Tyler, son of the President, in addressing the Huguenot Society of Charleston said, "I cannot but remember that in my father's management of the government of the Union which settled so many important questions, he had the assistance of two of South Carolina's greatest sons, Hugh S. Legare and John C. Calhoun."

Calhoun who had been Vice-President in 1825 and 1828, died in 1850. This city witnessed his funeral obsequies and interment in St. Philip's western churchyard. Robert Barnwell Rhett was sent to Congress, but resigned in 1852. W. F. DeSaussure followed Rhett and he was succeeded, in turn, by Judge Josiah H. Evans. After Hayne's great debate with Webster, slavery became a recognized political issue between the North and South. Hayne had read law with Langdon Cheves, and was admitted to the bar before attaining his majority; when Cheves was called into public life, Hayne succeeded to his great lucrative practice. Hayne rests beneath a marble monument erected by his widow, in the eastern part of the cemetery of St. Michael's Church. It was Hayne's desire that the South should be connected with the West that gave birth to his dream of the Blue Ridge Railroad.

In May, 1846, war was declared against Mexico. President Polk called for 50,000 volunteers for twelve months' service. South Carolina immediately organized a regiment, known throughout its brilliant career as the Palmetto Regiment. Shortly after the call the policy of the Federal Government was extended and it was determined not to receive any volunteers for a shorter period than the duration of the war. The Palmetto Regiment promptly volunteered "for the war." One of the first companies, if not the first, to respond was a company raised in Charleston at the suggestion of Mr. Lewis F. Robertson. A meeting was held at the residence of William Blanding, in Logan street, forty persons attended; a company was organized at a subsequent meeting at Masonic Hall. William Blanding became Captain, A. M. Manigault, first Lieutenant, Lewis F. Robertson, second Lieutenant and Ralph Bell was elected junior second Lieutenant. The City Council equipped the company and it was mustered into the regiment F. It covered itself with glory from the landing at Vera Cruz, in March, 1847, until the fall of the Mexican capital, September 14, 1847, when death had thinned its rank from ninety-six to forty members. The first American flag to float over the walls of Mexico was that of the Palmetto Regiment, presented to them by the city of Charleston. Upon the return of the remnant, City Council arranged for a public reception and dinner and presented each of the commissioned officers with a handsome sword and the non-commissioned officers and privates with a silver medal. A few officers received gold medals from the State.

One of the handsomest churches in the city, Grace Episcopal, was erected in 1847. In 1849 the limits of the city were extended westward to include that part of the town to the North and West of Boundary street.

Governor Thomas Bennett owned large property between Bull and Boundary now Calhoun, west of Smith as far north as Radcliffe, extending west to what is now Lucas street. A deep creek came in from Ashley, near the foot of Bull street, and a flood gate controlled the waters near that point. Ponds extended northeastwardly up as high as what was then "Pointsett's Grove" above Radcliffe street, between what is now Rutledge Avenue and Coming street and extending to Cannon street. Rutledge street between Bull and Cannon street was a causeway with a 40 foot bridge, under which the water flowed twice a day northward, to admit the passage of timber rafts. There was a similar arrangement on Calhoun street.

A few houses did sentry duty in this thinly settled region. At the corner of Smith and Calhoun streets was an old house from which Governor Middleton was buried, when the entire military force of the city paraded. It was a gallant sight as the uniform required red ostrich feathers in the caps and ball buttons on the uniform. The crimson flag of the company was surmounted by an eagle.

Churches constructed between 1840 and 1857 in the portion of town above Calhoun street include St. Luke's Church on the corner of Charlotte and Elizabeth, St. John's Chapel, corner of Hanover and Amherst, known as Hampstead, and Spring Street Methodist Episcopal Church, one of the best and handsomest in the city. During the Civil War it was used as a storehouse by the Confederate Government.

The Lafar family owned the tall brick house at Calhoun and Rutledge street when Calhoun street ended there. When the street was opened the portico was left standing as it is

THE PENNY POST,

ESTABLISHED BY AUTHORITY OF THE

Post Office Department,

IS NOW IN ACTIVE OPERATION.

☞ Persons can have their Letters taken to any portion of the City or Neck, by requesting their Correspondents to direct to the Street and Number of the House in which they reside.

NOTICES, COMMUNICATIONS,
INVITATIONS, &c.
DISTRIBUTED WITH DESPATCH.

Branch Offices.

G. F. COLE'S, 127 King-street.

CLEAVELAND'S, 250 King-street.

W. STEELE'S, corner King and Liberty.

R. W. BURNHAM'S, 343 King-street.

G. FOLLIN'S, 167 Meeting-st., (opposite Charleston Hotel.)

JOHN G. MILNOR'S, Vendue Range.

And COURT HOUSE, at Sheriff's Office.

Rates established by Congress, 2 cts. per Letter.

JOHN H. HONOUR, Superintendant.

Post Office, Charleston, 1849

NOTICE OF THE ESTABLISHMENT OF THE
PENNY POST, 1849

THE OLD "SLAVE EXCHANGE"

today. The residence of J. E. Adger (now the Franke Home) occupied the site of a cottage with extensive grounds where had resided the Honorable J. B. Campbell, whose wife was a daughter of Governor Bennett. St. Francis Xavier Church occupies the site of the summer cottages of one of the Alston family.

Beyond Ashley Avenue Edward Sebring built a fine residence, now the property of the Aimar and Duval families. During a wave of total abstinence Mr. Sebring, it is said, permanently sealed a supply of wines in the attic. William Gregg's gardens extended back to Mill street. In 1897 the property was in the possession of the Rutledge family and is now the home of Julius Anderson. The old Bennett house is now used as a home for nurses. On Ashley, once Lynch street, is a frame building, built by a member of the Ball family, who was lost in the wreck of the steamer "Pulaski." It was occupied later by the Haynes, and there Paul Hamilton Hayne the poet was born. On the opposite corner was Corbett's house, later F. J. Pelzer's home, now the Julian Williams' home. West on Bull street was a Simons house which still stands. But now the land is filled up around the open pond which was once the swimming-hole of the neighborhood boys. Houses in the neighborhood belong to this period and some are of an earlier date.

Despite politics, life in Charleston was proceeding happily enough. The Horticultural Society was holding exhibitions, the new bridge on Charleston Neck (at the junction of now Chappel and Washington streets) was bringing Mazyckboro closer to the city, when Thaddeus Street, Robert Martin and Edward Carew were the commissioners appointed for the bridge. "The Marine School" was being provided for by Mayor Charles MacBeth, who thus forwarded the work of Parson Yates. The Citadel Square Baptist Church was in course of erection, and under Mr. Kendrick's pastorate the buildings, designed by Messrs. Jones and Lee in Norman style of architecture was begun.

In 1860 four candidates were in the field for election to the Presidency. The Republican party, which held its convention in Chicago, May 16, advanced Mr. Lincoln. The Democratic candidates were Stephen A. Douglas of Illinois and John C. Breckinridge of Kentucky and Joseph Lane on the platform which had been rejected at Charleston. The Constitutional Union Party nominated Mr. Lincoln who received the highest number of votes, Douglas stood second, Breckinridge, third, and Bell of Tennessee, fourth.

The effect of Mr. Lincoln's election was to fill the South with alarm. South Carolina assembled and passed an Ordinance of Secession on December 20, 1860, by which she repealed the ordinance in which she had ratified the Constitution in 1789. By February 1, 1861, Mississippi, Florida, Alabama, Georgia, Louisiana and Texas followed suit. Delegates from these states met at Montgomery, February 4, 1861, established a government, named it the Confederate States of America and chose Jefferson Davis of Mississippi for President and Alexander H. Stevens of Georgia, Vice-President. Memminger and Robert Barnwell Rhett of Charleston proved energetic and able leaders in the Secession movement. Rhett nominated Howell Cobb of Georgia, who was chosen President of the Montgomery Convention.

A complete account of this chapter in the annals of Charleston must be left to the general historian. An outline of events which transpired from 1860 to 1865 show the civil government of the city continuing without material interruption. Francis H. Pickens of Edgefield, who had been a former representative in Congress, was elected Governor. His administration was marked by the greatest excitement that South Carolina had ever known and the residents of the city of Charleston were the observed of all observers. On December 17, a Convention of the People of South Carolina, called for the purpose of withdrawing that state from the Union, assembled at Columbia; and because of the prevailing small pox, the convention adjourned to meet in Charleston, in the St. Andrew's Hall. Notwithstanding the fact that Caleb Cushing was despatched to South Carolina in behalf of the President, an Ordinance of Secession was passed at one o'clock, declaring South Carolina to be a free and inde-

CHARLESTON

MERCURY

EXTRA:

Passed unanimously at 1.15 o'clock, P. M., December 20th, 1860.

AN ORDINANCE

To dissolve the Union between the State of South Carolina and other States united with her under the compact entitled "The Constitution of the United States of America."

We, the People of the State of South Carolina, in Convention assembled, do declare and ordain, and it is hereby declared and ordained,

That the Ordinance adopted by us in Convention, on the twenty-third day of May, in the year of our Lord one thousand seven hundred and eighty-eight, whereby the Constitution of the United States of America was ratified, and also, all Acts and parts of Acts of the General Assembly of this State, ratifying amendments of the said Constitution, are hereby repealed; and that the union now subsisting between South Carolina and other States, under the name of "The United States of America," is hereby dissolved.

THE

UNION

IS

DISSOLVED!

AN "EXTRA" ISSUED BY THE *MERCURY* TO
ANNOUNCE THE ADOPTION OF THE
DISSOLUTION ORDINANCE

ATTENTION! MOULTRIE GUARDS.

ATTEND A DRILL OF YOUR CORPS, THIS AFTER-NOON, at 5½ o'clock, on Citadel Green, and To-Morrow Evening, at 8½ o'clock, at Military Hall.
By order of Capt. PALMER.
August 8   1   W. D. McMILLAN, O. S.

ATTENTION!

IN PURSUANCE OF BRIGADE ORDERS NO. 55, AND Regimental Orders No. —, the Corps will assemble, in undress uniform, at the Citadel Green, for Drill, This Afternoon, at 6 o'clock, and on Mondays, Tuesdays, Thursdays and Fridays of each week, until further orders, at the same place and hour.
Defaulters will be returned to Court Martial.
By order of Capt. G. L. Buist: B. C. WEBB,
August 8   1   O. S. P. G.

ATTENTION! GERMAN HUSSARS.

YOU ARE HEREBY SUMMONED TO APPEAR IN Summer Uniform, at Citadel Square, This After-noon, at 5 o'clock, for Squadron Drill. By order of Capt. Theo. Cordes.   J. D. WULBERN, Clerk.
N. B.—Absentees will be reported to Division Adjutant General A. H. Brisbane, as per order from Headquarters.
August 8   1

ATTENTION!
EMERALD LIGHT INFANTRY.

ATTEND A MEETING OF YOUR COMPANY THIS Evening, at Military Hall, at 8 o'clock. Members will be punctual, as business of importance will be submit-ted.   PATRICK WALSH,
August 8   1   Acting Secretary.

MARION ARTILLERY.

ATTEND A REGULAR DRILL OF YOUR COMPANY at the Gun Sh-d, This Evening. Roll will be called at 10 minutes past 8 o'clock precisely.
          ROB'T MURDOCH,
August 9   1   First Ser.eant.

ATTEND DRILL OF YOUR COMPANY ON CITADEL GREEN, This Afternoon, at 6 o'clock, in Black Pants and Linen Jacket.
By order of Capt. B. G. Pinckney.
August 8   1   T. MORRITT HASELL, O. S.

ADVERTISEMENTS CALLING COMPANIES TO ATTEND DRILLS

pendent republic, which was adopted at Institute Hall in the evening. The rest is history.

The sentiments of the country were still greatly divided as Mr. Lincoln prepared for his inauguration. His cabinet, formed with a view of uniting the Union men, was, with the exception of Seward and Chase and one other member, made up of men from the border states, whose policy was one of watchful waiting.

Major Robert Anderson, then Commander of United States Military Defenses in Charleston harbor, a West Point graduate who had served in Florida in 1838 and fought in the Mexican conflict, was a citizen of Georgia, who held there land and slaves in his wife's name. His appointment by the United States Government was therefore considered a friendly gesture toward the South. He was immediately welcomed by the socially elect of Charleston, whose sentiments changed however when it was found that reclamation work was being pushed forward at Moultrie, which it had been understood, was "only to be prepared for a vigorous defense, should such a defense become necessary." Feeling that his command was occupying an untenable position if a force should be brought against it by the Confederates, Major Anderson determined late in the evening of Christmas day, 1860, to occupy Fort Sumter as soon as he could obtain means for so doing without exciting suspicion. The nominal defences of Charleston harbor included Fort Moultrie, Fort Johnson, Castle Pinckney, Fort Sumter. South Carolina committed itself to a pledge that while the Federal garrison in Charleston harbor was not reinforced property of the United States would be left undisturbed.

To this policy they adhered notwithstanding the excitement which prevailed in the vicinity of Charleston when it was reported on November 28 that the United States steamer "James Adger" was bringing six hundred men to strengthen the garrison at Moultrie. The North was warned, December 7, that should the Government attempt to send more troops to strengthen the forts, the catastrophe of war would be precipitated. The *Courier* of December 8 announced that a reinforcement of the United States garrison would be considered a declaration of hostilities. *The Mercury* declared on December 13 that an attempt to strengthen the garrison would be a hostile demonstration by the Federal authorities and just cause for war.

The United States Secretary of War, ad interim, January 3, 1861 stated that Anderson was "apprehensive of the safety of his command, for the insecurity of the fort, and had reason to believe that the South Carolinians contemplated or were preparing to proceed to a hostile act and desiring to prevent a collision and the effusion of blood, evacuated Fort Moultrie, spiked the cannon, disabled some of the carriages and removed to Fort Sumter." His change of base threw Charleston into great excitement and embittered the feeling that had taken possession of the public mind. The act was looked upon as a violation of the mutual agreement. It has been made a subject of doubt and bitter controversy whether or not Major Anderson had "tangible evidence of a design" among Carolinians "to proceed to a hostile act," before he resolved to retire from Fort Moultrie, and whether or not Anderson's removal of the garrison was the result of instructions from Washington.

After this act, R. W. Barnwell, J. H. Adams and J. Low, South Carolina commissioners, withdrew from Washington. The President declared that he had not ordered Anderson's move, but refused to order him back to Moultrie or to withdraw the troops from Charleston Harbor.

Startled and almost stunned by the intelligence that Anderson had evacuated Moultrie, set it on fire, and had taken possession of Fort Sumter, Charleston awaited the outcome of these questions as Anderson's retirement from Moultrie became known to Governor Pickens.

Of two of those so intimately concerned in the movements of those times it may be remarked that death itself is a great nullifier. Near the last resting place of Robert Y. Hayne, in St. Michael's Church yard, is the grave of James Louis Petigru. Hayne alone was a coastal plainsman of all the men nationally concerned in the nullification movement. Calhoun

FORT SUMTER. PRESENT VIEW

THE OLD CITADEL
While garrisoned by Colored Troops after the Confederate War

MAIN BARRACK BUILDINGS, THE NEW CITADEL, HAMPTON PARK

See Page 203

and Jackson were from the upland Scotch-Irish settlements, and Petigru from the French settlement at Abbeville.

The stone in St. Michael's Churchyard, erected by Mr. Petigru's daughter, Caroline Carson, says that he confronted life with "antique" courage and death with Christian Hope and that his eloquence was the protection of the poor and wronged, while his learning illumined the Principles of Law.

BOOK V

THE CONFEDERATE WAR PERIOD, 1861-1865

CHAPTER XIII

ANDERSON evacuated Moultrie on December 25th and 26th, 1860. In the City the Custom House was reopened under the State Flag on Friday, December 28. On Sunday the Palmetto Guard took possession of the United States Arsenal. Fearing a Federal attack on Moultrie, and there being no cartridge bags ready, the ladies of the city worked during the rest of the week to supply the deficiency.

After Anderson evacuated Moultrie, it was immediately occupied by the Marion Artillery, Lafayette Artillery, Washington Artillery, German Artillery, all under the command of Lieutenant Colonel W. G. DeSaussure. It was put in order, strengthened, and its guns remounted. Under the command of Colonel R. S. Ripley, Moultrie took a prominent part in the reduction of Fort Sumter on the 12th and 13th of April 1861.

On December 27, 1860, a detachment of the First Regiment Rifles, South Carolina Militia, commanded by Colonel J. J. Pettigrew and Major Ellison Capers, and composed of the Washington Light Infantry, the Carolina Light Infantry, and the Meagher Guard, embarked on the Steamer Nina, landed at Castle Pinckney, scaled the walls with ladders and took possession of the fort, then occupied by a United States working party. It was garrisoned by the Zouave Cadets, under Captain Chichester, and later a number of Federal prisoners taken at the battle of 1st Manassas were kept here. Major Stevens, Commandant of the South Carolina Military Academy, was sent to Morris Island with fifty cadets, two hundred negroes, and several cannon, and Charleston experienced the first act of war on January 9, 1861, when the transport steamer "Star of the West," carrying several hundred men and supplies of food and ammunition, attempting to relieve Anderson at Fort Sumter, was stopped and turned back by the firing of the Battery on Morris Island. Disregarding a warning shot the "Star of the West" had hoisted the United States Flag and continued her course. Five rounds were fired at her in quick succession, two of which took effect. At the sixth discharge, Moultrie having also opened fire upon her, she lowered the flag and steamed out of the harbor.

Events followed in rapid succession. Major Anderson, demanding of Governor Pickens whether or not he had authorized the firing on a transport bearing the United States Flag, was answered in the affirmative. Governor Pickens summoning Major Anderson to surrender Fort Sumter to the state authorities received Anderson's refusal, coupled with an offer to refer the matter to his government. Governor Pickens acceded to the request and dispatched Honorable Isaac W. Hayne to Washington, with power to act for the State. Protracted negotiations brought no satisfactory result, and the answer of Mr. Holt, Secretary of War, left little hope of an amicable settlement. Mr. Buchanan's administration came to a close under these perplexing circumstances, and Mr. Lincoln took office. The seven Southern states that linked their destinies with that of South Carolina fixed their eyes upon the Palmetto State, around which the fortunes of the South revolved.

On March 3, 1861, a native of Louisiana, a West Point graduate, classmate of Generals Hardee, Wayne, Johnson, Reynolds, Stevenson, Trapier, and Sibley of the Confederate Army, and McDowell, A. T. Smith, Granger, Barney and McKinstry of the Federal Forces, and a fellow Soldier of Anderson's in the Mexican War, arrived in Charleston to take command of the Confederate Forces. Beauregard had been in charge of the Lake defenses in Louisiana and of the erection of the Custom House in New Orleans. In 1860 he was appointed Superintendent of West Point but only filled the position for a few days: resigning his commission, he entered the Confederate service with the rank of Brigadier

General and was sent to this city. Inspecting the harbor defenses Beauregard altered the previous plan of concentrating all guns and mortars at Moultrie and on Cumming's Point on Morris Island and prepared for active measures against Sumter, which loomed defiantly in the distance. This city was thronged with men who desired to be among the first to strike a blow in a cause in which their lives, and more, were involved. Many who had answered the first call of their State had already endured privations and exposure on the sea islands, where they had worked as privates side by side with their own slaves to erect the coast defenses. Among these privates were planters and their sons and some of the wealthiest men of South Carolina.

Fifty thousand Carolinians voted for secession. Seventy-five thousand stood for it on the field of battle. Mr. James L. Petigru alone in South Carolina failed to secede; this was the spirit which animated Charleston when General Beauregard arrived to put into operation plans for a defense of the city and harbor. With scant, inadequate resources, for nearly two years Beauregard held miles of most vulnerable coast against formidable and always menacing land and naval forces of the U. S. A.

Major D. R. Jones, Assistant Adjutant General, Captain S. E. Lee, Captain S. Ferguson and Lieutenant Sydney Legare of the Regular Staff, with Messrs. John L. Manning, James Chestnut, Jr., William Porcher Miles, J. A. Gonzales, A. B. Chisholm and Colonels I. T. Wigfall of Texas and Roger A. Pryor of Virginia, constituted Beauregard's military family at the time, and Charleston's reception of these gentlemen afforded Mrs. Chestnut an opportunity to express, in her "Diary from Dixie," her opinion of various members of the General's military household and other notables who gathered around Beauregard's headquarters at the Charleston Hotel.

Beauregard began a bombardment of Fort Sumter on April 12, 1861. The sound of a signal gun fired from Fort Johnson, before daylight, passed like an electric shock through the length and breadth of the town, rousing even the heaviest

THE BOMBARDMENT OF FORT SUMTER, AS SKETCHED FROM MORRIS ISLAND

ST. FINBAR'S CATHEDRAL. BURNED IN 1861
See Pages 176 and 223

sleepers. The whole community made its way to East Battery and from its walls and adjacent houses with strained eyes or with aid of opera glasses and telescopes watched the two-day battle which ensued. Every home had sent its youth to war and there was scarcely an onlooker who had not at least one son in the fight. The first shot sped aloft, displayed its arch of fire, burst over Sumter, and fell crashing into the center of the parade as Beauregard commenced action. Every battery was in play by five o'clock. For two hours Anderson failed to reply, but at seven, committing his flag to the war in which, it is said, "his heart was not", the guns of Sumter spoke at seven and fired slowly and sullenly until nightfall. Having no ammunition to waste, Anderson fell silent until the morning of the thirteenth, when the presence of the Federal fleet outside the bar inspired continued resistance. Anderson's fire was directed, mainly, towards Moultrie, Stevens' Iron Battery on Comming Point and the Floating Battery.

In the thick of the bombardment a thin spiral of smoke was seen to curl up from Fort Sumter. A detachment from Company B, under Lieutenant Alfred Rhett, at Moultrie had thrown forty rounds of red hot shell from an eight-inch columbiad and had set fire to the barracks on the fort. In spite of this Sumter responded at long and irregular intervals to the Confederate guns.

Game to the core themselves, the Southerners could not but appreciate the critical position of their opponents, and carried away by their own enthusiasm, mounted the parapets and cheered Major Anderson at each successive discharge that came from the fort, while deriding and hooting the timorous inaction of the Federal fleet.

Matters reached a crisis when Beauregard, fearing that with the barracks on fire some terrible calamity might befall Anderson and his garrison, and being informed that the United States flag no longer floated over the fort, dispatched three aides with offers of assistance to Major Anderson, who thanking him for his courtesy declined to accept assistance and stated that the flag had fallen.

It was hoisted anew, but did not fly for long and a white flag of surrender soon appeared.

The surrender wrought a change in the harbor in a few moments. Steamers with fire engines were dispatched to the fort. The garrison gathered on the wharf to breathe the fresh air, numbers of little sailing boats were to be seen darting like sea-gulls in every direction, conveying gentlemen to the islands to see their friends.

As soon as the surrender was announced, the bells of the city commenced to ring and in the afternoon salutes of the "magic seven" were fired from the cutter "Lady Davis", the School Ship and the Cadets' Battery in honor of one of the most brilliant and bloodless victories in the records of the world.

Major Anderson appointed twelve o'clock to give up the fort and the Governor, his wife and suite, with General Beauregard and suite and many other military men, went down on board a steamer, whence they witnessed the ceremony of raising the Confederate and Palmetto flags.

An unfortunate explosion, caused by carelessness, occurred within the fort while Anderson, saluting the United States, retired. Four men were wounded and one, Private Howe, was killed. Those whose wounds were mortal were brought to Dr. Chisolm's hospital in Charleston. The private, Howe, was buried with military honors at Fort Sumter, where he fell. Parson Yates held the service, which was attended by a part of the Palmetto Guard. Anderson repaired to the Federal fleet. General Beauregard then entered the fort, which, in obedience to orders from the Confederate Government, he had successfully reduced.

It is said General Beauregard abstained from meeting Major Anderson, his former friend and professor, now his defeated foe, "lest his presence might add to the distress and mortification of a gallant officer."

Charleston celebrated the surrender of Fort Sumter by a grand fête given by Mr. Bull at Ashley Hall. Hundreds of the city-people and out-of-town folk attended, and, though the band played delightfully, the guests seemed more inclined to walk about and see General Beauregard and other "celebrities" than to dance. Wade Hampton was seen, and those who did not know him recognized him by his curious voice. Many of the ladies wore "jockey's caps" and "Renfew hats," some of which were of black velvet with white plumes, others white, with black plumes. The effect was very stylish and distingué and afforded variety to the scene out under the moss-draped oaks of the old estate.

In Charleston, though the presence of many officers gave promise of much gayety, the St. Cecelia and Jockey Club societies determined to give no balls and expectant debutantes were greatly chagrined at a season being scored against them in which they had no enjoyment. But as the horses had already arrived, the Jockey Club decided after all to give their annual three days' meet in February. On the last day a celebrated race between Albine and Planet was run. The ordinary excitement of the racing was enhanced by sight of every day acquaintances dressed in uniform, and plain "Mr." transformed to "Captain" or "Colonel".

The up-country troops were ordered to assemble in Charleston to entrain for Virginia, and every day brought hundreds of men and anxious mothers, wives and sisters who followed them. The graduating class of Cadets received their diplomas from the Calliopean and Polytechnic Societies. The speeches at the Hibernian Hall and the Cadets' Ball were held as usual, though pleasure was dampened by the stern atmosphere of war. The Citadel commencement was omitted, as Major Stevens and many of the officers were on duty. The Cadets received their diplomas, after which many enlisted and served in the Confederate Army until death or the conclusion of the war.

Lincoln fulfilled his threat of blockading the port by sending, on May 11th, the "Niagara" to Charleston, with twenty-four other fine vessels. The "Niagara" could use either steam or sail and was probably the fastest ship in the United States Navy. She carried twelve guns, was manned by six hundred men, and was equipped with provisions, implements and munitions of war. She had warned off two or three vessels from bringing provisions to Charleston. True to type, Charleston women made the best of the situation and marketing became a "function". City housewives were now unable to procure what they would choose. Meats were high, but vegetables which were usually sent to the North at that season were naturally retained and were abundant. Fresh butter rose to fifty cents in consequence of the price of hay, and everyone determined to give it up as a luxury. The pinch of war began to be felt, but the Home Guard was still in the city and several small entertainments were arranged to give excuses for social gatherings. A flag was presented to the Marion Artillery and also one to the Washington Light Infantry Volunteers. The latter was given by Mrs. Ancrum, the daughter of William Washington, and worked by the ladies of that family echoed the famous Eutaw flag episode of the Revolution.

On August 21st Brigadier General R. S. Ripley was assigned by the Confederates to the command of the First Military District of South Carolina. The lighthouse in the harbor perpetuates his memory.

In October, former U. S. Senators Mason and Slidell escaped the blockade and reached Cuba on their way to England as commissioners. They hoped to awaken the cotton-spinning interests to the fact that if the blockade of Southern ports continued their supply of cotton would be cut. It is said that Fanny Kemble Butler, the wife of Pierce Butler, whose plantation in Georgia was the home of this famous actress, where she openly rebelled against the institution of Slavery, (upon the subject of which she published a book, that led to a divorce from her husband), so influenced English men of note and through them the general public that Britain never formally recognized the Independence of the Southern States although secretly inclined to do so. Mason and Slidell were captured by Capt. Wilkes (U. S. Navy) but eventually were released to England.

On October 26th the Confederate steamer "Nashville" escaped from the harbor and successfully ran the blockade. The blockade-runners now became the only outside source of supply for the Confederates, who either lived upon what they could raise or did without. Before the contest was over delicately reared women were wearing homespun or used the satin covers from furniture and curtain materials of their once splendid homes. Home-made or prunella shoes became all the style, home-made dyes colored the home-made dresses. Hats were constructed from palmetto leaves and straw, candles made from myrtle berries gave light at the simple entertainments and food was sometimes scarce, but through it all the women preserved their culture and emerged the same imperturbable ladies that they were when the Confederate war broke out. Blockade supplies were distributed from the "Bee Block", which still stands in fine condition on Bull Street between Ashley and Rutledge Ave. Here the ladies of the town assembled—the bon mot of the period when depreciation of currency had set in being that they brought their money in a basket and carried their supplies home in their pockets.

The steamer "Hattie", a Clyde built boat owned and operated by Captain H. S. Lebby, was the last blockade-runner to leave and enter this port. Her powerful engines enabled her to give the Yankee gunboats the slip when she crept by through the fog and darkness of night. She brought ammunition and medicinal supplies all during the war. At least three battles were fought with munitions for which the Confederates had waited and which were landed safely by the "Hattie". Plot after plot was formed at Nassau to get hold of her but none of them were successful, for she slipped in and out like a phantom, taking desperate risks but attended by good luck.

Lincoln's call for troops had been met by a corresponding call from Jefferson Davis. First blood was shed when Northern troops were opposed in the streets of Baltimore by a mob on April 19, 1861. General Winfield Scott was in command of the Union forces and General J. E. Johnston of the Confederate. Mr. Seward, U. S. Secretary of State, viewed the first military movements in the mountains of Western Virginia with satisfaction and promised that the war would be over in ninety days. But the battle of Bull Run, which occurred on July 21st, put another complexion on the matter.

It was then that Lincoln, calling for five hundred thousand men, blockaded the southern ports and persuaded Congress to set seriously about raising money for the army and navy. General Scott retired and General George B. McClellan being placed in command of the Federal forces organized the Army of the Potomac at Alexandria in preparation for a second advance. The Confederacy spent the summer and autumn of 1861 in organizing the army of Northern Virginia under Beauregard.

It has been carefully estimated that out of the 291,388 white persons in South Carolina in 1860, the State sent 75,000 of her men into the field, while an additional 10,000 served in military companies and as home defenders. The State had on the firing line a man or boy for every three persons in her borders. In the strife which broke alike the past power and the future hopes of this State no absolutely accurate record is obtainable of the sacrifice in man power. The records of many companies show over thirty per cent killed and wounded and many more permanently disabled.

Out of a white population of fifty thousand (one half to two thirds of whom were women and children) Charleston furnished 23 Infantry Companies, 11 Artillery, and 8 Cavalry Companies, and a large home guard composed of older men, young boys, and a few men whose knowledge of the topography of the section was considered invaluable and necessary to the officers in command in this section. It may truthfully be said that such a large part of her adult male population saw active service that the city was in mourning from Manassas to Bentonville. The Charleston troops and Bonham's and the up-country troops received their baptism of blood at Bull Run. Kershaw men dipped in crimson the flag which had been presented to them in front of the Charleston Hotel and many of the boys who had marched away in the moonlight to the music of a military band that night now behaved themselves like seasoned veterans responding to the battle cry of their leader, and stemmed the tide of battle.

Troops departing from Charleston were frequently escorted to the depot by the Cadets and the Carolina Light Infantry with a band of music. The soldiers who expected to disband and be able to seek their friends and say farewell, were often marched directly down, far beyond the station, to where cars were waiting for them. But the crowds followed even to the depot yard, where a dense mass collected, although nothing could be seen but the occasional gleam of bayonets by the dim lantern here and there and a banner as it was carried in. The captains gave short speeches —and these were followed by farewells and cheers—and then the troops were gone! and probably but few returned. But this was only the beginning! The end no man could see!

On November 5th General Robert E. Lee, who had resigned from the U. S. Army at the time of the formation of the Confederacy, was assigned to the command of the Department of South Carolina, Georgia and East Florida. On November 7th, the Federals began operations against the coast, when the battle of Port Royal was fought. The Confederate fleet consisted of an old river-steamer which was Tatnall's Flag Ship and three tugs. The Federal fleet consisted of four steamers, a frigate, five sloops of war, twenty-five gun-boats, and seventeen sailing vessels which brought in 12,000 troops. William Tecumseh Sherman, who had been stationed at one time on Sullivan's Island and had many friends in Charleston, was in command. Traditions say that his fury against the south arose from the fact that he had courted and been rejected by a Charleston belle.

By the conquest of Port Royal, the Federals secured a base of operations from which to harass the entire seaboard. Numerous small expeditions were sent out to destroy the railroad between Charleston and Savannah. At Pocotaligo and Coosawhatchie the Federals were defeated by a handful of Confederates. Nevertheless the whole low country was ravaged, the plantation houses destroyed, the inmates terrorized and the estates plundered and pillaged. All hope of supplies from this source was destroyed. The latest news, which was brought by a blockade runner, was that the Federals intended attacking the coast in three places. In case of an alarm, it was arranged to toll the city bells fifteen times, five times in succession, and General DeSaussure ordered all the companies as far as Upper St. Johns to take their positions in readiness to move at a moment's warning. The city had fortified herself upon lines quite similar to those used during the Revolutionary War and the War of 1812. Commercial wharves were pulled down to make way for a battery; one was placed near Vanderhorst's wharf, and Boyce's became a shipyard where an iron clad gunboat was constructed.

Central wharf once the head and the front of the cotton trade where of a morning, 20,000 bales were stored in the holds of ships from the Indies, from Liverpool, Havre and Bremen, which carried goods for Fraser & Company to Europe, was selected by engineers for the site of a large battery to carry a monster gun. Blocks of buildings were removed and the docks partially filled to provide proper support for the giant gun. At White Point a battery mounting four guns was erected.

On November 16th, Captain Duncan N. Ingraham, whose father had served aboard the "Bon Homme Richard" with John Paul Jones, was assigned to duty as flag officer of the Confederate Naval Forces around Charleston. The city was calling into service her iron workers, to construct boats to be used in the war and cannon for defense of the city.

Charleston became crowded with refugees who came empty handed from the ravaged sea islands only to undergo the great fire of December 11th, which broke out on the northeast side of town. The fire, of incendiary origin, started in a shed next to Russell's machine-shop and spread to Cameron's foundry, where an immense number of rifled cannon, shot, and shell were stored, and destroyed. The fire swept the city from the Cooper to the Ashley. Streets between East Bay and the Charleston Hotel were burnt out. The hotel was saved with the stores on Hayne and Market streets. From thence it leaped to the south side of Market and swept everything before it. The theater, Apprentices Library, Art Gallery, Circular Church and the Institute Hall perished. The collection in the Art Gallery was entirely destroyed. The square on which the Mills House stood was saved, but the whole of the other side of Queen was consumed down to the old Roper Hospital. Fourteen houses were blown up to save the hospital, Medical College, Marine Hospital, Jail, Workhouse and other public buildings, which otherwise must have been destroyed. It was here that Federal Prisoners were confined during the War.

The greater part of King Street on both sides below Enston's store (corner of Market and King) down to the Quaker Church was destroyed. Reaching Broad Street, where some of the finest private residences in the city were situated, the fire burned only on one side of the street, leaving the Izard and Rutledge Houses, but destroying the Cathedral, which had been filled to overflowing with the silver, clothing, furniture, books and valuables of scores of people who believed the building fireproof. The pavements were loaded with the belongings and bedding of the refugees, who cowered beside their goods in despair, while others went hurrying along, clutching articles of value, seeking safety in the North West side of the town.

The spire of the Cathedral towering over everything, caught fire. Arch after arch fell in and still the Cross glittered and burned high over all until at last the roof caught and the Cross fell as the city was wrapped in a wall of fire from river to river.

CHAPTER XIV

THE first year of the war closed with much of the city in ashes, the people sadly in need, and the Federal fleet blockading the harbor and sinking obstructions in Maffit's Channel off Charleston bar. 1862 was a year of comparative peace in Charleston itself although numerous engagements were taking place on the sea islands adjacent to the city. General Lee, who had been in Charleston as Commander of the Southeastern Division, was called to Richmond and Major General J. C. Pemberton was placed in command of the Confederate forces of South Carolina and Georgia, Major General D. Hunter being the Federal officer for the South. The engagements on the sea islands caused further influx of refugees and on May 5 martial law was proclaimed in Charleston by the Mayor.

Through a fatal oversight as to its strategic value, Coles Island, which commanded the entrance to Stono river, was abandoned May 12, and on the 20th the Federal gun-boats gained entrance to the back door of the city, harassed James Island and finally possessed themselves of Folly. Union troops forced an advance across James Island, and on June 8th a skirmish in the rifle pits before Secessionville occurred, after which skirmishing continued until June 16th, when at the battle of Secessionville on James Island seven thousand Union troops assaulted the works garrisoned by Colonel T. G. Lamar and seven hundred and fifty men and were defeated. Brigadier General Johnson Hagood led the advance movements of the Confederates. His son, General Johnson Hagood, U. S. A., served on Pershing's staff in the World War. His wife is Miss Smalls of Charleston. The success at Secessionville was due to the fighting qualities of the men and the coöperation of the Charleston Battalion commanded by Lieut. Col. P. C. Gaillard, who held the Federal forces in check. His command included the Sumter Guards, the Calhoun Guards, Charleston and Union Light Infantry. Although wounded, Col. Gaillard fought on until reinforced by the Eutaw Regiment under Col. C. H. Simonton, which had marched three miles at the double quick, and the Louisiana Battalion under Lieut. Col. McHenry. Today Lieut. R. W. Greer of Charleston, who served in the Washington Light Infantry as part of the Eutaw Regiment, is the sole survivor of his command at Secessionville. Other troops which participated in this brief, bloody and spirited affray who lost heavily were companies A, D, E, G, I, K, of the 22d Regiment; Companies B, I, of the First Regiment of Artillery and Companies G, K, of the 24th Regiment. The fight caused many heartaches in Charleston. Captain Henry C. King of the Charleston Battalion, who fell while leading his men to victory was only one of many who gave their lives that day.

The Union troops evacuated James Island on the first day of July. In the middle of August martial law in Charleston was suspended. Pemberton was superseded by General Beauregard, who had returned from Virginia, and Brigadier General R. S. Ripley, a brilliant and able officer never properly valued, was placed in command of the First Military District. It has been said that Ripley was not popular, and that therefore scant heed was given to his sage counsel to fortify the end of Morris Island, which lay adjacent to Folly Island. Some small effort was made to defend this vulnerable place but no adequate fortification was placed there. The discussion of this aspect of the defense of Charleston harbor is a moot question in military circles.

The city was bearing its share of war. Necessities were sky high, money was depreciating. The State had contributed to the Confederate Army some of its most efficient and brilliant commanders. Many Charleston girls became the brides of those who left to serve on the fields of Virginia, some of whom, alas, never returned.

Milledge L. Bonham, native of Edgefield, graduate of the S. C. College, veteran of the Seminole and Mexican wars, had represented South Carolina at Washington from 1856 to 1860. In 1861 he commanded a South Carolina brigade, afterwards led by J. B. Kershaw. Bonham was elected a member of the Confederate Congress at Richmond, after the Battle of Manassas, and left the army to become the second Confederate War Governor of South Carolina; from which state he showed great energy in sending men to Virginia and the Mississippi valley.

Lieut. Generals Richard H. Anderson, Stephen D. Lee, Wade Hampton, James Longstreet (appointed from Alabama) and Daniel H. Hill (from North Carolina) were all born in South Carolina. Benjamin Huger of Charleston, J. B. Kershaw of Camden, M. C. Butler of Edgefield, and P. M. B. Young (the latter appointed from Georgia) were Carolina born and served as Major Generals in the Confederate Army. Other South Carolinians serving as Brigadier Generals include: Hamilton P. Bee and L. T. Wigfall (appointed from Texas; Pinckney D. Bowls and James Cantey (appointed from Alabama); Zachariah C. Deas, E. N. Law, and John Bratton, who was forced to flee to Canada for refuge after the war on account of his activities in the Ku Klux Klan. Other Brigadier Generals from this state include Ellison Capers, who became a Bishop in the Episcopal Church, James Chestnut, A. D. C. to President Davis, Thomas F. Drayton, John Dunnovant, Stephen Elliott, Jr., N. G. Evans, M. W. Gary, S. R. Gist, A. H. Gladden, D. C. Govan, Maxcy Gregg, Johnson Hagood, John D. Kennedy, E. M. Law, A. R. Lawton, T. M. Logan, Samuel McGowan, Abner Perrin, J. Johnston Pettigrew, John S. Preston, R. S. Ripley, R. R. Ross, J. H. Trapier, J. B. Villepigue, W. H. Wallace. Of the thirty-eight South Carolinians who rose to the rank of Brigadier-General, Charleston furnished James Conner, Thomas F. Drayton, S. W. Ferguson, Micah Jenkins, A. M. Manigault, C. H. Stevens and Bainard E. Bee.

Brigadier General Bainard E. Bee, of Charleston, who gave the name "Stonewall" to General Jackson, lost his life at Manassas in 1861. His body was escorted to this city to rest in state, before being carried to Pendleton for interment. Colonel Bartow's body was brought with that of his companion-in-arms from Virginia. Charleston men who lost their lives in this same engagement were brought home to rest at Magnolia. Colonel Bartow is buried in Savannah. A funeral car was sent with a military escort to Florence, and when the illustrious dead arrived in the city flags of the forts were flown at half-mast and guns were fired hourly from six to sunset, in their honor. At the northeastern depot the cortège was met by the dragoons as an escort of honor, and the German Huzzars and the Mounted Guard guarded the procession on its journey through the streets, where all business was suspended. The city guard marched on either side of the hearse, with trailing arms, and various companies paid their last respects with a salute of three volleys.

In giving a list of those Carolinians who served in various capacities in the Confederate Army or in other official capacities the name of Christopher G. Memminger of Charleston is linked with G. A. Trenholm as first and second C. S. Secretary of Treasury. Both were from Charleston and both left handsome homes. John M. Huger and Lewis Cruger were Comptroller and Solicitor. Mr. Huger, from Charleston, was a member of President Davis' staff.

Lucius Bellinger Northrop of Charleston was the first Commissary General of the Confederacy. His brother Claudian Bird Northrop's son was the late beloved Roman Catholic Bishop of this Diocese. His name is variously written. His baptismal certificate signed by the Rev. Mr. Gadsden of St. Philip's Episcopal Church reads: "Harry Pinckney Northrop." His tablet in the cathedral reads, Henry Pinckney Northrop, and his signature was usually made in the form of his initials. The roll of South Carolina's officers is completed with the names of F. R. Lubbock, A. C. Myers as first, and A. S. Lawton as second Quartermaster Generals; T. S. Rhett, Bureau of Ordnance, Samuel P. Moore, Surgeon General, and Colonel John Preston of the Bureau of Conscriptions.

In January President Lincoln ordered a general advance of land forces. Grant and Foote forced General A. S. Johnston to surrender Fort Donelson, Johnston lost his life at Corinth, Miss., April 6. Farragut opened up the Mississippi and

General B. F. Butler, nicknamed the Beast, was in control
of New Orleans. Carolina troops were fighting in Virginia, and it was from the Charleston troops that typhoid
took its dread toll. The Commissariats, unprepared for such
an emergency, were provided with medicine and nourish-
ment every week, sent from Charleston.

It was difficult to obtain accurate information about either
the whereabouts or condition of friends, as Beauregard would
allow only those who were going to join the army to go on
to Manassas. The Carolina regiments were continually on
the move.

Lincoln now seized Mr. Robert Mure of Charleston, a
prominent Scotch merchant, who was accused of bearing dispatches, as he was about to leave for Europe. He was thrown
into prison with many other Confederates accused of political
crimes and left to suffer with cold, hunger and disease. He
was not released until 1865.

George Trenholm & Company operated the first steamer
to run from Liverpool to Charleston. Seventy thousand
pounds were paid for her. The cargo was valued at three
hundred thousand dollars and in consideration of the
number of privateers swarming the seas, it was "deemed
prudent" to put two rifled cannon on board. She sailed
under British colors and papers and Charleston looked
eagerly for her arrival, as she would bring supplies for the
Confederacy.

In Charleston, the women redoubled their efforts. The
Ladies Volunteer Aid Society, of which Miss Hesse Drayton
was Superintendent, and Miss Emily Rutledge Secretary and
Treasurer, raised a thousand dollars and, with twelve managers, bought cloth, cut garments which were distributed to
the 192 members, and then collected the completed garments at quarterly meetings. These were sent to the troops.

Mrs. George Robertson and Mrs. Snowden formed the
Soldiers Relief Association to send clothes, comforts and necessaries to the sick and the wounded, and ladies interested in
the Y. M. C. A. sent hospital supplies to Virginia. There was
work to do at home as well. Troops were continually pass-

ing through town. Towards the end of the war Major Willis established a rest-room for soldiers. Some of the State troops were: The S. C. Artillery, which included the "Light Batteries of Bachman, Brooks, Beaufort, Calhoun-Preston, Chesterfield, Ferguson, Palmetto, Gist Guard, Johnson's, Lafayette, Boyces, Pee Dee, Marion, Mathewes, Santee, Tupper's, Vigilant, Rifles, Ward, Washington (with Hampton) Winder's, and four heavy regiments. The Light Battalions: German, Lamar and Palmetto, from A through K, and three heavy battalions, The First, Lucas' and Alston's.

On March 8, 1862, the Confederates took the sunken U. S. frigate "Merrimac", rechristened her the "Virginia", sheathed her with railroad iron, gave her an iron prow with which to ram her opponent and sent her out with two gunboats to destroy the "Cumberland" and "Congress", and disperse the U. S. fleet blockading James River. Although victorious, the "Merrimac" was driven to cover the next day, when the newly constructed, turreted, iron-clad Union boat, the "Monitor", appeared. The result of these first great encounters between iron-clads was to revolutionize the ideas of naval warfare and cause all great powers at once to construct boats of iron and steel. Several Charleston men, serving as volunteers in the 18th South Carolina Regiment (Gregg) then stationed at Norfolk, Virginia, took part as volunteers in this venture—Riddock, Harlow, Truesdall, Anderson, Waldeck, Stevens, Callahan, Deery, Hopkins, Ring, Sanders, Savage, Skerritt and Whelan.

In Charleston the new idea was eagerly welcomed and the new iron-clad rams, "Palmetto State" and "Chicora", each mounting four guns, were completed, and put on duty in the harbor. Pilot Isaac B. Relyea, one of the city's ancient mariners, says that the steam tug "James Gray", purchased by the ladies of Richmond and presented through Governor Pickens to the Confederates under the name "Lady Davis", sailed for Charleston under Lieutenants Thomas B. Huger, William G. Dozier and John Grimball, took no part in defending Sumter in April 13, 1861, but as a privateer under Lieutenant Pelot, annoyed the blockading fleet, captured a

last extremity. The effort to take it by a land approach over James Island had failed at the Battle of Secessionville, June 16, 1862. By the concentration of ironclads, gunboats and transports in the Stono and adjacent waters, it became evident that a combined land and naval attack was now contemplated by the Federals.

The sole object of the occupation of Morris Island, as stated by General Gillmore, was the demolition of Sumter as preliminary to the entrance of the ironclads. That accomplished, it was thought the gate to Charleston would be thrown open to the Federal troops and the "Cradle of Secession" would fall. Holding a position thought to be of secondary importance to the security of James Island, which *must* be secure beyond peril of surprise and capture, Morris Island was but lightly guarded.

Shortly after the Battle of Secessionville, Captains F. D. Lee and Langdon Cheves of the Confederate States Engineer Corps planned, on a spot designed by nature for defense, the fortification known as Fort Wagner, which occupied a position three-quarters of a mile to the South of Cummings Point, near Fort Johnson, at a place where James Island narrows to a strip of land about two hundred and fifty yards wide, between Vincent's Creek on the west and the ocean on the east, and distant about two thousand feet from high sand hills. Fort Wagner was erected on a strip of land that had an alternating width of from twenty-five to forty yards at high tide, along which attacking sappers and miners would have to build their approaches. An unsuccessful attack was made upon it early in the new year (1863). Time presently showed the value of this defense.

On January 31 three ironclads, under Flag Officer Ingraham, attacked the blockading squadron, disabling two vessels which surrendered but escaped later. On February 13, three cotton-laden steamers ran the blockade and one entered from Nassau: March 7, the fortification of the southern end of Morris Island was begun. On the 28th, General D. Hunter of the Union Army occupied Folly Island, which had been left unprotected after the abandonment of Coles Island.

On April 7, 1863, Fort Sumter, commanded by Col. Alfred Rhett of the First South Carolina Artillery, bore the brunt of the attack by the iron-clad squadron under Rear-Admiral Dupont. This squadron numbered eight turreted vessels and the new "Ironsides." In two hours and a quarter the entire squadron retired completely worsted, after firing one hundred and thirty-nine shots from twenty-three guns. More than half the vessels were badly damaged and one went down early the next morning. Less than half of the guns of the fort were engaged, firing eight hundred and ten shots. The masonry in a few places was injured, but by the following day the fort had repaired its few serious damages and was ready to renew the fight.

By June 12, on the Islands, where scouting expeditions had taken place, Hunter had been relieved and Brigadier General Gillmore was now in command of the Federal force. Dupont had been relieved by Rear-Admiral Dahlgren. Gillmore established himself on Folly Island, crossed over to the northern end of Morris, erected a tower which commanded a view of the surrounding country, harbor and city, and "placed" a battery with forty-seven pieces of artillery, which remained undiscovered by the Confederate pickets on Little Folly Island. His intention was to capture and occupy Fort Wagner, erect breaching batteries against Fort Sumter, destroy its defensive powers, and thus remove the most formidable obstacle opposing the entrance of the Federal fleet into the harbor.

The entire effective Federal force in the State was 17,463. The force employed on Morris Island did not vary much from 11,500, and it was aided by a powerful fleet of iron-clads. Confederates on the island numbered only 1,600. This force was reduced at times to less than 1,000 men, divided between Fort Wagner and Battery Gregg; nor could the force have been increased in any emergency to any practical extent, on account of limited transportation at command and the exposed landing at Cumming's Point.

Fort Wagner had also proposed to play an important part in the expected attack by the ironclads of the Federal Fleet on Fort Sumter; but this intention, it is believed, was defeated through treachery and the plan to blow up the Union fleet by wires from Wagner was never accomplished.

The crisis approached. On July 9-10, Capt. C. F. Haskell commanding a Confederate night scouting expedition from Morris to Folly, discovered a flotilla moored in the inlet ready to transport troops. The next day 3,000 Union troops descended upon Morris Island and, assisted by four monitors, captured the Confederate works at the southern end, where the light-house now stands.

On July 11, General Strong led the Federal assault on Battery Wagner, which was met by Colonel Graham, commanding the Confederate Garrison. The Confederates lost 12 men, the Federals, 339: Such was the strategic position occupied by Battery Wagner. General Gillmore in conjunction with Rear-Admiral Dahlgren, commanding the naval forces made a successful descent upon the Southern end of Morris Island, menacing batteries Wagner and Gregg, the outposts of Fort Sumter, on the Northern end of that island. Fort Sumter took part in the defence of these works until August 17, on which day General Gillmore opened his breaching batteries of the heaviest rifled cannon, all but demolished the fort in seven days, but did not silence the Confederate guns until the sixteenth day of the bombardment. On August 1, Gillmore began the construction of the Marsh Battery, near Wagner, called the "Swamp Angel", and the Union forces were reinforced by 3,000 additional troops.

CHAPTER XV

ON FRIDAY July 10th, 1863 the real attack against Charleston had begun. Union forces opened fire from their batteries on Folly Island against Confederate breastworks commanded by Captain J. C. Mitchell upon the extreme South end of Morris Island. The Confederates had previously contrived to obstruct the passage of the inlet across from Folly by a row of piling, which the Federals had discovered and destroyed. During this engagement 70 Federal guns kept up a fast fire from works of uncommon strength against small open works defended by 6 small guns. The Federals, assisted by four barges, crossed the inlet and at 9 o'clock landed a large force, which was continually increased by fresh arrivals. Captain Mitchell was obliged to fall back after Lieutenant John Bee was killed and Captain J. Ravenel McBeth and Lieutenant G. Heyward were captured. Mitchell himself was captured but rescued by his handful of men. Colonel Graham's regiment, which now fought with Mitchell, formed for battle across Gregg's hill to Vinegar hill, where in the sand hills they were joined by the 21st Regiment under Major McIver, and Nelson's battalion. Fiercely fighting, the Confederates retreated to Battery Wagner with a loss of 16 officers and 300 killed and wounded, among them Captain Langdon Cheves, designer of Battery Wagner, and his nephew Charles Haskell. The enemy, whose loss was uncommonly heavy, followed up their advantage by an assault at daylight, in which they were repulsed with a loss of 130 prisoners, 95 killed and many wounded.

On July 14th at midnight, emerging from Battery Wagner, Major Rion and two or three hundred men made an attack upon the Federal rifle pits three-quarters of a mile away. The sally, which completely surprised the enemy, was a success: 40 Federals were killed and a number taken prisoner.

The long and desperate defense of Wagner is second only to that of Sumter. Battery Wagner was garrisoned by

1,600 Confederates, unrelieved, serving in rotation, six hundred at a time, reduced at last to four hundred fighting men; yet the Battery never surrendered to the 11,500 troops, continually reinforced and assisted by eight monitors and five gun-boats. The story is one of heroism, endurance and desperate defense on the part of the Confederates and superb courage by the attacking Federals. A Federal officer says, "The artillery fire of Wagner was very troublesome, as the rebel riflemen had formed a lodgement in a deep ridge of sand in our immediate front, and with the aid of those in the fort itself, maintained an accurate and fatal fire of musketry. Frequent attempts were made, at this and other times, to employ the full sap in our advance with varying success." The Parapet on the left of the parallel was very slight, owing to the scarcity of material, and a section fell with each ball that penetrated it.

The sap roller was a cylindrical basket stuffed with fagots, which the sappers constantly pushed before them, while securing their flanks by a parapet thrown up as they advanced or by the use of baskets of brushwood, called gabions, resembling barrels in size and shape, placed in position and filled as the sap roller advanced. The account, written from a Northern viewpoint continues: "It now appeared to all that no further progress could be made until the enemy's sharpshooters were driven from the ridge in our front. After an unsuccessful attempt, the task was eventually accomplished by the Twenty Fourth. A portion of that ground which we (Federals) had captured had been thickly planted with wooden torpedoes by the Confederates." July 11th saw the first, and July 13th the second assault on Wagner.

Showing the deadly accuracy of the Confederate sharpshooters, the writer, a Federal officer, says: "A colored corporal was killed by one of the wooden torpedoes and his body, denuded of clothing by the explosion, was deposited face downward upon another a few yards off in a position which was exposed to the view of the enemy's sharpshooters. Here it remained two days before it could be removed."

Union troubles did not end here. Many of the men who

had fallen on the eighteenth were buried at this point and the sappers were continually uncovering their remains. The effect on the morale of the troops was very perceptible. Meanwhile it was discovered that the Confederate torpedoes could be handled with safety if a small augur hole was bored through them and their bursting charge well moistened with water. July 18th had witnessed a combined land and naval bombardment of Wagner with 42 siege- and field-guns and mortars, 6 iron-clads and 4 gunboats throwing 14 shots per minute. Brigadier General Gillmore moved 3 brigades forward to the assault: the first and second, being engaged, were repulsed with loss of 1500 to 2000 men. There was no doubt of success in the minds of the Federals, who knew that not five hundred men were left in Wagner. Said the soldiers, "We'll sleep in Wagner tonight," and many a poor fellow did sleep the sleep that knows no waking. Language has not the power to describe the horrors of the night succeeding the assault of September 6. The shattered Federal column reformed within their lines. It is said that only six hundred out of four thousand answered the roll call. Briefly told the enemy in front made no impression on the fort, but continued to advance his lines until his last parallel was but a stone's throw from its sandy walls. Every day the Federal fleet threw immense volleys of shot and shell at the fort. A large number of missiles reached the mark. From July 18 to September 8 eight monitors and the "Ironsides" frigate fired over seven thousand pieces of artillery at this small earthwork. Their position enabled them to enfilade it and they swept it from one end to the other. The shots burst in and around the works, tearing up the ground, throwing tons of earth high in the air. The gunners from the "Ironsides" handled their 11 inch guns to such advantage as to drive the Confederates to their bomb-proofs, where the stifling heat, scarcity of water and flies, attracted by the fearful surroundings in stinging swarms, caused great and terrible suffering. No aid could be dispatched to the garrison, which was now reduced to less than four hundred fighting men. The incessant fire of the enemy guns, the rumbling and shaking of the earth, the lack of sleep, all told on the defenders. To add to the horrors of the situation, land batteries now poured their concentrated fire into Wagner, the earth of which was so scattered as to close the sally ports with sand and leave the wood-work of the casements exposed.

On the nights of September 6, 7, the Confederates evacuated in the dead of the night, so quietly that the Federal sentries suspected nothing. The Union forces renewing the attack next morning continued to fire until at last the deathly quiet of Battery Wagner impressed itself upon them and investigation showed that the fort was evacuated—not conquered.

Confederate Doctor T. Grange Simons, a participant, described the nerve-racking horrors of the siege, under a burning summer sun, with little water to drink and the incessant falling of shells into the fort, and the ceaseless quivering of the structure under the impact of the missiles as "nothing less than Hell." Could words, coming from a Charleston gentleman of the old school, who was universally respected, be stronger? "Yet," he added, in his letter to General Irvine Walker, "not a man faltered."

With Wagner out of the way, the attack upon Sumter was renewed. In April the fort had borne the brunt of the attack launched against it by the Federal fleet of nine vessels, when Sumter's garrison of 550 men was under Colonel Rhett of the First South Carolina Artillery. The fleet had advanced under Dupont, and steamed up to within two thousand yards of Fort Sumter, which they attacked, but from which they were forced, ultimately, to retire, leaving parts of the fort a mass of crumbling ruins. During the engagement the more adventuresome commander of the "Keokuk" advanced to within seven hundred yards of the fortress.

In two hours and thirty minutes five out of the nine vessels were disabled and the "Keokuk," afloat all night, sank the next morning at her anchorage. Sixteen of her crew were wounded, but none killed during the encounter. Her armament was removed by a select body of Confederates, one of

THE U. S. STEAMER KEOKUK, WHICH OPERATED IN CHARLESTON HARBOR

IN WHITE POINT GARDENS DURING THE CONFEDERATE WAR
From an Original Photograph

A STREET SCENE IN CHARLESTON, 1866

By Courtesy of the *News and Courier*, Special Editions

the guns placed in Battery Bee, Sullivan's Island, and the other, mounted en barbette on Fort Sumter, formed with an eight-inch columbiad the last serviceable gun finally fired from the crumbling walls of the fort.

The Artillerists exhausted by fatigue and exposure, were needed at other points. Major Elliott was sent down to Sumter where he had repaired the shattered walls, filled the officers' quarters on the gorge with bales of wet cotton held in place by sand, had torn up the streets of Charleston and thus secured cobblestones with which to build his inner defense. General Gillmore's success at Morris Island inspired Admiral Dahlgren to demand the surrender of Fort Sumter, which he did on the morning of the 7th of September. Thomas Jordan, Chief of Beauregard's staff, addressed a communication to Major Stephen Elliott in command at Sumter, directing him to inform the admiral that he may have Fort Sumter when he can take and hold it; that such demands were puerile and unbecoming; and that no further flags of truce would be received from him or General Gillmore until they satisfactorily explained the firing on flags of truce from "these" headquarters on several recent occasions.

It was conjectured that the Federals would attempt to take Sumter by assault and a garrison composed entirely by riflemen, was sent down. The conjecture was justified when Dahlgren on the night of September 9th attempted to force the surrender of the fort by sending a fleet of barges against the berm and gorge face of Sumter.

Sentries on the parapet who signaled with three rockets were answered immediately by fire from Johnson; Moultrie, Battery Simkins and the gunboat Chicora concentrated upon the barges as the Charleston Battalion in the fort, under Captain Blake, poured a rapid fire into the black mass moving on the water.

The foremost barge reached the ledge and entered upon its work with gallantry and resolution, but was met with brave resistance by those defending the fort. After a short encounter the storming party retreated in confusion to the base of the fort. The other barges fled in haste, but the attacking party of 13 naval officers and 102 men were captured along with four barges and three flags—among them the ensign which floated from the parapet while Major Anderson was Commandant of the fort. Sumter had repulsed the fleet in April, withstood the fire from land batteries on Morris Island, and resisted the barge attack; she was now to experience her first great bombardment—of which there were three. It commenced on August 17th and lasted until the 23rd.

By the 22nd only four guns were able to "speak". The main flag-staff had been shot down and replaced over and over again, but the flag still floated from the crest of the gorge. Five monitors now joined in the attack and fifty well-placed shells were landed near the western magazine. The danger from an explosion had been lessened by withdrawing over thirty-five thousand pounds of gunpowder but the menace was still very great, and the fort replied with six shots from its last two guns. During the week the fort, which had received over five thousand shots, was all but demolished, and Moultrie garrisoned by South Carolina Infantry under Colonel Wm. Butler, again came to the rescue of Sumter, as she had done in the engagement of April 7.

After General Gillmore's descent upon Morris Island, July 10th, 1863, Moultrie took part at long range in the defense of that island until its evacuation by the Confederates on September 6th, 1863.

On September 8th, Fort Moultrie, supported by the Island Batteries, was heavily engaged with the ironclad fleet, and particularly the "Ironsides" frigate.

On October 26th, 1863, the second heavy bombardment of Sumter was begun from the evacuated batteries Wagner and Gregg and others on the Northern end of Morris Island, aided by the squadron, and was continued without intermission for forty days and nights, until December 6th, 1863.

On July 7th, 1864, the third heavy bombardment commenced, reaching its height on the twentieth instant, when Captain Mitchell, commander of the fort was killed on the southwest parapet. Captain John Johnson, engineer in charge, was wounded and succeeded by Lieutenant E. J. White—on the 22nd day of the siege.

On July 21st, Captain T. A. Huguenin, First South Carolina Infantry, succeeded Captain Mitchell in command of the fort. The bombardment continued with some decline of fire until the first week in September or upwards of two months; after this desultory firing was kept up until the evacuation of the fort. The fort was struck over seventeen thousand times during the war. On account of the ingenious devices evolved and used by the Confederates from Stevens battery, and the iron clad floating battery, the torpedoes and other mechanical contrivances, the War of Secession will be the object of special study to the historian, sociologist, mechanic and philosopher of the future as well as to the casual reader.

The Confederates were making valiant efforts to decipher Union signals. Augustine Smyth wrote to his aunt, Miss Janie Adger: "August 3rd, 1864, St. Michael's steeple, Sunday morning: Here I am in church it is true, and in one of the high seats of the synagogue to boot, but I have to be preacher, choir, congregation and sexton too, for that matter, for there is not a soul here but myself."

From 1863 on, Gillmore was shelling the city and the lower part of town was practically deserted; grass grew in the streets and houses were closed. Frequent fires resulted from the shells and the volunteer fire-department strove to extinguish the flames. But as soon as fiery tongues shot into the air, illuminating the sky, Gillmore redoubled the shelling. Watchers of the Confederate Signal Service, from the bath-house pavilion or stationed in the tower of St. Michael's steeple, could see the blockading fleet, the grim and silent walls of Sumter, and on Morris, Folly and James Islands the white tents of the two armies.

The Federal fleet remained in the outer harbor, viewing the spires of Charleston over the low hills of Morris Island. The Swamp Angel at Cumming's point kept up ever and anon an ineffectual fire at St. Michael's Church steeple and other points in the city.

A balloon was constructed by the Confederate Signal

Corps in the hope of getting a better view of the blockading fleet than could be obtained from St. Michael's steeple. The balloon was made of silk and filled with gas at the gasworks on Charlotte Street. Captain Joseph Manigault, commanding the Signal Corps, chose Augustine Smythe as his best man to make the ascension; but all came to naught. The balloon was not strong and burst during the inflation. When the airship, the "Los Angeles" flew over Charleston in 1929, Count Zeppelin recalled the fact that he had helped to fill balloons here during the Confederate War.

An iron ring was being drawn around the city as Gillmore continued to shell the town. On August 16th, the U.S.S. launch "Pawnee" had been destroyed by a torpedo and five days later the new frigate "Ironsides" was attacked by Confederate torpedoes.

Both history and romance lie behind this simple statement. The history of a new invention and the romance of those adventurous souls who manned these two types of torpedo-boats used in and about Charleston. One, constructed by Samuel Easterby under the supervision of its inventors Dr. St. Julien Ravenel and Capt. Theodore Stoney, was called the "Little David" by Mrs. Ravenel, who thus contrasted the cigar-shaped torpedo-boat with the giant "Ironsides". Several successful excursions were made by the "Little David", none more so than that of October 5th, when Lieut. Glassell of the Confederate Navy attacked the "Ironsides". Torpedoed and damaged but not destroyed, this vessel was taken to Port Royal for repairs and never appeared again off Charleston bar.

James H. Tombs, engineer of the small craft, says that the "Little David" struck the "Ironsides", exploded her torpedo against the side of the great vessel and then lay helpless under the quarter of the frigate, her fires quenched by the great volume of water caused by the explosion. Lieut. Glassell and the fireman, James Sullivan, swam off towards the enemy's ship, which all this time was directing a heavy fire upon the helpless torpedo boat. The pilot, Walter Cannon, remained in the Little David, and Mr. Tombs who had leaped overboard, swam back to the torpedo boat. There, in spite of the heavy fire of the enemy, he rebuilt his fires enough to move the machinery and, eluding the Federal ships, brought his little vessel back into the harbor in safety.

As some of the "grannies" of the Confederate Navy did not sanction these new fangled contraptions, the service of torpedoes was not formally legalized by the Confederate Congress until some time later, when a bureau was established at Richmond with a special corps of officers and men enlisted and trained for this warfare.

Another type of torpedo-ram, known as the "Fish Boat", was built at Mobile and sent to Charleston.

Unlike the "Little David," which was intended to float just below the surface of the water, the principle of the Fish Boat was to dive and torpedo the enemy beneath the surface. Fins attached to either side were used to depress or elevate the boat, which was under the command of Lieutenant Dixon, Company E, 21st Alabama Volunteers, who perished with his crew and boat when she sent the "Housatonic" to the bottom on February 17th, 1864. The "Fish Boat" with all aboard, including commander and crew, Arnold Beeker, C. Simkins, J. A. Wicks, F. Collins, —— Ridgeway, (all of the South Carolina Navy, and Corporal C. F. Carlson of Capt. Wagener's Battery of Artillery), also went down. When the "Housatonic" was raised many years later, the torpedo boat was found alongside of her with eleven of her dead in the sunken craft.

Prior to this attack upon the "Housatonic" the submarine fish had made several trial excursions in Charleston Harbor which proved disastrous. At one time she lay alongside the steamer Etiwan at Fort Johnson. The steamer moved off without notice and the fish boat went to the bottom with her manholes open. Captain Page, who was in charge, together with Lieutenant Hooker, escaped, but the rest of the crew of seven men were drowned. Shortly afterward the boat was raised and the bodies recovered.

The next experiment was made near Adger's wharf, when a dive from which she did not rise was attempted and nine men were lost. She was subsequently raised and it was found that her propeller had become entangled with an old hawser. It was some time after this, when most people had lost confidence in the boat, that Captain Dixon made his attack. The service was of the most desperate character; officers and crews staked their lives in every attempt that was made. Four crews lost their lives during experiments, yet volunteer crews were ever ready to step aboard these strange craft.

The Swamp Angel, which swept the lower part of the City, produced a feeling of awe and dread in the Charlestonians who elected to remain throughout the siege. Watchers from roof or steeple could see on Morris Island the burning fuse of the shell as it left the great gun, mounted toward the zenith and began its downward course just as the sound of the gun reached the city. Then came the terrific screeching of the descending shell, growing louder and more loud until with a cry of *"where is you"* it struck, to explode with a deafening concussion, or failing to explode, bury itself in the earth.

To offset the demoralizing effect of the Swamp Angel an immense gun was stationed at the intersection of South and East Battery. It was thought that no vessel could withstand a shot from this monster, but at its first trial the gun burst from an overcharge, and the concussion damaged the houses near it more than did the earthquake of 1886.

At present it is difficult to reconstruct the physical aspect of the city in that part now occupied by White Point Gardens and the houses on the water-side of South Bay. It ended at old Ashley River Breakwater near the present intersection of South Battery and Lenwood Street. Dr. Rhame's house occupies the southeastern corner of old Hunter's Point, next to Mr. Langdon Cheves' house adjacent to the Henry Frost and the Wilkinson homes—adjoining the Larsen-Lucas home. The Booker and the Allen house, occupied by St. John Lawton, are all modern. The only very old house on the block is now the home of Mr. Henry Trezvant Williams, (39 South Battery), a retired business man, the commander of the Confederate veterans (Camp Sumter) and a deep student of their history.

The modern Fort Sumter Hotel was recently built on a former water-lot. There South Battery formerly ended and there the Princess Louise landed when on her visit to this country in the gay eighties or nineties.

In 1863 and 1864 many spirited engagements took place on the Islands near Charleston. The last of any great importance, in which the Southerners gained a decisive victory, took place at John's Island on July 9, 1864.

In Charleston the streets were almost deserted. As many as could leave the city had refugeed to the up country, which was considered safe. The military situation in Virginia may be gathered from the fact that during the spring the Union and Confederate armies were in plain view of each other from the heights above Fredericksburg. Lee, tied to Richmond, had overthrown every army sent against him, while in the West, Bragg, free to move about, continued to give ground before the Union army.

In May, the Confederates, under Lee, won Chancellorsville by dividing his small army, getting the Federals between its two wings and then attacking with both wings, compelling the Federals to retreat. This success to the South was overshadowed by the death of T. J. (Stonewall) Jackson, killed by his own men through a mistake.

Shortly after Chancellorsville, Lee, attempting to relieve the South by invading the North, marched across Maryland into Pennsylvania and engaged the Federal forces under General Meade at Gettysburg in the most terrific battle ever fought on the American continent. Pickett's brilliant charge up Cemetery Hill on the third day promised for a few brief moments to turn the tide of battle. But after the Federal lines were reached and a Confederate flag placed there, the withering fire forced the men in grey to retreat. The fortunes of the Confederacy were on the wane. The South, which had begun the contest firm in the belief that they were equally prepared with men, guns, ammunition and supplies to finish the contest, realized at this time that their man power was all but exhausted. Every male from sixteen to sixty was under arms, and supplies diminished as the blockade tightened and the neglected fields of the southern plantations failed to yield their harvests. Makeshifts of every conceivable kind were employed. It is difficult to believe the accounts of the straits to which people were reduced.

Yet the morale of the southern women never slackened. Those in the city worked day and night to secure pitiable little delicacies for the sick and wounded, while those on outlying plantations cultivated as best they might the fields. Dr. Francis Peyre Porcher wrote his book on the resources of the southern fields and forests in an effort to bring out the medicinal value of the common plants growing in the South from which medicine could be made for the Confederate hospitals. Colored people seemed then, as now, to be able to live "Out of the Creek," and brought fresh produce to the City to sell to the Federal prisoners confined in the Jail or the convalescents at Old Roper Hospital.

In December, 1864 A. G. Magrath, a talented lawyer of Charleston and a former Judge of the United States District Court, was elected Governor of South Carolina. No Governor ever assumed the administration of the affairs of a State under less favorable circumstances. Its resources were exhausted. Business was suspended; plantations were abandoned; men were in the army and their families were at home, nearly starving. It would seem incredible that during this period, from 1860 to 1866, which included the school age of an entire generation, amid all the discouragements and distractions of war life, there still went on a sort of prolongation of the old-time system of education for the boys and girls. But the reader of any one of a score of the memorials of life in the South during the fighting years may picture the devices and schemes employed for schooling the children through which the old love of letters was maintained and civilization preserved.

During the actual continuance of the War, the women of the eleven Confederate and four border states shouldered the upper side of civilization. For the first time in the history

of this section women who as mistresses of the old plantations had cared for the sick, the old and the ignorant among
the slaves, and as heads of large households had taught the
servants to churn, cook, sew, weave, clean house, read, and
attend church, now stepped out of the alleged retirement
and "carried on" while the men fought.

Still the Confederacy struggled on. Grant's victories in the
west had cut off troops and supplies from points west of the
Mississippi. Shilo, Vicksburg and Chattanooga followed in
quick succession. The part played by South Carolina troops
can be read on the stone markers placed in the Military Park
at Chickamauga.

Charleston men were giving a good account of themselves
in Moultrie, Wagner, Sumter, and on the nearby islands, and
in engagements on the battlefields of the Confederacy—
wherever "Johnny Reb" was meeting "Billy Yank." The
troops of South Carolina did gallant service at the Battles of
Chancellorsville, the Wilderness, Spottsylvania Court House,
Winchester, Hatcher's Run and Appomattox in Virginia;
Gettysburg in Pennsylvania; Bentonville and Fort Fisher in
North Carolina; Lookout Mountain, Chickamauga, Atlanta,
Knoxville and Franklin in the west.

The Western Campaign coincided with Grant's movements in Virginia, where he had gone. General Sherman
moved from Chattanooga toward Atlanta, which in 1864
became the scene of activities resulting in the destruction of
Hood's Army and the commencement of Sherman's victorious
March to the Sea. He started in the middle of November and
arrived at Savannah on December 21, 1864, where, in communication with the Union fleet, he described the Confederacy as "nothing but a shell", and stated that he was ready
to march Northward. This march began on February 1, 1865
and on the 16th Sherman reached Columbia, South Carolina.

On February 17, 1865, Mayor Macbeth of Charleston
sent to inform the U. S. General commanding on Morris
Island, that the Confederate authorities had evacuated the
city. Charleston was then immediately occupied by the
United States forces and held under military rule.

On April 1, 1865, Lee made his last stand in Virginia. The Union Army entered Richmond April 2nd, and on the 9th General Lee surrendered to General Grant. When General Robert E. Lee bade farewell to his defeated soldiers, saying, "Go home and cultivate your virtues", he struck the keynote of the higher American civilization for sixteen great states. President Lincoln (re-elected 1864, and beginning his second term on March 4, 1865) visited Richmond and walked with his son along the desolate streets. He appointed a day of thanksgiving for the end of the war, which would be celebrated on the day on which four years before Fort Sumter was attacked. A party went to Charleston where Henderson again raised the U. S. flag over the ruined fortress. In 1931 a flag-pole was erected on Fort Sumter in memory of Major (later General) Anderson, and at the same ceremony the Charleston Chapter of the Daughters of the Confederacy placed a bronze tablet on the Fort to the memory of the Confederate soldiers who had taken and held it. Andrew Murray of Charleston has provided for a monument on South Battery to the Confederate dead.

On April 14, President Lincoln was assassinated and an attempt was made against Secretary Seward. This tragedy is said to have deprived the South of a friend and to have increased the bitter feeling of hostility toward the Confederates. On April 26, General Johnston surrendered to General Sherman and on May 8th President Davis, who had fled with his Cabinet, was captured and placed in prison in irons. In addition to the general field line- and staff-officers serving from Charleston in the Confederate service in the President's family, was Colonel John M. Huger, A. D. C., with the rank of Colonel of Cavalry. Memminger was first Secretary of the Treasury, and he with Honorable G. A. Trenholm, the second, was imprisoned with the Governors of the Southern States in Fort Pulaski, where they were guarded by negro troops. The Confederacy was dead.

Chapter XVI

MAYOR McBETH had been requested by the retiring Confederates to abstain from informing the Federals of their departure as long as possible, stating that they did not think that the Union forces would learn of the evacuation until the Monday morning. As a precautionary measure a sentinel had been placed in the steeple of the Orphan House. This look-out reported at ten o'clock a boat flying the United States flag coming to the City. The Mayor dispatched the Clerk of Council in another boat to inform the enemy that the Confederate forces had left. The boats met, the message was given and the Federal troops very soon began to take possession of the city. The population, white and black, preserved order during the evacuation and the approach of the Federals, and the police were respected and obeyed until the order putting the city under martial law appeared. The next day the Navy took possession of Fort Moultrie and Castle Pinckney and a volunteer party of ten men from Morris Island planted the United States Flag on Fort Sumter.

With the surrender of the city came the inevitable consequences. The order which evacuated Charleston destroyed the last hope of southern success. The consequences of its loss were irreparable. The fall of the city sounded the knell of the "Cause."

General M. C. Meigs, U. S. A. said of Charleston, "Its defense ceased only when, after a siege almost unexampled since the invention of artillery, for duration and persistency, the approach of a powerful army from the Mississippi Valley rendered any further resistance entirely hopeless. Then the armed Rebel force abandoned the town, destroying such stores as they could. There was no capitulation, no surrender by which any of the extreme rights of captors were modified or abated, in the giving up of an equivalent. The place was defended to the last extremity and the whole town is a conquest."

On the twentieth of February 1865, cotton stored at the wharves of Lucas Mill, ready for the blockade runners, was fired, and the residence of the French Consul was consumed with all the jewels and possessions of French citizens. A large amount of cotton that had been piled in the yards of the North Eastern Railroad was also fired and resulted in a fearful explosion in which more than one hundred and fifty people were injured. Provisions left in the depot had been informally turned over to the city authorities for the poor. These rushed to the scene of the fire, not knowing that gunpowder in cartridges was stored there. The depot blew up, fell in, burying men, women and children in the ruins, and firemen forced to retreat left the fire unchecked. The Federal officer offered to aid in extinguishing the flames now raging in several places in the city.

Meanwhile a fire on East Bay destroyed other buildings, among them the large school of Madame Du Pre, and the Blake Block on Meeting street. The Confederate ironclad steamer "Palmetto" was blown up with a concussion heard all over the city. The superstitious affected to read as a symbol of coming events the cloud of smoke which took for an instant the form of a palmetto tree and then disappeared.

> "Hushed is the roll of the Rebel drum,
> The Swords are sheathed and the cannon dumb,
> And fate with a pitiless hand has furled
> The flag that once challenged the gaze of the world."

The physical condition of the city, already bad, was rendered doubly so by these fires. Refugees pouring in found the hotels injured if not destroyed; doors of the Mills house were open to the world; the windows had lost their glazing and were boarded up: sixteen shots had struck the building. The Charleston Hotel had several great holes in its walls. The churches had not escaped. St. Michael's had been repeatedly struck, and all other churches in the lower portions of the city were wrecked: many bombs from the iron throat of the Swamp Angel had fallen amongst them. The lower part of the city had especially suffered from the shells thrown into it by the distant Federal guns. Some of these shells took effect at the office of the *Mercury*, in Broad street, entering the roof, passing into the chimney and in exploding, dumped several car loads of brick-bats, mortar and soot into the editorial room, of which it smashed the windows and splintered the doors. The *Courier*, in Bay street, had not escaped damage. A shell went through the roof, falling down through the floors, ripping up the boards, breaking the timbers, jarring the plaster from the walls, exploding in the second story, rattling all the tiles from the roof, bursting out the windows, smashing the composing-stone and opening the whole building to the sunlight. Another shell dashed the sidewalk to pieces and blew a passage into the cellar wide enough to admit a six-horse wagon.

Near the *Courier* office the Union Bank, Farmers and Exchange Bank and the Charleston Bank, all costly buildings, fitted up with marble mantels, floors of terra cotta tiles, counters elaborate in carved work, with gorgeous frescoing on the walls, were destroyed. The oaken doors were splintered, the frescoing was washed from the walls by rain, the desks were smashed to kindling wood, the cornice-work dropped from the ceiling to the ground, the tiles were scattered, the marble mantels shattered and the plate glass windows lay in a million fragments upon the floor when the city was evacuated.

In January 1862, the three banks held six hundred and ten thousand dollars' worth of the seven per cent State stock issued under the Act of December, 1861. By the end of the War, Confederate currency was spoken of as "Representing nothing on God's earth now but the hopes of a nation that perished."

After the occupation the Mayor who called on the commanding General retired after being refused admittance. The next day the streets of the city were filled with furniture and lined with pianos, mirrors, bedsteads, etc. Every unoccupied house was entered and all furniture seized as derelict. All cotton and original packages of goods from foreign ports were seized. Every vehicle and work-animal was taken for military purposes.

Corporal squads of black troops were sent throughout the city to tell servants that they were free. Others visited unprotected homes, demanding turkeys and chickens wherever found. To the everlasting credit of many of the colored people be it recorded that in very few instances did the faithful slaves show any rude behavior to their erstwhile owners. In several instances negro families moved into and occupied the homes of their white friends and thus preserved these places from being pillaged and destroyed. Later these homes were returned to their rightful owners after their owners had complied with the military requirements and taken the oath of citizenship. The recital of the experience of one family will serve as an illustration of what went on. The story has been preserved, along with a hundred similar documents, in a book gotten out through the initiative of the Charleston *News and Courier* in a volume entitled "Our Women in the War." Women refugees coming into the city had attempted in many cases to wrap the corn and rice left on the plantations in carpets and fetch these provisions into the city as some scant provision for the future. One such refugee, writing from the country, says: "Just one week afterwards my youngest sister was born. Hearing that Sherman, with his dreaded army was advancing towards us we prepared for flight, as it was impossible for a handful of delicately nurtured women and children to remain unprotected in a house upon an isolated plantation, exposed to the depredations of the lawless band that infested the outskirts of the army.

"We could depend upon but few of the negroes for assistance, excited and rendered insubordinate as they were by rumors of their approaching emancipation; there were two faithful slaves, however, who were of inestimable value then and afterwards; who followed us to the city and remained with us until peace was declared and our father restored to our family. We accordingly arrived in Charleston with the barest necessities of life.

"No pen can describe the hurry and confusion that prevailed on every side. Shortly after our arrival, (it was the night before the evacuation,) the burning of the Northeastern depot and New Bridge took place. After this ensued many weeks of the bitterest privation and want.

"At this time many families were in such a destitute condition a kind of commissary was established by the Yankees, and tickets were given to those who were known to be in need; these tickets when presented at the commissary, drew salt pork, grist, rice flour, vinegar, etc., and for weeks these supplies were the sole support of a great many persons.

"At one time, for nearly two weeks, mother passed her nights in a large chair placed against the door of our bedroom, neither undressing nor lying down for the night's repose during the two weeks, subjected at all hours to the visits of armed men, who roamed at will about the house and were only with the greatest difficulty prevented from intruding upon us. My mother was protected from further invasions by lodging a complaint with the provost marshal, who treated her with the utmost courtesy and consideration, and after requiring her to take the oath of allegiance, which at first she was loath to do, immediately took measures to prevent a recurrence of the annoyance.

"One of my aunts, a lady of more timid disposition, was not so fortunate; she allowed the soldiers to search her entire premises and actually to open her trunks and wardrobe, and stir up their contents with the point of their bayonets."

On another occasion the house of a friend was invaded by a tumultuous mob of idlers, who thronged the streets and with not a few soldiers threatened to break up the furniture and commit other outrages. The ladies in a state of extreme alarm took refuge in the upper portions of the house. An elderly lady who was present, hastily directed one of them to go out by the back stairs and seek assistance as quickly as possible. She then advanced to the head of the front stairs, which they threatened to ascend and commanded them to stay out of the upper part of the house.

"Suddenly," she says, "a faltering was visible in those below, and turning she perceived a Yankee officer in full uniform beside her. He at once commanded the crowd to disperse and threatened to take the number on the caps of the soldiers present to report at headquarters. They at once slunk out of the house, and the remainder, disheartened by the turn affairs had taken, speedily took their departure.

"Some of the officers of General Hatch's staff were ordered to collect all the property which had been deserted by its owners and confiscated to the United States Government. My mother occupied the house of a gentleman who had 'refugeed' to the up-country, and on their rounds they paid us a visit; after conducting them from room to room, she paused with her hand upon the door of our chamber. 'Sir,' said she, turning to the officer in command, 'this is my sleeping apartment; I give you my word of honor that every article in it belongs exclusively to myself.' I may say just here, that it was our good fortune in after life to meet this gentleman again. Indeed, my father and himself became warm friends, despite their difference of opinion, politically."

No pen can ever produce with completeness or sufficient vividness the actual state of things which surrounded every household in the State and City during those twelve years of bitter humiliation that ensued, between the fall of the Confederacy and the election of Hampton. Years of insult, of struggle against poverty and privation, of anxiety, of danger and of universal distress and anguish, all borne with patience and self-restraint.

To the almost wholesale destruction of property was added the sudden emancipation of four million slaves, as yet incapable of freedom, who were naturally intoxicated with the new found "liberty", interpreted to mean "forty acres and a mule" as a gift from the Government, and liberty to roam in uncontrolled idleness. In the words of an intelligent colored man in the city, it was "like giving a little child a valuable watch to play with." The colored race had also to reconstruct its ideas of life, to assume heavy duties and obligations and to plunge into an economic struggle for which they were ill prepared.

After hostilities had ceased the paroled soldiers of the Confederacy returned to their desolate homes, bearing with them the solemn promises of the United States Government that they would there be protected in their property rights, citizenship and their rights of person.

Had not Grant allowed the Confederates to keep their horses so that they would be able to put in a crop with which to carry themselves and their families through the winter, famine would have stalked through the land over which not even a crow could pick a living after Sherman's "March To The Sea." Starvation stared into the eyes of the weary soldiers returning from the army, finding plantations neglected and overgrown in weeds; no cattle nor work-animals; houses burned and slaves set free. Industry was in ruins and agriculture prostrate. Instead of money there were only crushing obligations. Property and labor were both gone.

In October, Mayor Macbeth assembled the Council and communicated to them that he had been informed from Federal military headquarters that there was no objection to his immediately resuming his functions as Mayor of Charleston in all matters in which no conflict would arise with the Military Commander of the department of South Carolina. The Mayor and Council therefore resumed their duties: but under constant supervision by the military authorities they found that only a partial exercise of their proper functions was left them. October 17, 1865, the Mayor was informed that the military authorities were prepared to turn over to the City Council the collection of city taxes, except for the trades of liquor, powder and arms.

P. C. Gaillard, who served as Lieutenant Colonel of the Charleston batteries and had lost an arm at Battery Wagner, was elected Mayor to succeed Mr. Macbeth.

Honorable B. H. Perry, by authority of Andrew Johnson, was appointed Provisional Governor and issued an ably written proclamation which was received with enthusiasm by all, with hopes of rescue from what seemed to be absolute ruin. Civil government was restored, a convention of the people was called, and on October 18, 1865 James L. Orr of Anderson was elected Governor and the State believed that it was once more in the Union. South Carolina was to learn that not only was she not a State, but that she was territory conquered by the United States and subject to the control of Congress only. William D. Porter of Charleston was elected Lieutenant Governor. The Legislature passed an act known as the "Black Code," which discriminated between whites and blacks as citizens; provided separate courts for the trial of all civil and criminal cases and did not give the negroes the ballot nor the full right of citizenship. President Andrew Johnson had vetoed the 14th Amendment which gave voting rights to the negroes while denying them to a large number of Southern whites.

"So far from embodying a spirit of defiance or any purpose to evade the conditions imposed by the victors, the Legislature of South Carolina was in the main conscientious and straightforward in an effort to bring some sort of order out of the social and economic chaos which a full acceptance of the result of the war and emancipation involved. To distrustful Northern minds such legislation very easily took the form of a systematic attempt to relegate the freedmen to a subjection only less complete than that from which the war had set them free. None of the men elected to Congress were allowed to take their seats. There was a rude awakening from the dream caused by Perry's proclamation and Orr's election and some years had to pass before South Carolina could be called a State." So says a well known writer.

When certain merchants of Charleston petitioned for a return of their property, General M. C. Meigs wrote to President Johnson, "To return this property to the original, disloyal owners, would, it seems to me, give a shock to every earnest and loyal man." Refusing to destroy a prostrate nation, state or city, President Johnson, like General Grant, had wisdom as well as compassion, and his reply shows that, though defeated, Charleston was still regarded by some in the North as having rights. The property was restored to the claimants. It was this attitude of mercy that helped cause President Johnson's impeachment. Fraser and Company were the great cotton merchants whose property was returned. The Fraser home was on E. Bay.

In 1876 when the Reconstruction Act was passed, the Honorable State of South Carolina became by order of the United States Congress "Military District No. 2", and negro troops with white officers were put in entire control of the people. Each military district was put under command of a Federal General. A convention was to be held in every State. Negroes were given the right to vote for delegates and sit as members. This convention was to form a constitution. If acceptable to Congress, and if the legislature elected ratified the 14th Amendment, the State would be re-admitted into the Union.

The Union Generals in command of the districts removed the Governor and other State officials, appointed army officers to fill their places and held the elections. When the Federal armies occupied any part of a State, many who lived there abandoned their homes and moved to the nearest town lines. The negroes left the plantations and collected around the camps, where they had to be taken care of. In 1865 Congress created the "Bureau of Freedmen, Refugees, and Abandoned Lands." The commanding general managed the bureau for each State, while in each county, agents were appointed to look after the freedmen. These local agents were taken from the commissaries' and quartermasters' department of the Federal army. Their control over the negroes was great, and they were responsible for much political trouble that followed, because they assumed and exercised extraordinary powers, when under the Reconstruction Act, many of them were appointed to fill county offices. They organized the negro voters, and secured their own election to State and County offices. Many of these came South, bringing their only property, the wearing apparel which they carried in their carpet bags, for which reason they were called "carpet-baggers." Many of them were notoriously corrupt and dishonest, and became rich soon after being elected to office. Wherever they gained control exorbitant taxes were levied and enormous public debts accumulated. Under these "constitutions," when framed, carpet-baggers and negroes were State officers and members of the legislature.

In this city, to which large numbers of country negroes had flocked, the entire police force was in the hands of the negro party and its leaders. Soon the Mayor and Aldermen, the Chief of Police, the police-officers and men, showed that they were bitter partisans of the blacks; many were recently emancipated slaves. The first Federal troops to occupy the city had been white men, but with the employment of colored troops the plight of the city became desperate.

When the so-called Black Code was passed by the last white man's Legislature in 1865, the Radicals sounded a shrill note of alarm. In Congress, Wilson, Sumner and other extremists took up the cry. Military government in Charleston was re-established under General Sickles, whose headquarters were in a handsome house on Charlotte street, now the home of Mr. Sottile, from whence he issued orders banishing several patriots to the Dry Tortugas south of Florida. Sickles gave way to Canby, who ordered, in November, 1867, an election to be held for securing delegates to a constitutional convention to be held January 14, 1868, resulting in the election of 124 delegates, of whom 76 were colored and 48 white, who were roughly classed as Republicans, "natives" and "newcomers," or "scallawags" and "carpet-baggers." The residences of twenty-three whites were given as South Carolina, nineteen elsewhere, two from England, one from Ireland, one from Prussia, one from Denmark and one "origin unknown." Of the seventy-six negroes, fifty-nine gave South Carolina as their previous residence, nine gave eight different states, one Dutch Guiana and six did not know from whence they came.

The convention was in session two months, framing a constitution modeled after that of one of the great Northern states, which met the requirements of the war amendments of the National Constitution and which, with few amendments, governed South Carolina for twenty-seven years, including the nineteen years following those when the whites resumed control of the state government in 1876.

From 1865 to 1869 the State was under both civil and military government. Orr's position as governor, to which he succeeded Perry, was more than anomalous, it was undefinable.

For the prevention of aggressions on the part of the negro race under the vile leadership of Northern adventurers, which would have lead to bloodshed, "Rifle Clubs" were organized in Charleston, which soon had branches over the state. Their influence was felt throughout the critical period, when white supremacy was a thing of the past and negroes were in control. Little information concerning the rifle clubs other than that of word of mouth or the pamphlet issued by Major Theodore G. Barker has ever been printed concerning these sub-rosa movements by Charleston men. Newspaper accounts furnish few definite detailed accounts of political activities.

The papers were to play a large part in the drama for the preservation of civilization in the South. Colonel Thomas Young Simons, born within sound of St. Michael's bells, graduate of Yale, lawyer, member of the Legislature, raiser of two companies and Captain of one (the Charleston Light Infantry, later Company B-27 Regiment), became editor of the *Courier*. Great names issue from the list of city reporters —Sparnick, John Moroso, Molone, T. W. Miller. The *Mercury* also reappeared. It was founded by Monford and bought by Henry Laurens Pinckney in 1823, when it became a representative of the free trade and state rights party. Pinckney was succeeded by John A. Stuart, and he by Colonel John E. Carew, who retired on January 26, 1856. The *Mercury* was then purchased by Colonel R. Barnwell Rhett, Jr. in 1857, after his kinsman and part owner of the *Mercury*, William R. Taber, was killed in a duel in defence of a series of articles which had appeared in the paper. Timrod, De Fontaine,

Selby were all well known writers who had been connected with the publication.

It was an event of importance when the Charleston *Mercury* made its reappearance under Colonel R. Barnwell Rhett, Jr., who was soon assisted by Captain F. W. Dawson, possibly the most brilliant light that has ever shown on the journalistic field of Charleston.

In its career 1867-68, the *Mercury* made history when it employed its trenchant pen in its reports of "The Ring-streaked and Striped Convention." Some of the history of the *Mercury's* crusade against the Reconstruction Convention is well known, but the inside history and the purpose of the crusade has never been published. The scheme was to make any attempt to establish a mongrel government in South Carolina a stench in the nostrils of the public, and to make the odium of being a member of the mixed body too great for the white members to bear. The paper carried detailed stories of the lives of those who were members of the Convention.

The *South Carolina Ledger*, put forth by Tim Hurley with Allen Coffin, as editor, stated that their paper would be devoted to the interest of "Free Labor and General Reform." "Free Lunch and General Graft" would have been nearer the mark, said a Charleston wit. The paper's motto was: "First the blade and then the ear, after that the full corn in the ear." Mr. King in his history of the press observes that "Before the (y) ear filled, the dream of Mr. Hurley had flitted away." Perhaps Tim used the juice of the corn to fill himself and wasted the "(y) ear."

The *Missionary Record* was the sanctimonious name which R. H. Cain and A. J. Ransler, the Lieutenant Governor, gave to their South Carolina Republican Paper. The *Free Press* and the *Charleston Advocate*, when they suspended, left, according to Mr. King, "no blank in nature."

What was known as the "Outrage Mill" was established for the purpose of working up the raw material of false reports into political capital, to be used to maintain in power the Republican Party.

Charleston learned to accept conditions, not with the stolid defiance of the savage, nor the stoic fortitude of the philosopher, not yet with the cheerful acquiescence of Christians, but with the patience of patriots.

All was not gloom. Even in the sad days of reconstruction, youth refused to be denied wholesome recreation. The young people took every possible chance meeting, and every group of three or four couples was an opportunity to dance. Starvation or cold-water parties came into fashion. The larger houses were gathering places for these impromptu affairs. In some of these houses pianos had been left untouched by the soldiers and any girl who could play was accounted a great belle. Many a pleasant hour was spent at the Frank Porcher house, the DeSaussure residence, the Ravenel drawing-room or the hallway of the Holmes' house, or any other homes of the old social set. The first big dance was given by the young men at the Heyward house at the corner of Legare and Lamboll streets. When there the young people met and danced on the waxed floor or promenaded on the wide piazza nearby and enjoyed their simple refreshments of lemonade.

Many of the old houses were now occupied by their former owners and before very long a semblance of the old social order began to appear: two years after the evacuation found Charleston enjoying formal balls again. The only public balls were those given by the Cotillion Club, held in the South Carolina Halls, which had a fine waxed floor. A good band was forthcoming but the refreshments were characterized as mild. Then the St. Cecelia Society revived it and it was determined to give two balls. This was a great event in the life of the young ladies and every one began to think about ball dresses.

After the War Madame Du Pre's school was burned. Now many others were opened in the city and conducted by ladies of the community; among these Mrs. Alston's school occupied the present Pelzer house on Meeting street. Another fashionable school was that of Madame Talvane, kept behind the brick walls of the house until recently owned by

Mr. B. F. Allston, that goes by the name of the Simonton house, or the "House of the Sword Gates," and is now the property of President Lincoln's granddaughter.

Tradition has it that the high walls were erected after one of the girls had so far forgotten herself as to elope with the man of her choice. Another tradition has it that after the Civil War this school was closed by the lady then at the head of it rather than receive the daughter of General Sickles. Mrs. Alston was more kind to the poor, lonely, delicate, little girl and received her as a student, saying to a patron who objected that she could remove her daughter if she objected to the presence of the child.

There had been another fashionable school, kept at one time in Legare street in the Smythe house on the western side of the street, known to earlier people as the Heyward house, and in which a ghost is said to walk. The school was kept by Miss Datty, who later moved to a house in Glebe street just one door north of Wentworth, and there conducted a boarding-school, facetiously called "The Nunnery of St. Datty."

In 1867 phosphate rock had been discovered near Charleston. Money, no less than knowledge, has power, and Charleston partially owes her emancipation from the intolerable conditions of the Reconstruction days to the applied scientific knowledge of her distinguished sons who developed the phosphate industry, when the rice fields no longer yielded their golden grains, nor fields of cotton made "imitation snow under the clear blue Southern skies." Many substantial Northern men, hearing of the returning prosperity, came to the city. Money was unearthed from stockings and other hiding places. As commerce returned the city took on an almost normal, brisk business aspect.

Meanwhile, little Charleston children, all unaware of the sleeping volcano over which they lived, rolled their hoops on the Battery, skipped rope in the sunshine, or fished from the bathing-house bridge, went to school and church sedately and enjoyed life thoroughly, as it was a tenet of Charleston life to refrain from casting responsibility upon a child.

BOOK VI

RECONSTRUCTION

CHAPTER XVII

THE popular attitude of the average uninformed North- erner toward the South had been voiced on the three hundred and ninety-second day of the Siege of Charleston, when Parson Brownlow made a speech in New York, saying he wanted to see "Richmond and Charleston captured by negroes alone, commanded by Butler, and when we come out of the war we will come out with 500,000 or 600,000 of the best soldiers who have got their hand in and would as soon have their hand in a little longer as not. Then I am in favor of giving old England a turn. We can whip the Southern Confederacy; we can take in France and England and the whole civilized world and I want to carry it on till we whip out all of God's creation." South Carolina was "Whipped" for twelve years.

In 1860 the State's taxable property, exclusive of slaves, was $316,000,000 and the annual taxes $392,000. In 1871 the property value was $184,000,000 and the taxes $2,000,- 000. The public debt of less than $7,000,000 in 1868 became nearly $29,000,000 by 1871. During Radical rule "the State House was refurnished; clocks cost $600.00; looking glasses, $600.00; window curtains $600.00 to $1500 apiece; benches were replaced by $200.00 sofas; chairs which had cost $1.00 were thrown out and those worth $60.00 substituted; $4.00 tables by $80.00 tables; $10.00 desks by $175.00 desks; forty cent spittoons by $14.00 cuspidors."

"Chandeliers were bought that cost $1500.00 to $2500.00 each. Each legislator was provided with Webster's Un- abridged Dictionary, a $25.00 calendar inkstand and a $10.00 gold pen. Railroad-passes and free use of the Western Union Telegraph were perquisites of the office. Under the committee rooms, forty bedrooms were furnished each session, and the legislators, upon leaving and going home, carried the furniture with them. Day and night in the State House, at restaurants and bars, the legislators refreshed themselves and their friends at state expense, with delicacies, wines, liquors and cigars. A Speaker of the House who lost $1,000 on a horse race was the next day voted by the House a gratuity of $1,000."

One Governor and his cohorts were spoken of as Ali Baba and his forty thieves. South Carolina, the head and front of the old South, was being swept by a political revolution as radical as the emancipation of the slaves in 1865, from which the so-called third estate emerged, held power and has figured in state and city affairs and will continue to figure as time goes on.

In the European sense, there never was a Southern aristocracy. After the Civil War the ruling class became the leading class in spite of Federal domination. But in the American sense there always was a dominant class, composed of able, politic and persistent and ambitious men.

Until 1865 the most prominent object of interest to students of social science in the Southern states was the relation of the upper and under classes of society, the slave holder and the slave. After 1865 Civilization itself was on trial in South Carolina, where "Bills made by the officials and legislators and paid by the state, reveal a strange moral sense and a strange mixture of objects, from liquors, wines, cigars, baskets of champagne, hams, oysters, rice, flour, lard, coffee, tea, sugar, suspenders, linen-bosom shirts, cravats, collars, gloves, (masculine and feminine) by the box, perfumes, bustles, corsets, velvets, stockings, chignons, chemises, gowns, garters, fans, gold watches and chains, diamond finger rings and ear-rings, Russian leather workboxes, hats, bonnets; to, in short, every article of furniture and house furnishing from a full parlor set to a baby's swinging cradle, not omitting a $100.00 metallic coffin, all being bought and charged to the State Expense."

As the leading city in the state Charleston felt that her

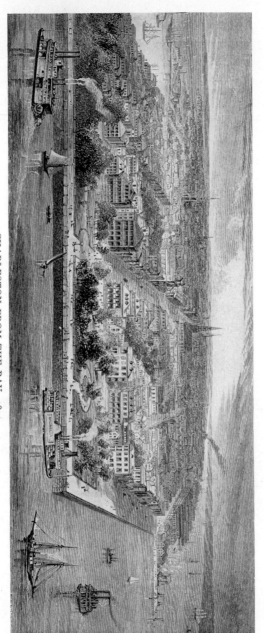

CHARLESTON FROM THE BAY, 1873

CHARLESTON DURING THE RECONSTRUCTION PERIOD
Looking Westward down Broad Street from St. Michael's Steeple

doom was sealed and white supremacy at an end unless some remedy could be devised. Daylight began to dawn when in May, 1871 a convention of the tax payers of the state was held at Columbia, over which Honorable W. D. Porter, of Charleston, presided. Though the protest framed by the convention accomplished nothing visible, yet it linked men together in the desperate effort to rid the state of radical rule. White men but bided their time to strike. In club-house, hall and armory, they awaited the signal of Hampton's will.

James S. Pike, of Maine, a strong anti-slavery man before the war and a consistent Republican, visited South Carolina in 1873, and his remarkable book "The Prostrate State" was perhaps the first intimation to the Northern mind of the doings of reconstruction leaders. After him came Dr. E. Benjamin Andrews, whose masterful pen pictures showed what crimes were being committed in the name of free government. Since these pioneers, historians and novelists have found South Carolina between 1868 and 1876 a rich field for exploration.

The oath as prescribed by law had disfranchised almost the entire white population. The revelation of the wrongs done to all reached at length the ears of the National Government, but by that time the trouble was past curing. The former slaves, elated at their elevation to power, were easily incited to rash and insolent acts. The Ku Klux Klan in the up-counties had only made matters worse, and Major Merrill, commanding officer of the U. S. troops had collected $15,000 in rewards, offered for every person arrested "with evidence to convict" who belonged to this organization. Several citizens had been convicted and sent to the penitentiary at Albany.

Affairs continued in a more or less demoralized condition for several years, and many of the white citizens held aloof from any participation in the political affairs of the State until the election of General Wade Hampton as Governor in 1876. The legality of his election was questioned, and it seemed for a time that the issue might result in a serious disturbance of the State, but it was smoothed over chiefly through the personal influence of General Hampton and the high regard in which he was held by all classes of citizens.

A record of events occurring in the city from the beginning of 1876 shows the negroes meeting at White Point Gardens in January and endorsing the election of Whippet (negro) who had been appointed Judge of the Circuit Court. The Federal Governor, Chamberlain, refused to sign the commission, and gave great offense to the radicals, who incited the negroes to overt acts and kept the colored population in a state of great unrest.

A large fire, supposed to be of incendiary origin, broke out, destroying a great deal of property near Warren and St. Philip streets, but sparing the fine house built by Mr. Aiken at the southeast corner of King and Ann streets; nor did it make headway toward the eastern part of the town, where the fine Aiken house adorned that part of the city and gave name to the row of brick houses to the north of Aiken Park. These still stand, filled with rich treasures of art and furniture.

The flames spared also the James Gadsden house, recently destroyed to make way for a filling station on Meeting and Ann Streets. Mr. Gadsden was minister to Mexico and arranged the Gadsden Purchase. The First Memorial Association of America met in this house.

The white men of the city were once again allowed to assemble in agricultural societies and the changing attitude of the North toward Charleston was demonstrated by the fact that on February 22, 1876, the Old Guard of New York paraded with the Clinch Rifles of Augusta and the Washington Light Infantry of Charleston in celebrating Washington's birthday. Whom Charleston would destroy, she first invites to deliver addresses. The Federal Governor, Chamberlain, made, by invitation, many speeches in the city and elsewhere in the state. About this time, the rascality of the Radicals caused the failure of their bank in Columbia and a suit against Niles G. Parker, State Treasurer. But matters became worse before they were mended. Negro Radicals were told to "empty the saddles" of the Democrats riding to vote and leave the evidence on the ground. This is echoed today in the instructions given by some owners of sea islands to their overseers to shoot trespassers.

General James Conner, Captain F. W. Dawson and General E. W. Moise and a host of other Charlestonians took a leading part in ridding the State of Radical rule. General McCrady made the suggestion of forming younger men into a political society, the membership to be limited to men under forty years of age, in order to eliminate the stock politicians. Mr. Moffett, the first president, met with death by a sudden fall from the window of his home on the southwest corner of St. Philip and Vanderhorst streets. Mr. Henry T. Williams was elected president. Nothing was to be contrary to the Constitution of the United States. When John A. Wagner, a member of the association, became Mayor the German interests were secured.

Neither time, space, nor knowledge permit of an extended story of the devious political moves whereby a split was made in the ranks of Charleston Republicans, whereby a bargain was made with Mackey, and the election of Mr. Cunningham, whose term of office as Mayor marked the beginning of better things for Charleston, accomplished.

The able, brilliant and best minds of the city were enlisted. F. W. Dawson, editor of the *News and Courier* lent the support of his facile pen and charming personality as well as the columns of the paper to the movement. C. R. Miles, George D. Bryan, Joseph Barnwell and men of like caliber began to form themselves into small groups. Armories were kept open and men always at call. Chamberlain appealed to the U. S. Government. Black troops were sent down under General Kuger. President Grant issued a proclamation commanding the white clubs to disperse. After the Old Guard departed a riot occurred on King street and in the clash between the races several persons were seriously injured and one man killed. Other riots and fires occurred.

On September 10, 1876, Governor Chamberlain and Mayor Cunningham issued proclamations forbidding the carrying of weapons and commanding peace. The Republican Convention followed and the Irish citizens in mass-meeting assembled (as did the Germans a fortnight later) endorsed the Democratic platform and candidates. Negro riots at several places in the state proclaimed that the state was threatened with a serious situation.

Greatly to the surprise of Governor Chamberlain, on October 25 Judge A. G. Magrath and General W. G. De Saussure, representing the citizens of Charleston, appeared before him and asked that troops be sent to certain sections of that county, where they said the negroes were exhibiting an ugly feeling towards the whites. The troops were sent and in several instances were welcomed by the citizens as being some sort of protection for themselves and families against the negroes, who under the exciting influences of the most desperate Radicals were a terrible menace to life and home. A demonstration occurred on the Wando river, near Charleston, at the DuBose home, where DuBose Heyward's grandmother was living.

The Democrats nominated Wade Hampton for Governor and a full State ticket. Then came the memorable "Red Shirt Campaign" of 1876. "Hampton or Military Rule," became the slogan, and Hampton, a son of Charleston, won! It was an interesting coincidence that the U. S. lighthouse on Morris Island flashed its first signal on October 21, 1876.

Then began again a dual government: the Radicals, claiming that Hampton had been elected by fraud, held possession of the State House and all of the offices, in which attitude they were backed by the United States troops and the authorities at Washington. There were two governors with their individual sets of legislature in South Carolina.

State elections occurred on November 7 and on the eighth a bloody riot happened in Charleston, during which fifteen whites were wounded and Mr. E. H. Walter was killed; in consequence of which the white schools were suspended and did not open for several days. Negro riots occurred near Orangeburg and Lawtonville and conditions were desperate. Federal troops occupied the State capital as the state continued under double rule of Democrats and Republicans.

On December 18 Governor Hampton made a demand upon Chamberlain for the possession of the executive office, state seals, etc. This was followed by a tax levy by the Chamberlain administration and was countered by a mass meeting of the Charleston taxpayers to support Hampton. The New England Society's annual dinner provided an additional opportunity for a display of the sentiments of those of Northern birth, who upheld the Democratic ticket and stood for white supremacy, as did a reception tendered by the Washington Light Infantry, to General N. P. Banks.

On December 23, the Radicals adjourned under the euphonic announcement: "Adjournment of the Constitutional House and of the Senate and Mackey House."

The Radicals were without money. The Democrats were able to conduct the affairs of State with money furnished by taxpayers and proceeded to carry on the State institutions while the Radicals sat in the State House and waited, like Micawber, for something to turn up.

The dual government was broken up on April 11, 1877, when Mr. Chamberlain withdrew and Governor Hampton entered the State House.

When Rutherford B. Hayes was elected President of the United States one of his first acts was the withdrawal of the United States troops from the State House, thus returning the government of South Carolina to her own people and Charleston gave Hampton—her son, born in his grandfather Fitzsimmon's home, the old Rhett house on Hasell street—a royal welcome on his visit to the city of his birth.

Men had planned and labored for a grand ovation, youths had given themselves up to military enthusiasm, fair women had worked with eager fingers day and night, children had danced with glee, and even tottering infants lisped, "Hooyah f'r Hampton."

Upon the occasion of the unveiling of a monument in the South, the orator of the day, Henry Watterson, said, "I have declared that we are one people. No air lines, nor water lines, not isothermal lines, separate us into geographic fragments, all the good on this side, all the bad on that." The war ended nearly 70 years ago, but a decent Northerner said in 1890, "I do not know what New Boston with her 500,000 people, would do if suddenly overwhelmed by an avalanche of the 700,000 South Carolina negroes, marshaled by Gen. B. F. Butler, in a solid colored contingent, to capture the city government, administer its vast interests, handle its twenty million debt, and, in public affairs, represent it to the world. I fancy the weight of the meeting would there prevail, by some of the numerous methods by which an Anglo-Saxon community everywhere, in the end, manages to put inferiority on the back seat and land the management of vital affairs in the upper story."

Others might take the attitude toward the whole question that Lord Greville assumed toward the passage of the "Church acts" when he said to one who wished to discuss the subject: "Sir! You are of one opinion, I am of another and a life-time of talk would not be long enough to change my opinion."

Although the State was stripped of many beautiful things, yet a peep behind the scenes reveals that very many beautiful possessions found their way back into the hands of their proper owners.

The city possesses its fair share of Fraser's miniatures. Mr. J. Alwyn Ball, of Charleston, made a valuable contribution to the Gallery in 1920, by the gift of several specimens of Fraser's work, one being a Self-portrait of the artist. The Strobel miniatures owned by Dr. Martin are also in the Art Gallery. Fraser, a catalogue of whose work is found in the *Courier* of February 13, 1857, made over three hundred portraits during his long life. Examples of the work of other miniature painters still to be found on the walls of Charleston houses are Parisen, Canter, Hill, Lavelle, Peter Henri, Jarvis, Smith, Weaver, Chollet, Belzons, French, Bounetheau, DeBeaux, Curtis, Labatat and Rabuske.

Miniatures were followed by "The Papyrotomia" or gallery of paper cuttings—likenesses made by Masters Hubbard and Hankes. Cromwell "took" likenesses of every description, at Mr. Bross' Washington Inn, on Sullivan's Island, near the landing where, according to an advertisement, he painted profiles elegantly on Super Royal Bristol paper.

Portraits painted by Thomas Sully are found in many private homes of the city, and the Carolina Art Association possesses several examples of his work. Among others are the portraits of his sisters Mrs. Middleton and Mrs. Porcher. The Hughes, Rutledge, Vanderhorst, Cheves and Mitchell families possess examples of the work of Sully, who left, among others, portraits of James L. Petigru and one of his sister Miss Petigru, who became the wife of Governor Robert F. W. Allston. Further examples of his work are listed in his recently discovered register of portraits from 1801 to 1871. A long and interesting list might be made of the works of Charles Peale, James Earle, Samuel F. B. Morse, Thomas Coran, Mr. Marchant, John B. Irving, William Williams, Flagg, Thompson, Langlois, and other artists who worked here. Some of these were or are native to the city while others are visitors who open studios here. The German artist Meyer painted here his most interesting work, a group of the fire-fighters of the city, which hangs in the Mayor's office. The Bogle brothers painted here in the forties, and after the Confederate War, Carter, Stolle, Beard and Chapman, who did some fine views of the city. Modern native artists include Leila Waring, Marguerite Miller, Elizabeth O'Neill Verner, Fannie Mahon King, Mrs. LaBruce, Mrs. Minnie Robertson Mikell, May Paine, Eola Willis, who represented the city at the Paris Exposition, Mrs. Arthur Rhett, Miss Alice Huger Smith, Miss Amey Allen, young E. S. Dingle, a painter of nature, examples of whose work promises to rival in value that of Audubon, Emma Gilchrist, E. H. Jennings, Max Buhrman, and Robert Whitelaw. Alfred Hutty, a painter and etcher of national note, has founded an art colony, and a home here. Older Charlestonians sat for their Silhouettes to Mr. Brown, a native of the city, and ancestor of the Mikell family. Prints here were made by Leech, and engraved by Wollett and Smith. Engravers were Kenan, Bonner, Heliger, Coram, Borde, Egan and Richards.

The literature of the city, which includes the work of Elliott, Legare, Simms, Hayne, Timrod, Clough, Snowden and a host of lesser literary lights, who wrote under their own or under assumed names (and the cry is "still they come") has been enriched by the various writers of today, including John Bennett, DuBose Heyward, Herbert Sass, A. Sprunt, the nature writer: Beatrice Ravenel, Peter Gethings, Josephine Pinckney and Samuel Gaillard Stoney, whose work has received recognition. Bennett's "Madam Margot," and Heyward's "Porgy," have become national literary figures. Silversmiths include Askey, Atmar, Austin, John Bering, Bevin, Boudo, Bock, Brander, Butler (Chas.), Carrel, Vernal Cart, Chapman, Courtonne, Darby, J. Ewan, W. H. Ewan, Eyland, Finlayson, Gaultier, Geissendanner, Gowdey, Gregg, Harris, Heron, Harper, Jacques, Janiver, Kershaw, Kanapauge, LaRoussitur, LeNormant, Mood, Maille, Miller, Martini, McKean, Michel, Monk, Meurset, Morgan, Minot, Petrie, Purse, Richardson, Rouse, Rutherford, Benjamin Rutledge, Enos Reeves, Sarrazin, Spear, Smith, Spring, Sonenery, Taylor, Daniel Trezvant, Thomas You, Daniel You, Vane, Veree, Westermyer, Willkings, Wightman, Winckler, and Whilden.

BOOK VII

FINIS

CHAPTER XVIII

IN WRITING the history of Charleston after Hampton's election, the record shows representative white men assisted by the more moral and intelligent representatives among the colored people in charge of affairs. A Court of Claims helped to stabilize conditions when the State assumed the financial burdens and deficiencies left from Radical times. Hampton was re-elected Governor, which position he resigned to become United States Senator from South Carolina. His last public service was that of United States Commissioner of Railroads.

In 1876 the Centennial Fair in Philadelphia gave the first joint exhibition of the resources and wealth of the whole country, North and South, and telephones and electric lights, destined to bring the country closer together, were shown for the first time.

In the State, Comptroller General Johnson Hagood and Attorney General James Conner, both of Charleston, accomplished wonders in stabilizing the resources of South Carolina. Superintendent of Education Thompson rescued the system of public education from the wreckage into which it had fallen during the war. In this he was seconded by Charleston authorities, whose efforts are embodied in the fine system of public schools of Charleston. The city moreover, benefited from the policies of Governor Simpson, who built railroads, deepened rivers, drained swamps, reclaimed lands and developed general industries.

As South Carolina is an agricultural district the new State Department of Agriculture undertook to look out for farming, teaching new methods of rice culture, the care of live stock. The phosphate concessions, immigration and the lien laws were regulated by Simpson. He resigned the Governorship to accept the position of Chief Justice of the State Supreme Court and Thomas B. Jeter filled the last three months of his term. He was succeeded by Johnson B. Hagood who is rated as one of the best governors in the long roll of those who have served the state. Charleston owes it to him that the Citadel developed into a large military college.

The war had left the country and city with many helpless and dependent children. Dr. Anthony Toomer, Mr. Porter and Mrs. Amaryllis Snowden each founded schools for the education of the sons and daughters of Confederate soldiers. Mr. Porter secured the United States arsenal for his boys, and Mrs. Snowden arranged for her girls the use of a hotel on Broad street which still bears the name of the Confederate College. Several other societies to help the widows and orphans of destitute soldiers were organized. The Ladies Memorial Association of today is typical of these societies and of the personalities and spirit of those who founded them.

The Confederate War could not, and did not, destroy the love of beautiful things in the citizens of the cultured city, nor all of the fine mementoes of the older days. This city has been repeatedly described as being wedded to the past, but Charleston's phosphate industries and naval stores loomed large in the State's resources, and by 1880 cotton was again passing in large quantities over her wharves. Drays heavily laden with cotton in bags rumbled over the cobble stones of East Bay to dump their loads at one of the numerous compresses going at full blast during the season, when masts of sailing vessels, waiting to be loaded at the wharves, looked like the trees of a forest. At one mouthful the modern steamer engulfs the load which formerly required a number of small sailing vessels. The tonnage of today far exceeds that of 1880, but lacks the romantic aspect of the days of sailing ships when East Bay was crowded with picturesque crews from foreign vessels and various ship chandlers catered to the sailors: little shops put out signs showing goats perched on barrels quaffing foaming

SOME PORCHER POSSESSIONS SAVED FROM DESTRUCTION
By Courtesy of Miss Virginia Porcher

HEADINGS OF TIE-RODS USED IN BUILDINGS AFTER
THE EARTHQUAKE
See Page 276

CITY HALL

glasses of beer, out of which flowed the words, enticing to the males of the day, "Ales, Wines, Liquors, and Cigars."

The fisheries of the State centered around the city, and the long nets of the fisher-folk hung outside the walls of the market in picturesque drapery, while interesting establishments at the foot of Market street were the rendezvous of the sailors of the "mosquito fleet" who sail, every day, rain or shine, for the Black Fish Bank, many miles across the bar.

Superintendent of Education Honorable Hugh S. Thompson was elected Governor in 1881. His term saw the completed and successful reopening of the Citadel, which in 1865 had been seized and occupied until 1878 as a garrison by the Federal forces. Colonel J. P. Thomas, father of the present Episcopal Bishop of lower Carolina, was elected superintendent when the Academy opened in 1881 with one hundred and eighty students. It has grown so large that entirely new buildings have been erected at Hampton Park on the Ashley river.

The erection of the jetties at the mouth of the Mississippi river turned the attention of Charleston engineers to a possible method of disposing of silt brought down the rivers and deposited, which resulted in similar works being built at the mouth of Charleston's Harbor.

Cleveland's election placed a friend of the South in the White House. He signified his interest in Charleston by a visit to the city when Honorable George D. Bryan was Mayor.

In 1885 a cyclone unroofed several houses, damaged others, and terrified the inhabitants of the city. On the evening of August 31, 1886, when the bells of St. Michael's chimed the third quarter after nine o'clock, the sound rang out over a scene of utter calm, shattered a moment later by an earthquake, which caused great property loss and killed and wounded several persons. Fires flared up in twenty places at once and several large buildings were consumed. The streets were piled with debris and fallen houses. The negroes, who thought the end of the world had come, dropped into primitive terror and for weeks kept the city in an uproar. The property-loss amounted to $6,000,000, as great damage was done to private and public buildings, churches, stores and residences. Much of this loss was borne by individuals but the nation rallied to the relief of those who were destitute. Thousands of dollars were sent here in money and supplies to the Mayor to be distributed. The greater part was donated by New York, Massachusetts and Pennsylvania. After this calamity many of the old buildings were pulled together by tie rods and fastened with turn buckles run through the buildings and capped with screw heads of various designs.

During the tenure of office of J. P. Richardson, the "Farmers' Movement", headed by Benjamin R. Tillman, first appeared, and the submerged Third Estate made itself felt in Politics. The Tillman movement split the State into hostile camps, and in Charleston to be a "Tillmanite" was a term of reproach to certain elements of the community. In the main Tillman proved a friend to the city and by the time that he died he had won the respect of even his bitterest enemies. He was then chairman of the United States Committee on Naval Affairs, under Josephus Daniels, after having served as Governor of South Carolina. Perhaps the most interesting feature of Tillman's régime is the remarkable "dispensary system" which taxed intoxicants to defray the expenses of State institutions, including the schools, asylums and penitentiary.

During Governor William H. Ellerbee's term, the price of cotton, the tax situation and the irritating dispensary law were all forgotten when on February 15, 1896 the United States ship "Maine" was destroyed in the harbor of Havanna, with two hundred and sixty-six of her men. The Columbian Exposition of 1893 and the Atlanta Exposition of two years later had aided the acquaintance of one section of the country with another: Mr. McKinley's administration had done nothing to disturb this growing sense of unity, which became permanent with the destruction of the "Maine." The capstan of the vessel stands on the East end of White Point Gardens of Charleston's Battery, erected there through the efforts of Victor Blue Camp, Spanish American War Veterans of Charleston.

Charleston rallied to the call of the bugle and formed several companies for service during the War with Spain. Again the streets of the city echoed to the tramp of troops who came from the up-country or reached here on transports. Local companies were raised and Edward Anderson's Battery went into training on Sullivan's Island.

The sea story of this city would include vessels that brought settlers, Spanish galleys, pirate ships, Sir Peter Parker's fleet, the "Saucy Jack," the "Star of the West," the "Little David," and the boats of the Spanish American War, whose names were romantic and whose size was sufficient to draw the attention of the government to Charleston's harbor and cause the Navy Yard to be founded here.

Some of the larger boats that came into Charleston waters were the "O. B. Dam" (rechristened the Grand Duchess) bringing the 3rd Wisconsin troops, the "Mobile," with the 16th Pennsylvania and the 6th Illinois troops aboard. The "General Miles," the U. S. Cruiser "Columbia," and the press dispatch-boats, all of whom "discovered" Charleston.

Prizes of war brought here were the Spanish vessel "Rita", later the Spanish bark "Maria Dolores", a small British steamship "Newfoundland", the "Mayflower," and the "Olinda-Rodriques." The "Newfoundland," condemned by the prize commission, was ordered by Judge Brawley of the United States Court to be sold, but "The Manoubia", also brought into Charleston waters was later released by order of the War Department.

Charlestonians of today recall that warehouses were turned into barracks for western troops. All of the work that was done within the city, looking to the comfort and welfare of the troops, was prophetic of the coming year of 1918.

Charleston now ranks as a world-port. The controlling depth of the channel is 32 feet mean low water, with a tidal range of more than five feet, making it possible with few exceptions for the largest vessels in foreign trade to enter and leave safely. The entire Atlantic fleet has twice anchored in the harbor and it is a frequent practice for such giant battleships as the U. S. S. "Arkansas" and sister vessels to proceed to pier-head berth at the municipally owned Union Pier.

Immediately following the Spanish War the city realized renewed prosperity, which increased when the resources of the State were set forth at the Interstate and West Indian Exposition held in Charleston, 1901-02. During the years when Governors Clinch Heyward and Martin F. Ansel occupied the executive chair, all industries of the state, including water and electric power were developed and Governor Heyward instituted a movement bringing the system of interior waterways in direct connection with the coastal waters, thereby opening the South Atlantic Seaboard to trans-Atlantic service.

Charleston was once more on her way to being the chief port of the South Atlantic section. The truck-farms of Charleston began to expand and cotton once again crowded the streets of the city.

During the last few months of Governor Cole L. Blease's second term the World War closed the high seas to export movements and thereby threatened the cotton-producing states with disaster; and with them, South Carolina and Charleston, her port. In January, 1915, Mr. Blease resigned the governorship, and when Governor Richard I. Manning took office in January 1915 the World War was in progress. Disaster did not occur: the State reached her maximum productivity along manufacturing and agricultural lines. Cotton, which formerly had "no price" now reached the peak price of twenty cents and Charleston flourished.

In the summer of 1916 two South Carolina regiments and a troop of cavalry of the National Guard were sent to El Paso, Texas, to serve along the Mexican border. Their service was but a foretaste of the great war in which South Carolina troops, as part of the United States Army, participated during Governor Manning's second term. In October, 1917, some American troops were for the first time put into the trenches on the French front.

No history of Charleston would be complete without a mention of liberty-loans, war-stamp campaigns, war-camp community service and public-health work put through, and of how The Young Men's Christian Association, the Young Women's Christian Association, the Knights of Columbus and the Council of Catholic Women all rallied to the cause of caring for the thousands of soldiers and sailors who mobilized here. The Red Cross organized the women of the city into a compact body of workers to carry forward garment making, nursing and canteen and transportation services. The recreational facilities of the town were taxed. The efforts of the city were advanced by the National Council for Defense. Several prominent women were members of it, and functioned as officers of the nation, state and city.

The National Guard of the State played a great part in the war. When the history of the conflict is written the Thirteenth and Forty-second Divisions, which served in the A. E. F. will be placed among the immortals. When the Armistice was effected and news of its signing was flashed to the world, the citizens of Charleston arose from sleep and trooped by thousands through the dark streets to meet on Marion Square and hear the good news proclaimed by Major Tristam Tucker Hyde, then Mayor, whose sons were both commissioned officers. When the South Carolina soldiers came home, Charleston was the place of debarkation. By authority of the War Department, sixteen companies of State Reserve Militia have since been organized in South Carolina.

No attempt has yet been made officially to classify or list the Charleston men who took part in the World War. It would require several years' effort in Washington to cover this subject properly.

Governor Manning had said, "Before I assumed the office of governor an order had been issued disbanding the National Guard. Among the first of my official acts was the issuance of an order declaring the previous order null and void, and re-establishing the National Guard of South Caro-

lina." A few months later the forces were drafted into the
U. S. Army. When the U. S. entered the war on April 8,
1917, the armed forces of this state under the name of the
National Guard consisted of the 1st and 2nd Infantry Regiments, the Charleston Light Dragoons, Troop A Cavalry,
Co. A Engineers, a battalion of Coast Artillery and a field
hospital unit.

The selective draft called men between twenty-one and
thirty-one years of age, who were sent to the camps for military training. South Carolina men served in the 20th, 42nd,
and 81st Divisions. The State supplied, also, many officers
and men to the Navy and the Marine Corps. When the call
came for officers at the beginning of the war, many men
volunteered and were sent to officers' training camps. Those
who received commissions were placed in various divisions of
the United States Army.

South Carolina contributed heavily to the armed forces of
the nation. A great many South Carolina boys were assigned
to the Eighty-First or Stonewall division of the National
Army—better known by reason of its emblem, as the Wild-
cat division. Organized units predominantly South Carolin-
ian were: Headquarters troop, the One Hundred and
Eighteenth Infantry regiment, the One Hundred and Fifth
Ammunition train and a field hospital all of the Thirtieth
or Old Hickory Division, National Guard. One battalion of
the One Hundred and Seventeenth Engineers, together with
the regimental commander and the Lieutenant-Colonel in
the Forty Second or Rainbow division, National Guard.

An ambulance company in the Eighty-first Division, the
only volunteer unit in that organization, and one negro regiment with white officers, the Three Hundred and Seventy-
first Infantry, of the Ninety-second Division, National Army.

Original segregations of troops into the classifications,
Regular, National Guard and National Army, very soon became obscured through reorganizations, transfers and the re-
placement system. No adequate list has been made of the
South Carolinians who were medal winners; from Charleston
went Johnson Hagood, who served on General Pershing's

EXCHANGE BUILDING, CORNER EAST BAY AND BROAD STREETS. BUILT PRIOR TO
THE REVOLUTION

This view is taken from the Intersection of Broad and Church Streets

JAMES S. GIBBES MEMORIAL ART GALLERY

staff, was a Brigadier General, U. S. A., acted as Chief of Staff of the service of Supply of the A. E. F. He received a medal for exceptional meritorious and distinguished services.

Brigadier General Frank Parker commanded with marked distinction the Eighteenth United States Infantry, and later as brigade commander exhibited qualities of rare leadership, superb courage and unusual initiative. He received a medal for the services he displayed as commander of the First Division in the Argonne offensive in the Autumn of 1918.

The Distinguished Service Cross, similar to the Medal of Honor, is awarded for personal bravery. Charlestonians who received this award were: Sergeant Herman F. Bremer, for extraordinary heroism in action near Bellicourt, France, September 29, 1918. He was instantly killed. Julius C. Cogswell, a Citadel graduate, who had two brothers in the service, William and Vernon, was First Lieutenant, Company G, Sixth Regiment, U. S. Marine Corps, Second Division. Having been previously wounded in the bombardment of La Cenze Farm, France, he refused to be evacuated and handled his platoon with marked bravery and skill in an assault on a formidable machine-gun position, until seriously wounded on June 6, 1918. He received crosses from the United States and from the Navy.

James H. Holmes, of Charleston, Captain, Twenty-sixth Infantry, after having bravely led his company in three attacks near Soissons, France, July 18, 19—1918, was killed in a fourth attack, while charging an enemy gun.

Frank Johnstone Jervey, Captain, Fourth Infantry, for extraordinary heroism in action near Les Franquete Farm, France, July 23, 1918. Although wounded five times, when his company was suddenly fired upon by machine-guns while crossing an open field, Capt. Jervey remained in command of his company until he became unconscious.

Thomas M. Jervey, First Lieutenant, Ordnance Department, First Army, attached to Observation Group, Air Service, for extraordinary heroism in action near Louguyon, France, October 31, 1918.

Barnwell R. Legge, Major, Twenty-sixth Infantry, First Division, for extraordinary heroism in action near Verdun, France, October 5, 1918.

Francis K. Lesesne, Captain, Three Hundred and Seventy-first Infantry, for extraordinary heroism, in action, near Ardeuil, France, September 29, 1918. Painfully wounded in the arm by shell fire, Capt. Lesesne nevertheless remained with his company until his organization, two days later, had gone into reserve position, and he was evacuated.

Carl W. T. Prause, Second Lieutenant, Company I, One Hundred and Eighteenth Infantry, for extraordinary heroism in action near Vaux-Andigny, France, October 11, 1918.

Martin C. Rudolph, Captain, Eleventh Infantry, Fifth Division, for extraordinary heroism in action at Vieville-en-Haye, France, September 2, 1918, and near Cunel, France, October 21, 1918.

Edward L. Wells, First Lieutenant, Second Machine Gun Battalion, First Division, for extraordinary heroism in action near Exermont, France, October 4, 1918. Within fifty yards of the enemy emplacements, one of his three remaining men was killed and Lieutenant Wells was mortally wounded, but he had succeeded in indicating to those in the rear the location of the hostile positions, for which he was twice awarded posthumously, the Distinguished Service Cross. Captain Lawrence Gantt, Maj. Hardy Silcox and Colonel H. O. Withington, all of Charleston, served with distinction. It has been impossible to secure a complete list of those who rendered gallant service. The record included among others that of J. Buist Rivers. Marble tablets in the vestibules of several Charleston churches carry the names of boys from the congregations who served in the war, and the Citadel has mounted an impressive marble tablet giving a list of Citadel graduates who served. A border of Palmetto trees has been planted along the Citadel driveway in memory of Charleston soldiers, and the bridge that spans the Ashley river is called the Ashley River Memorial Bridge.

Charleston is a subtle place. No transient traveler can appreciate the many interesting things that are hidden in her

COOPER RIVER BRIDGE

THE CUSTOM HOUSE AND DOCK

past. She has always attracted interesting people. Mary
Baker Glover Eddy once lived here on Wentworth street.
O. Henry, the celebrated writer, was once a drug-clerk in this
city. Levine, one of the first to fly over the Atlantic, had
charge of some work near the Navy Yard soon after the
World War. A thorough search would reveal many other
interesting personalities who have lived here as transients,
Freemont, the father of Perdicardis and Sir Thomas Lipton.

As has been mentioned, Charleston has been accused of
being more interested in the past than in the present and in
the potentialities of the future. But this is no longer true.
Because of an unusual combination of natural advantages,
Charleston is the logical fuel port of the South Atlantic for
both coal and fuel oil, and ships to the South Atlantic find it
the most convenient port for bunkering, thus replacing New-
port News as the nearest coaling-port for ships in this range.

Charleston is now served by four railroads as well as by
many steamship lines, and today is adopting the motor-
truck method of distribution of South Carolina iodized products. She has a modern airport, sends airmail and passengers
and is in a fair way to become the Port of trans-Atlantic
service.

The Southern Railway has erected here the most modern
coal tipple south of Norfolk, and four large oil companies
have selected Charleston as a distributing center. Sixteen
large fertilizer plants are located here, the total output of
which makes Charleston rank as one of the world's largest
manufacturing points for commercial fertilizers, and here
also is found the country's largest plant for the manufacture
of woven asbestos, the factory of the General Asbestos and
Rubber Company. And the proximity of the city to the Cuban
ore fields and advantages in cheap transportation will
eventually bring steel plants and mills here.

Charleston is unique in that while the visitor to this city
is surrounded by modern conveniences, he walks in the un-
spoiled atmosphere of Colonial times. Modern hotels and
hostelries have been erected to care for the thousands of

visitors who make Charleston their annual mecca, winter and summer. Charleston is open to the four winds of heaven. Winds from the "dead men's feet" at the East, come to ripple the waters of the harbor and stir memories of significant events. Winds from the South, laden with a salt tang and sweet with odors of pine and myrtle, bring no echo of the "Swamp Angel's" hoarse challenge.

Persons of national prominence have recognized the delightful facilities of this region for country home life and sport, and have established at Yeaman's Hall, on a former colonial estate, a winter colony, whose members are eminently representative of the wealth, ability and prestige of the nation.

Winds from the West bring their quota of history, of the days when St. Andrew's Parish and John's Island were the abodes of wealthy planters, and tell of the Gardens where azaleas flash and flame through the dark trees to mirror themselves in those limpid pools, which Narcissus himself might haunt.

Charleston's beach-resorts add to the pleasure of the tourists, and three excellent courses give variety of play to the golf enthusiast, while yachting, hunting, fishing, motoring, air-planing, and other sports have been brought to a high stage of development. The city now has a free library.

Three national highways now serve Charleston, and its confining rivers are spanned respectively by the Ashley River Memorial Bridge and the giant Cooper River Bridge, nearly three miles in length. The headquarters of the Sixth Naval District and the headquarters of the Sixth Light House District are located here.

The presence of the destroyer-squadron every spring and autumn brings into Charleston, as their home port, thousands of sailors. The recreational and athletic advancement of Charleston has gone rapidly forward, as is evidenced by the municipal stadium, dedicated to the memory of General Johnson Hagood, and various playgrounds provided for both white and colored throughout the city. The Horse Show takes place annually at the Stadium and a Polo Field is in

CHARLESTON MUSEUM—THOMPSON MEMORIAL HALL

THE OLD AND THE NEW. BOUNDARY STREET, NOW CALHOUN STREET
From a Painting by A. C. Wyatt

course of construction. Additional civic recreational facilities used by the Charlestonians include a cinder-track unit in connection with the Johnson Hagood Stadium and a municipal swimming pool.

King Street is generally known as the fashionable promenade and shopping street, Meeting Street as the locality for the jobbing trade in dry goods, clothing, shoes, crockery, etc., and Broad Street for banks, lawyers, brokers, etc. The business part of Meeting Street is confined to the short area between Wentworth and Market Streets, supplementing itself with Hayne Street, while the wholesale grocery business is conducted on East Bay Street, contiguous to the wharves, where are found extensive cotton and shipping enterprises.

It is a far cry, adown the years, from the first settlement at Albemarle Point to the Charleston of today. No fictitious narrative, but vital, glowing history fills the years from 1670 to 1931, and the city and her surroundings are saturated with authentic story that springs like grass from her soil, and drips like dew from the eaves of her quaint beautiful buildings and runs through her roadways and streets, weaving a golden thread of romance through the years of her existence. Time and times have moved, just as the people moved from the ancient spot where the first settlers trod: and as they moved down the river to settle on Oyster Point so the river of time has come to the modern city and brought activity to this peninsula where Charleston stands, her own best memorial of the past.

Sometimes in the twilight when the sunset makes glamor on the Battery, Charleston becomes as unreal as a dream. But the land between the Indian rivers is real, and the sentinel palmettos stand silhouetted against the silver Indian rivers, now the Cooper and the Ashley. With the thought of the old Indian names, the past seems to rise and the opening scenes of the drama of the city are re-enacted, the closing acts of which will come when Judgment Day pulls down the curtain of creation and writes "finis" to Charleston's historic and romantic story.

INDEX

A

Abercrombie, James, 58
Adams, John, 178
Adger, J. E., 206
Aiken house, 266
Aimar family, the, 207
Albemarle, 32
Allen, Andrew, 70
Allen, John, 58
Alston, Governor, 185, 186, 189, 271
Amory, Jonathan, 60
Ancestral homes, 101-107, 170-172, 191, 206-207, 244-245, 261-262
Anderson, Maj. Robert, 209, 210, 212, 213, 215, 216, 226, 248
Arbuthnot, Admiral Marriott, 138, 140
Archdale, 55, 59
Art, 270-271
 family portraits, 271
 miniatures, 270
Ashe, John, 63
Atkins, Edward, 95
Aury, 184
Axtell, 56

B

Bailey, Joseph, 21
Bakers, the, 28
Ballentine, John, 94
Banks, Gen. N. P., 269
Barbadian influence, 19, 20
Barbot family, the, 106
Barnwell, Col. John, 73
Barnwell, R. W., 210
Bassett, Master, 189
Bassett, Nathan, 57
Beal, Othniel, 94
Beauregard, 213, 214, 215, 216, 217
 classmate generals, 213
 military family, 214
Bee, John, 58
Bell, Ralph, 205
Bellinger, Landgrave, 64
Bennett, Gov. Thomas, 206
Beresford, Richard, 76
Berkeley, Governor, 20
Bernard, Gabriel, 72
Black, Alexander, 197

Black Code, the, 258
Blake, Joseph, 55, 56, 61, 63
 family, 104
Blakeway, William, 81
Blanding, William, 205
Blease, Gov. Cole L., 278
Bohun, Edward, 60, 61
Bonham, Milledge L., 225
Bonnet, Steve, 78, 79, 80
Boone, Joseph, 70, 76
Boone, Thomas, 100, 112
Boones, the, 28
Bowen, Bishop, 69
Boyd family, the, 106
Bragg, 245
Breckinridge, John C., 208
Brewton family, the, 101, 104, 141
Brisbane family, the, 104
Broughton, Col. Thomas, 72, 76, 89, 93, 100
Bryan, Hon. Geo. D., 275
Buchan, Doctor, 58
Buist, Rev. Dr. George, 58
Bull, Col. William, 93, 95, 100, 121, 126, 153, 159
 family, 104
 house, 104
Bull, Mr., 216, 217
Bull, Stephen, 25, 53, 86
Burke, Aedamus, 160
Butler, Col. William, 240
Butler, Fanny Kemble, 218
Butler, Pierce, 160, 168, 174
 family, 104

C

Calhoun, John C., 186, 201, 204, 210
Calhouns, the, 93
Campbell, Lord William, 100, 104, 125, 126, 127
Capers, Maj. Ellison, 212
Capers, the, 102
Cardoza, J. N., 198, 204
Cardross, Lord Henry, 48, 49, 50
Carew, Col. John E., 259
Carey, Thomas, 60
Carson, Caroline, 211
Cartaret, 32, 87, 88
Chamberlain, 266, 267, 268, 269
Chancagnie, 103

287

44